SAUL DAVID is a historian and br acclaimed books include: *Operation* Book of the Year which was turne *Silent Warriors*, shortlisted for the M *Times* bestseller; *Devil Dogs*, a *Times* and *Daily Telegraph* History Book of the Year; and *Sky Warriors*, another *Sunday Times* bestseller. He co-hosts the *Battleground* podcast with Patrick Bishop.

'A very fine book . . . Saul David has both a knack with the pen and a nose for a thrilling tale . . . Masterly [in] style . . . Readers should exult in *The Force*, whose heroic subjects deserve to be forever remembered'
ALEXANDER ROSE, *Wall Street Journal*

'*The Force* brilliantly recounts the heroic exploits of the first US and Canadian Special Operations team. Every chapter is filled with harrowing adventure, life and death struggle, and bedrock patriotism. The amount of new cutting-edge research is impressive. A monumental achievement!'
DOUGLAS BRINKLEY, No. 1 *New York Times* bestselling author of
American Moonshot

'A riveting and harrowing account . . . An important, highly engaging work that is unputdownable'
Washington Independent, Books of the Month

'With impeccable research and a keen eye for detail, Saul David has brought to life the surprising story of the original band of brothers'
DOUG STANTON, No. 1 *New York Times* bestselling author of
Horse Soldiers and *In Harm's Way*

'A mesmerising read . . . A compelling tale of human valour, doubts, mistakes and victory, honestly told'
BING WEST, former US Assistant Secretary of Defense, *New York Times* bestselling author of *The Village* and co-author with James Mattis of *Call Sign Chaos*

'Told at soldier's-eye level, *The Force* is a gripping and awe-inspiring account of a storied unit and a legendary battle'

JOHN R. BRUNING, bestselling author of
Race of Aces and *Indestructible*

'With this riveting story of an unlikely group of men becoming elite soldiers and contributing to the Allied victory, Saul David brings us a superb tale, well told'

GREGORY A. FREEMAN, bestselling author of *The Forgotten 500*

'With his incomparable gift for storytelling, Saul David captures the brotherhood forged in war, the tragedy and chaos of battle, and the rich tradition of American tactical brilliance that these elite soldiers helped to launch'   DAVID M. REEL, Executive Director, West Point Museum

'Action packed . . . This thrilling tale will captivate readers'
Publishers Weekly

'The First Special Service Force created in 1942 was a unique elite unit . . . As Saul David makes clear in this stirring account of their heroics, they did much more than their share and established precedents for the US and Canadian Special Forces of today'

JAMES M. MCPHERSON, Pulitzer Prize-winning author of
Battle Cry of Freedom

'Compelling and well researched, *The Force* is an uplifting story of bravery, duty and honour, an account of men who found the courage to take on an impossible mission – and prevail against all odds'

HOWARD BLUM, *New York Times* bestselling author of
Dark Invasion and *The Last Goodnight*

THE
FORCE

THE LEGENDARY
SPECIAL OPS UNIT AND WWII'S
MISSION IMPOSSIBLE

SAUL DAVID

WILLIAM
COLLINS

William Collins
An imprint of HarperCollins*Publishers*
1 London Bridge Street
London SE1 9GF

WilliamCollinsBooks.com

HarperCollins*Publishers*
Macken House
39/40 Mayor Street Upper
Dublin 1
D01 C9W8
Ireland

First published in paperback in Great Britain by William Collins in 2024
First published in the United States by Hachette Books in 2019

1

A catalogue record for this book is available from the British Library

ISBN 978-0-00-870108-6

Set in Electra LT Std

Printed and bound in the UK using 100% Renewable
electricity at CPI Group (UK) Ltd

This book contains FSC™ certified paper and other controlled
sources to ensure responsible forest management.

For more information visit: www.harpercollins.co.uk/green

Contents

Contents

Plans for Operation Raincoat

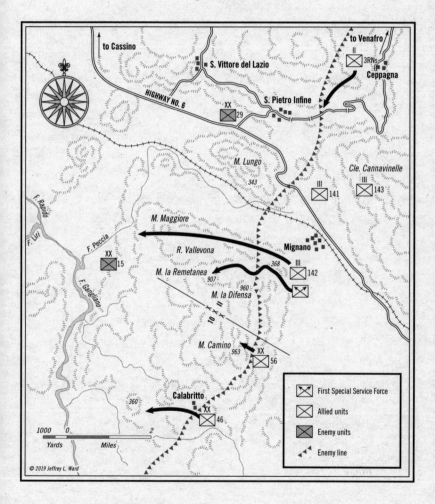

to Cassino

to Venafro

II 3RNs

Ceppagna

S. Vittore del Lazio

S. Pietro Infine

HIGHWAY NO. 6

XX 29

M. Lungo
343

Cle. Cannavinelle

III 141

III 143

M. Maggiore

F. Rapido

F. Liri

F. Peccia

R. Vallevona

Mignano

XX 15

M. la Remetanea
907

368

III 142

F. Garigliano

960

M. la Difesa

10 X II

M. Camino
963

XX 56

360

Calabritto

XX 46

1000   0   2

Yards   Miles

© 2019 Jeffrey L. Ward

First Special Service Force

Allied units

Enemy units

Enemy line

Prologue

"It seemed like the mountain was on fire"

As darkness fell on December 2, 1943, Captain Bill Rothlin, a no-nonsense former metalworker from Berkeley, California, ordered the 88 men of his company to shoulder their weapons and packs and begin the steep climb up Monte la Difensa, the keystone to a formidable German defensive position in southern Italy known as the Winter Line. Difensa's 3,000-foot-high summit was held by the crack troops of the 15th Panzergrenadier Division, veterans of the fighting in North Africa and Sicily, and all previous Allied efforts to take the position had failed: four weeks earlier, multiple attacks by two battalions of the US 7th Infantry had been repulsed with heavy casualties (91 dead and 538 wounded). Bloated American bodies still lay on the lower slopes. Now this mission impossible was being given to the First Special Service Force ("the Force")—later dubbed the "Black Devils" by the awestruck Germans—an elite unit of Canadians and Americans trained for winter warfare behind enemy lines.

Ten days earlier, an officer and a scout with Native American blood had reconnoitered the mountain. The only militarily feasible approach to the summit was thought to be via a gulley that ran up its eastern face. But the open terrain would expose an attacker to direct fire from the summit above and to enfilade fire from machine-gun nests that had been cleverly sited on a spur that ran down the mountain. So the scout suggested an alternative: to work around to the steeper northern face of the mountain and use ropes to scale the collar of near-vertical 200-foot cliffs that lay just below the summit. This assault route had two main advantages: it would allow the Forcemen to utilize their training as mountaineers and, more important, it was so steep it was unlikely to be defended. The final go-ahead was given after the Force commander had made a personal reconnaissance over the target area in his Piper Cub light plane. But he knew he was taking a big risk: if the Germans got wind of the attack before the men had scaled the cliffs, they would be caught in the open and cut to pieces.

The Force was made up of three combat regiments—each composed of two battalions—totaling around 1,650 men. Yet just a single battalion of 291 men was assigned to the initial night assault on Monte la Difensa. Its spearhead was Rothlin's company. Commanding the point platoon was a 26-year-old lieutenant from Appleton, Wisconsin. The son of a millwright, with film-star looks, the lieutenant was the first of his family to go to college. He had joined up as a private and trained as a medic, but his leadership potential was quickly recognized and he was persuaded to go through Officer Candidate School where, like Rothlin, he volunteered for a new unit specializing in "parachute jumping, mountain climbing and skiing."[1] Though put in charge of arguably the most unruly and ill-disciplined platoon in the Force—full of tough former miners, loggers and trappers—the lieutenant soon became something of a father figure to his young NCOs and privates.

Among them was an athletic and adventurous 18-year-old private from Saint-Lambert, Quebec, who had just finished Grade 9 when he lied about his age to join the Canadian Army in 1941. As he climbed on December 2, the young Quebecois was astonished by the number of Allied shells exploding on the upper slopes of the mountain and its neighboring peaks (where a British assault was in progress): 925 guns fired 22,000 shells in the first hour of the barrage, or 11 tons a minute. German guns were responding in kind. "Shells roared overhead in both directions like freight trains," recalled the private.[1]

Rothlin and his men reached the base of the northern cliffs and waited while the artillery continued its saturation shelling of the peak. "It seemed like the mountain was on fire," wrote a 19-year-old from North Carolina who had been facing a court-martial for striking an officer when he signed up for the Force. "I never saw a barrage like it during our whole time. You wouldn't think an ant could crawl out of it alive."[1]

It was well after midnight, and the barrage had lifted, when two scouts led Rothlin's men up the cliff. Encumbered as they were by packs, weapons and extra ammunition, the climb was only possible because the scouts had earlier fixed two rope lines to the rock face. Even with the help of ropes, the ascent up the dark, slippery slope was an exhausting and nerve-jangling experience. "The climb under combat load," noted the battalion's XO, "was incredibly difficult. Scrambling up cliffs with every foot and handhold doubtful demanded superhuman effort by men loaded with weapons, ammunition, radios and litters. To our ears, every rock displaced clattered downhill with sound magnified a thousand times and raised the question in our minds, 'Did the enemy hear this?' — a not very comforting thought."[1]

At the top of the cliff, the assault platoon dumped its packs while the two scouts searched for a route up the 200 yards of gently rising scree to the summit. It was 4:30 a.m. when one returned to say he had found it. By now the whole of Rothlin's 1-2 Company had made it up the cliff. Led by the scouts, they edged "along a narrow, rough and rocky path toward the German positions concentrated in a saucer-like area ahead of us." The young Quebecois could see the rocks of the peak silhouetted against the skyline. He knew that German sentries were just yards away. "We tried to make as little noise as possible," he wrote. "2 and 1 Platoons were close behind us."[1]

They were nearing the top when a German sentry shouted a challenge. He was shot by one of the scouts and, seconds later, the German defenders fired flares and swiveled their MG 42 machine guns and Schmeisser machine pistols to meet this unexpected threat from the rear. The stillness of the night was shattered by the roar of German machine-gun bullets, fired mostly blind but no less deadly for that as they pinged off rocks and sent lethal fragments in all directions.[1] "All hell broke loose," recalled a staff sergeant, as he and his men dived for cover.

It was 5:00 a.m. and still dark. The battle for Monte la Difensa had begun.

So how did this elite fighting force—made up of an assortment of men from two countries, all with unusual skills, who had spent more than a year preparing for a mission such as this in a remote location in the United States—come to fight on a barren hillside in Italy? The answer lies in decisions made at the very highest level of Allied planning by the US president, the British prime minister and their respective military chiefs. But first we must go back to a hot summer's day in 1942, when Force recruits started arriving at a former National Guard camp in the vast northwestern state of Montana to begin one of the toughest military training regimes ever devised.

1

Forcemen

With a blast of its whistle and a final hiss of steam, the train clanked to a halt in a dusty siding near Helena, Montana. It was just after noon on Thursday, August 6, 1942, and many of the 480 Canadian officers and men on board were bleary-eyed and grimy after the three-day journey from Ottawa, Ontario, a distance of just under 2,000 miles, though some had made the much shorter trip from Calgary in western Canada. Apart from occasional stops for exercise, the men had passed the time eating, playing cards and trying to sleep on the hard horsehair seats in the 14 "immigrant-style day coaches." Despite the discomfort, most had enjoyed the long trip across the flat prairies of central Canada, excited by what lay ahead.[1]

At dinner the night before, as they were about to leave the province of Alberta and cross into the United States, the officers had raised their glasses of port to toast their monarch, George VI, with cries of "God Save the King." They knew it would be quite some time before they returned to "British" soil—if ever.[2]

All had volunteered for the First Special Service Force, a joint Canadian/American para-ski unit that was being raised for a top secret mission behind enemy lines. The standard expected of recruits was very high: the Canadians had to be "active personnel" with "high physical standards," military trained and ideally possessing the "combined qualities of mountaineer, northwoodsman and skier." It helped to have a working knowledge of engines, and, given the fact that the lowest rank in the Force "would ultimately be that of sergeant," all recruits had to be "good NCO material."[3]

One of the Canadian officers who arrived that day was 27-year-old Captain Tom MacWilliam, a schoolteacher from the eastern Maritime province of New Brunswick. The youngest of six siblings, he had grown up on a farm in Fords Mills on the Richibucto River, 40 miles north of the city of Moncton. He did well at school and won a place at Mount Allison University in Sackville, one of Canada's finest, where he excelled at track and rugby and joined the Canadian Officers' Training Corps (COTC), receiving a second lieutenant's commission in the New Brunswick Rangers, a local militia battalion, in November 1939. It was also during his time at "Mount A" that he met his future wife, Harriet "Bobby" Robinson, just five feet two inches tall but iron-willed and extremely pretty.

MacWilliam was teaching at his old school, Mount Allison Academy, when his battalion was activated for war service in July 1940. For the next two years he was either on coastal outpost duty in small towns or villages, keeping a watch for German submarines, or attending various courses. In 1941, he and Bobby got married. A year later he was close to completing a company commanders' course at the Royal Military College in Kingston when he saw a notice requesting volunteers for a special parachute unit. He applied because he was "ambitious and wanted to make a contribution to the war effort, rather than sitting on guard duty." Though far from physically imposing—he stood just five feet eight inches tall and weighed 135 pounds—he was a talented athlete, deceptively strong, and had recently completed a ski instructor course. With born leadership qualities, he was just what the Force was looking for.[4]

Most of the ordinary soldiers on the train were poorly educated and unskilled. They came from families that had struggled to make ends meet during the depression of the 1930s and were typically streetwise, resilient and unsentimental. But there were exceptions. Twenty-nine-year-old Sergeant Percy Crichlow, for example, had been born in the sunny climes of Barbados, a British colony in the eastern Caribbean, and educated at Harrison and Codrington Colleges in Bridgetown, the island's capital, graduating from the latter in 1934 with a first-class honors degree in Classics. He was, therefore, something of a nerd and soon got a job teaching at the Lodge School on the east of the island. Unlike MacWilliam, his fellow teacher and future battalion commander, Crichlow was not an athlete. But he did have experience in soldiering, having served as a lieutenant in the Barbados Volunteer Force, a part-time unit that was deployed during the civil disturbances on the island in 1937.

Three years later, with France overrun and Britain threatened by invasion, Crichlow went to Canada and enlisted in the Victoria Rifles, determined to do his bit. But garrison and outpost duty across Canada were not what he had hoped for, and it was something of a relief when he heard the call for volunteers to join a parachute unit that would be trained in the United States and serve under American command. He put himself forward, easily passing the IQ and attainment tests he was set at Lansdowne Barracks in Ottawa. He was hardly the ideal recruit for the Force: a little too old and with no experience of outdoor living in harsh environments. But he had military experience, intelligence and obvious leadership potential. His interviewer gave him the thumbs-up, and he was right to do so. The mustachioed and slightly built Crichlow was tougher than he looked. Within days he was on the train to Helena.[5]

Also on board was a soldier Crichlow would come to know well: 22-year-old Private Joe Dauphinais, a handsome, broad-chested farm boy and former miner from Starbuck, Manitoba, who had been furious to be left behind when his original unit was posted overseas. So

Dauphinais made the best of it by qualifying as a diesel mechanic at a top school in Calgary before undertaking a course in mechanical engineering at the Canadian Army Trade School in Hamilton, southern Ontario. It was in Hamilton that the then Corporal Dauphinais volunteered for the Force, his mechanical expertise and mining background both counting in his favor. He was accepted, but not before he had been busted back to private for going on an all-night drinking spree.[6]

From a relatively well-to-do background, but one not unaffected by the economic downturn of the 1930s ("We were never allowed to put butter on bread"), was 19-year-old Jack Callowhill, the son of a manager at the American Can Company in Hamilton. Callowhill senior had fought with a Highland Scottish regiment in France in the previous war, reaching the rank of regimental sergeant major (equivalent to first sergeant in the US Army). His son was recruited into the Royal Hamilton Light Infantry by a schoolteacher who was also an officer in the reserves, first as a part-timer and then, after he turned 18 in April 1941, a regular. His chief motive was to "get out from under my family" and look "for a bit of adventure." The alternative was to get a job, but he hadn't excelled at school and his prospects were not good.

A likable fellow with an easy grin, Callowhill took life as it came, unlike his more intense elder brother Bill who, thanks to a football injury, was barred from the air force and army and eventually joined the Royal Canadian Navy. Also a decent athlete, short and wiry, Callowhill was stationed with his regiment in Quebec when he heard about the special mission in 1942. His decision to volunteer was more about relieving the boredom of garrison duty than because he was eager for combat. In Ottawa, once selected, he was told to put on his dress uniform, dump the rest of his kit and board a train for an unknown destination.[7]

The youngest soldier on the train was almost certainly Don MacKinnon from Saint-Lambert, Quebec. MacKinnon had left school after Grade 9 and was working in a "dead-end" job in Montreal when he was inspired by his father's World War One service, and the fact that his elder brother had just joined the Royal Canadian Air Force, to enlist a month before his 17th birthday. Tall and well built, he told the recruiting officer he was 19. It was easy to believe. The plan was for MacKinnon to join his unit, the Royal 22nd Regiment (the "Van Doos"), in England after he had completed his advanced training at Trois-Rivières. Instead, tired of waiting, he applied for and was accepted into the Force. It helped that he was an athletic daredevil who had ridden the ice floes on the Saint Lawrence River as a boy and who excelled at swimming, hockey, football and skiing.[8]

He and the other Canadian officers and men had volunteered for special service for an indefinite period, agreed to undergo training in parachute jumping and in "warfare under winter conditions," and would serve "wherever required." They were prepared, moreover, both to serve under and command officers and personnel from the US Army, and would obey their US superiors' orders as if they were Canadians of relative rank. Yet they would continue to be subject to Canadian military law and would receive Canadian Army pay and allowances, including parachute pay.[9] This last, seemingly innocuous point would prove to be a major bone of contention.

As MacWilliam, Crichlow and the others jumped down from the train and formed up in ranks of three, Canadian style, they were met by the astonished stares of their welcoming party, a small group of American officers and enlisted men,[*] who wondered: "Who the hell are these people?"

Some of the watching Americans were from the Force's noncombat Service Battalion, which had been formed several weeks before to provide cooks, bakers, kitchen porters, latrine workers, firemen, MPs, drivers, ammunition suppliers and parachute riggers—thus allowing

---

[*] Canadian NCOs and privates were known as "other ranks" or ORs.

the combat echelon of 1,200 men to concentrate on its mission. Others were destined, like the Canadians, for the three fighting regiments, and had come from across the continent and from every different type of US Army unit, including the Army Air Corps.

Among them was 24-year-old Second Lieutenant Bill Rothlin, a recent graduate of the US Army's Officer Candidate School at Fort Benning, Georgia. Born and raised in a middle-class detached home in Berkeley, California, Rothlin had completed both high school and a two-year nondegree program at the University of California's College of Agriculture at Davis before working for a time as a semi-skilled metalworker. In February 1941 he enlisted as a private and was posted to the 2nd Infantry Regiment in Michigan. By the time the 2nd Infantry departed New York for Iceland, en route to the United Kingdom, in April 1942, the tall and intelligent Rothlin, with obvious leadership qualities, had been selected for officer training at Benning. Though not due to complete his 17-week course at Benning until late September, Rothlin was among the first batch of 35 officer candidates who applied for and were accepted as new second lieutenants in the Force in mid-July. All had to report to the Force's base at Fort Harrison, Helena, no later than July 25.[10]

The notice posted at Benning and, among other places, Fort Ord in California and the Corps of Engineers Officer Candidate School* at Fort Belvoir in Virginia had asked for "volunteers for special training, which would include parachute jumping, mountain climbing and skiing."[11] Applicants then had to fill out a questionnaire detailing educational background, occupation and hobbies, experience of outdoor life and reason for applying to join the Force. One officer applicant, a former plant manager from New York State, wrote that he liked hunting, fishing and knife collecting and had spent practically all

---

* The Force actively recruited among the graduating classes of officer candidate schools because its commander, Colonel Frederick, did not want junior officers "conditioned by other commanders" (Hicks, *The Last Fighting General*, p. 71).

his life outdoors in the mountainous climate of the Adirondacks. He was, moreover, keen to get into action. His form was marked "Highly Recommended."

The successful applicants, Rothlin included, were then interviewed by a Lieutenant Colonel Ken Wickham, the Force's adjutant, who had traveled down from his office in Washington. One officer selected with Rothlin was handed a sheet of paper by Wickham and asked: "Lieutenant, is that your signature?"

"Yes, sir."

"You have just been selected for a special project called Plough and you have four hours to clear this post. You will report to the commanding officer of Fort Harrison located west of Helena, Montana."

Four hours later, Rothlin and the others were on their way.[12]

The rules laid down for American soldier volunteers were a little more specific. According to a letter sent by Wickham to military headquarters across the country, the Force was looking for single men between the ages of 21 and 35 who had completed three or more grades of grammar school and whose occupation or hobby included lumberjack, forest ranger, hunter, trapper, north woodsman (guide), game warden, prospector and explorer.[13]

Two of the men who answered the call were serving at Fort Ord on picturesque Monterey Bay, California, the headquarters of the 7th Infantry Division.[14] The eldest was 37-year-old Private First Class Howard Van Ausdale, a half-Dutch/half–Native American[*] gold prospector and sometime trapper from Arizona who had lived most of his adult life in the largely forested and mountainous northwest state of Oregon. Olive-skinned and classically handsome, with a straight nose, full lips and wide-spaced eyes, his black hair slicked back from a side parting, Van Ausdale looked more like a Latin film star than a soldier. He had enlisted in February 1941, later joining the 15th Infantry,

---

[*] Van Ausdale's mother was said to be a member of either the Apache or Yavapai tribe.

and though he was slightly older than the ideal Forceman, his teak toughness and familiarity with mountains and the wilderness made it impossible for the recruiters to turn him away.[15]

The other volunteer from Fort Ord was 26-year-old Ray Holbrook from Washington State. The eldest of four siblings, Holbrook had had a far-from-idyllic childhood. Thanks to his mother Etta's mental health issues, his parents separated in 1926 and later divorced. Ray and his younger brother lived either with their father or with relatives in Spokane, where Ray attended high school. After graduating in 1934, he worked for his father's lumber business in Inchelium, close to the Canadian border, supervising the cutting of trees and maintaining the machinery. In late 1940, more than a year before the United States entered the war, Holbrook joined the army. Perhaps he had seen the writing on the wall, or maybe he was just bored with manual labor. By the summer of 1942, the Force offered an exciting alternative to service with the 15th Infantry in California, and he took it. Square-jawed and stockily built, with light brown hair and dark eyes, Holbrook's one slight physical defect was his nearsightedness, which he wore wire-rimmed glasses to correct.[16]

Popular myth has it that many of the Force's US recruits were taken straight from army jails. This is not true. But a few, like 18-year-old Bob Davis from North Carolina, were given the opportunity to join the Force rather than face military justice. Davis had been rebellious since the age of 13, often in trouble with the police and rarely attending school. His only steady job before joining the armored corps had been as a bootlegger. He was facing a court-martial for striking an officer when he volunteered for and was accepted into the Force. Did his camp commander agree to drop the charges because he was glad to see the back of Davis? Possibly. But for every potential trouble-maker like Davis, there were many more recruits who joined for less cynical reasons. Once in, even Davis put up with the harsh training regime, because he enjoyed the feeling of "security and comradeship" the Force provided.[17]

2

"Where you from, soldier?"

As the two nationalities sized each other up, they were struck by the unfamiliarity of each other's uniforms. The American dress ranged from summer khaki to green herringbone twill, from the officers' distinctive pink pants and green tunics to the jodhpurs and high caps of the US Cavalry. One newcomer, reminded of the hat he had worn in the Royal Canadian Mounted Police, quipped: "Hey, I should have brought my old uniform."

Most of the Canadians were clad in their summer uniform of olive-drab (OD) shorts and short-sleeved shirts, puttees and black iron-shod boots. Their headgear ranged from stiff "wedge" caps perched over their right eyebrow to black berets (denoting armored troops). A few, however, were from "Scottish" regiments like the Black Watch and the Queen's Own Cameron Highlanders. They were wearing red and blue-green tartan kilts, sporrans and knee-length woolen stockings, their heads topped with either large, round, floppy tam-o'-shanters that looked like cowpats, or stiff glengarry bonnets edged in red-and-white checkerboard.

Formed up in column of threes, the new arrivals were set in motion with the order, "By the left, quick march!"[1] This was gobbledygook to the watching Americans, who always marched in ranks of four and off the right foot. Nor could they get their heads around the Canadians' gratuitously high arm swing. What many did appreciate, however, was the strangely discordant wail of the bagpipes at the head of the column. "Right there," recalled one officer, "I fell in love with the pipes."[2]

Half a mile up a rough track lay Fort Harrison, a former National Guard summer camp that would be the Forcemen's home and training base for the foreseeable future. "Dust was everywhere that hot August day," recalled one Canadian, "as bulldozers and construction crews labored over the airstrip for the C-47 jump ships, the parachute drying towers, packing sheds, mess halls, and roads."[3]

The rapidly expanding fort was located on a dusty plain three miles northwest of the state capital of Helena, a modest town of 10,000 souls that had been founded during the Montana gold rush of the 1860s. More than $3.5 billion of gold had been extracted from within the city limits during the first 20 years of the town's existence. By 1888 it had 50 millionaires, more per capita than any city in the world. Such a vast concentration of wealth had helped to pay for much of the town's impressive Victorian architecture, including the Cathedral of Saint Helena and the Montana State Capitol.

Despite the proximity of Helena—and the obvious risk that built-up areas posed for camp security—Fort Harrison was an ideal location for the Force: it was far from the main centers of population on the East and West Coasts; the flat prairie offered space to expand the camp and build an airfield for parachute maneuvers; and the peaks that fringed the plain, including Mount Helena, would prove useful for ski training, rock climbing and testing the special snow vehicle that was being developed exclusively for the Force. The fort itself was at an altitude of almost 4,000 feet, and physical exertion in such thin air was tough for the Forcemen, but they would reap the benefits when they returned to sea level.

Marched to an area close to the tent lines, the Canadians were "separated by twos and directed into individual company streets and to individual tents [square wooden bases topped with canvas]."[4] The plan was to mix them equally with Americans, four to a tent, and many found their new comrades waiting for them. Young Jack Callowhill, for example, was welcomed by a sergeant from San José Island in Texas called Clyde Spofford. "For a day or two," recalled Callowhill, "we were the only ones in there, and because he was more conversant with the American way of doing things, I asked him a lot of questions. He helped me to get my uniform and told me what I needed to do with various bits of equipment."[5]

Inevitably, as the two nationalities got acquainted, there was plenty of good-natured banter. "Where you from, soldier?" asked one American. "What outfit?"

"The Princess Patricia's Canadian Light Infantry."

"You got to be kidding. What in hell's that?"[6]

In general—because of the pervasiveness of American popular culture in Canada, particularly in the form of movies and radio—the Canadians tended to know more about the United States than the other way around. Some questions were inevitable: "Are you still paying taxes to King George?" But it did not take long for Americans to learn not to cast slurs on royalty, while the Canadians avoided criticism of US president Franklin D. Roosevelt.[7]

Young Don MacKinnon was put into a four-man tent that, with its neighbor, was formed into a section that included fellow Canadians from Alberta, Manitoba and Ontario and Americans from Massachusetts, Washington, Oregon and Illinois. There were "a lot of different accents and cultural backgrounds" and "minor conflicts and rivalries as people adjusted to each other." But they would not last, and by the end of that first month they were "working as a team."[8]

The Canadian officers were mostly assigned to tents with just one other occupant, usually an American. Each tent was equipped with a tiny wood stove that resembled "a vertical drainpipe with a hole at the bottom and a tin smokestack leading out through the top of the canvas." Though it was still summer, the high altitude of the camp meant that nights were chilly, and the stoves made the tents bearable. Captain Bill Becket was lucky enough to be the sole occupant of his tent and, "except for rare visiting officers from distant places," was alone in his "little canvas home."

A junior associate in a Quebec law firm, Becket had been working on a case on Prince Edward Island when his reserve battalion of the Black Watch was activated in September 1939. The following year, shortly after the birth of his first daughter, he wrote a memorandum on the need for a Canadian parachute unit that would be trained in the United States and used primarily for coastal defense. Nothing came of it until the summer of 1942, when the 33-year-old Becket, recently returned from attachment to a Canadian unit in England, was working as a staff officer in Prince George, British Columbia. A top secret message came through from district headquarters in Vancouver calling for volunteers for a US/Canadian parachute unit that would be trained in Helena, Montana. The Canadian portion would be known, for administrative and security reasons, as the 2nd Canadian Parachute Battalion (the 1st was undergoing training at Fort Benning, Georgia). Becket volunteered, only to fail the physical because of his nearsightedness. Fortunately he knew someone on the staff of Army HQ in Ottawa, who sent the following urgent telegram: "Captain R. W. Becket to be accepted irrespective of medical."[9]

Shortly after their arrival at Fort Harrison, Becket, MacWilliam and the other Canadian officers were introduced to the commander of the Force, Colonel Robert T. Frederick.[10] With his dark swept-back hair, chiseled good looks and pencil mustache, Frederick could have passed for a forties matinee idol. But there was something in the graceful, almost feline way he moved his body—one subordinate described him as "unusually fit, both muscularly and in coordination"—that suggested a man who would not be deterred by any physical hurdle. He had already given an indication of his prodigious courage by being the first Force officer at Fort Harrison to undertake the two jumps necessary for parachute qualification, and because the supply of jump boots had yet to arrive, he did so in ordinary shoes and after just ten minutes' instruction. Asked after the first jump if he had been nervous, he said: "Yes. But my aim was to lessen the qualms of others and let them know I wouldn't be sitting on my haunches."[11]

After a short pep talk by Frederick, the Canadian officers were given their assignments. Captains Bill Becket and Tom MacWilliam, for example, were put in charge of 1st Battalion, 1st Regiment (1/1st) and 1st Battalion, 2nd Regiment (1/2nd) respectively. Becket was surprised and delighted: a captain would typically command a company. But it made more sense when they were told that the Force would operate in small, heavily armed, eight-man sections and was only using terms like *regiment*, *battalion* and *platoon* to obscure its true purpose as a special operations formation. So whereas a US infantry regiment would be at least 2,500 men strong, the Force equivalent was just 417 officers and men. This meant that the strength of Becket's and MacWilliam's battalions was around 200 men, the same as a company of US infantry. Each battalion was subdivided into three companies, each company into three platoons, and each platoon into two sections.[12]

The first task for the newly arrived Canadian Forcemen was to complete the two jumps that would earn them their parachute wings. Incredibly, the man selected as the Canadian parachute instructor was Bill Becket. "I had," he wrote, "until my arrival in Helena, never seen a parachute. Apparently the Ottawa Canadians had labeled me 'Mr Parachute' because of my Memorandum." When he explained the situation to one of the US instructors, the man laughed and said, "Nothing to it. We are using a very abbreviated program—no towers like Fort Benning—so just watch me a few times on the training platforms and come up in the planes while we drop a few, and you will catch on. We'll qualify you right away and then you can help me up there by taking over a lot of the planes and getting the boys out."

Unsurprisingly, it was not that simple. After just a day's instruction, Becket was the first Canadian officer in his group of parachutists—known as a "stick"—to jump from a C-47 transport plane. The plan was to do one drop in the morning and the second that afternoon. But during the first he made the error of looking up at the officers behind him and missed the ground rushing up to meet him. Unprepared, he landed on one leg instead of two, heard a crack and felt a sharp pain. After gathering up his chute, he tried to walk off the tarmac without limping—but failed. He was spotted by a medical officer who sent over the "meat wagon" to take him to the hospital.

His heart sank as they cut off his parachute boot in the ambulance. A broken leg, he knew, would mean the end of everything he "had hoped for and worked for." All fractures were being sent back to their parent units because they would miss too much valuable training time. Already Lieutenant-Colonel J. G. McQueen, the senior Canadian and Frederick's deputy, had been cut from the Force strength after he fractured his ankle making a jump. Becket anticipated a similar fate. But fortunately for him, the break was clean and "without complications," and Frederick gave him permission to remain with the Force. Ten weeks later, still limping from the break and using two parachutes as a precaution, he dropped again and qualified.[13]

On the same day the main body of Canadians arrived at Helena, the US War Department's Bureau of Public Relations issued a press release with the title UNIQUE ARMY COMBAT UNIT INCLUDES CANADIAN CONTINGENT. It went on to explain that the new unit, known as the First Special Service Force, would be composed of men "skilled in all offensive operations—parachute, marine landing operations, mountain fighting and desert warfare" and would operate under the US Army's deputy chief of staff. Moreover, it would include Canadian troops, the first time in history they had "served as part of a United States Army unit," and would train at a camp in Helena, Montana.[14]

What the press release did not reveal, of course, was the nature and location of its secret and highly dangerous mission. Nor did it mention the fact that the "brains" behind the scheme was a brilliant if eccentric British educator and inventor who earlier that year had been appointed director of programmes to Vice Admiral Lord Louis Mountbatten's Combined Operations, the military organization tasked by British prime minister Winston Churchill with launching surprise attacks on the enemy-held coastline; or that Churchill himself was—and would remain—an active and enthusiastic supporter of the Force and its mission, a scheme code-named "Project Plough."

3

"Germany First"

In the early hours of April 4, 1942, a giant Pan American Boeing 314 Clipper flying boat left its mooring near Baltimore, taxied across Chesapeake Bay and lumbered into the air like a huge albatross, setting a course for Bermuda in the Caribbean, the first leg of its journey to the United Kingdom. Among its handful of VIP passengers was Harry Hopkins, confidant and chief advisor to US president Franklin D. Roosevelt, and the US Army chief of staff, George C. Marshall. They were on a secret mission to London to discuss Allied strategy with Winston Churchill and his military chiefs.

This contingency planning had begun as early as July 1941, five months before the Japanese attack at Pearl Harbor, when President Roosevelt instructed his military to gauge the "over-all production requirements to defeat our potential enemies." The detailed report, known as the Victory Program, was mostly compiled by Lieutenant Colonel Albert C. Wedemeyer—who was also on the mission to the UK—and submitted in September 1941.[1] It concluded that America would need to put approximately 10 million men in uniform (7.4 percent of the US population of 135 million): 6.7 million men for the army; 2 million men and 26,000 combat planes for the air force, and 1.25 million men and 869 ships of all types for the navy. It also stated that half the total manpower would be needed to defeat the Germans on continental Europe, a campaign that could not begin until full mobilization was complete in July 1943. Implicit in this conclusion was a "Germany First" strategy: an acknowledgment that Germany's conquests had made it largely self-sufficient in resources, and therefore Japan's defeat would not lead inexorably to Germany's downfall. The opposite was true for Japan, in that a victory over Germany would allow the US and Royal Navies to blockade the home islands and starve Japan into submission.[2]

Soon after the surprise Japanese aerial attack on the US naval base of Pearl Harbor* on December 7, 1941, Churchill and his chiefs again crossed the Atlantic to meet with the shocked Americans in Washington and coordinate Allied plans at a conference code-named Arcadia. It confirmed the broad "Germany First" strategy (agreed at the "ABC1" Anglo-American staff talks in early 1941); accepted the American proposal that each theater of war should have a single Allied commander; agreed to coordinate shipping and to try to keep China fighting; and to direct the war set up a Combined Chiefs of Staff (CCS) Committee in Washington with Field Marshal Sir John Dill, the British former chief of the Imperial General Staff, or CIGS, as the permanent representative of the British Chiefs of Staff (BCOS).

On the question of how to defeat Germany, however, there was less agreement. Churchill preferred a "peripheral" strategy whereby Germany was contained by blockade, bombing, small raids and an attack on North Africa, until it was sufficiently weakened by its efforts in Russia for a knockout blow on the Continent. Roosevelt was broadly in agreement. But his chief political and military advisors—

---

* The attack sank four US Navy battleships and badly damaged another three.

notably Henry Stimson, the septuagenarian secretary of war; George C. Marshall; and Dwight D. "Ike" Eisenhower, the deputy chief of the War Plans Division (soon to be renamed the Operations Division)—were convinced that only the earliest full-frontal assault on Germany via France would keep Russia in the war. Marshall's only slight concession was his conditional support for an Allied landing in North Africa in early 1942 if Vichy France, which controlled most of the northwest coast, was prepared to cooperate. This, he knew, would help to prevent the Germans from gaining control of the Middle East's oil fields.[3]

Apart from the welcome news that a combination of bad weather and desperate Russian defense had prevented the Germans from capturing Moscow in early December 1941, the initial outlook for the new alliance was grim. On December 10, three days after Pearl Harbor, the battleship *Prince of Wales*, pride of the Royal Navy, and the battle cruiser *Repulse* were sunk by Japanese planes off Malaya. The Japanese advance into Southeast Asia—launched on December 8—soon seemed unstoppable: Hong Kong fell on Christmas Day, 1941; the fortress island of Singapore, at the southern tip of the Malayan Peninsula, on February 15, 1942, with the loss of its 85,000-strong garrison (causing Churchill to lament that the numerically superior defenders "should have done better");[4] and Rangoon, the capital of Burma, on March 7. Meanwhile, American troops under General Douglas MacArthur were hard pressed by the Japanese in the Philippines (the last 10,000 US–Philippine troops surrendered on May 8), British and Commonwealth troops were retreating in North Africa, and British India was being destabilized by internal dissent from Mahatma Gandhi and others in the form of the "Quit India" movement.

For Marshall, these theaters were largely a sideshow. What mattered was continental Europe, and the obvious route into it, via Britain, was France. In early March he asked Eisenhower, the new chief of the Operations Division (OPD), to draw up invasion plans. Ike came up with three: Operation Bolero, the shipment of 30

divisions—500,000 men—and 3,250 aircraft to Britain as preparation
for an invasion; Operation Roundup, an assault on the French coast
between Le Havre and Boulogne by 5,800 planes and 48 infantry
and armored divisions (with the British contributing almost half the
planes and a third of the troops) by April 1, 1943; and Operation
Sledgehammer, a smaller-scale operation to establish a bridgehead of
just five divisions (half American, but with the British providing almost all the air cover) at Cherbourg, Normandy, in September 1942
to take the pressure off the Russians and keep them in the war.[5]

It was to present these plans—known collectively as the Marshall
Memorandum—to the British, and hopefully receive their approval,
that Hopkins, Marshall and the others had set off from Baltimore
in the huge Clipper flying boat. As secrecy was vital, the mission
was code-named Modicum and its members were all given aliases:
Hopkins, Marshall and Wedemeyer, for example, were respectively
Mr. Hones, Mr. Mell and Mr. White.

After a frustrating two-day pause in Bermuda while one of the
Clipper's four engines was replaced, the Modicum party took off
again on April 7 and took 20 hours to cross the Atlantic. They landed
at Lough Erne in Northern Ireland and breakfasted at the seaplane
base before boarding an eight-seater transport at a nearby airstrip for
the short flight to Hendon Aerodrome, north of London, escorted part
of the way by RAF fighters.[6]

Landing at 1:00 p.m. local time on Wednesday the 8th, they were
met by Winston Churchill and his chiefs of staff, including General
Sir Alan Brooke, the irascible if talented Ulsterman who in December
1941 had replaced Dill as CIGS, and Acting Vice Admiral Lord Louis
Mountbatten, the chief of Combined Operations and a full member of the BCOS Committee since early March. The presence of the
British prime minister on the tarmac was a measure of how important
the British regarded the mission, and his welcome of Harry Hopkins,
Roosevelt's personal envoy, was particularly warm.

A 51-year-old harness-maker's son and prominent social reformer from Iowa, Hopkins had been a close friend and political collaborator of the president since 1928. He was an enthusiastic backer of the series of federal programs, public works projects and financial reforms known as the New Deal that Roosevelt's administration had introduced in the 1930s as a response to the Great Depression. So indispensable did he become to the president that in 1937, after the death of Hopkins's second wife from cancer, he was invited to live at the White House. He had been there ever since. Hopkins's official title was US Secretary of Commerce with responsibility for the Lend-Lease program that from early 1941 had provided Britain, and later the Russians and the Chinese, with vital military aid that would be paid for after the war. In that capacity he had met Churchill the previous year, and the two hit it off immediately. Churchill, noted his private secretary, "gets on like a house afire with Hopkins, who is a dear, & is universally liked."[7] He was also unwell, having recently survived stomach cancer, and cut a sorry figure with his long neck and gaunt features. But the fact that he had not allowed his physical ailments to deter him from traveling on such an important mission made Churchill more appreciative still.

The welcome over, the Americans were driven past bomb-damaged streets and into central London, where rooms had been booked for them at the luxury Claridge's hotel in Mayfair. While the three juniors were given the afternoon off, Hopkins and Marshall went to 10 Downing Street to brief the prime minister on the Marshall Memorandum and the need for a major Allied offensive in Western Europe as soon as possible. "Only there," noted the memorandum, "could their combined land and air resources be fully developed and the maximum support given to Russia."[8]

After Marshall had presented the broad outline of his memo, Churchill's encouraging response was that he had told his chiefs that "in spite of all the difficulties, he was prepared to go along."[9] He was even more effusive in a letter to Roosevelt, describing the memorandum as a "masterly document" and adding: "I am in entire agreement in principle with all you propose, and so are the Chiefs of Staff...If, as our experts believe, we can carry this whole plan through successfully, it will be one of the grand events in all the history of war."[10]

Marshall was delighted with Churchill's response, feeling that the prime minister had gone "a long way" and that he, Marshall, had "expected far more resistance than he got." In truth, Churchill and his chiefs were very concerned about the prospect of a premature invasion of Europe that was unlikely to have, in their view, any impact on the war on the Eastern Front, while, at the same time, the loss of landing craft would probably delay a major invasion still further. They were, as a result, extremely skeptical about the prospects of Operation Sledgehammer and even an early Roundup. But Churchill was not about to admit this to the Americans, because he feared that if they knew the British were not wholly committed to an early invasion of Western Europe, they might abandon their plans for Operation Bolero—the buildup of troops and materiel in Britain—and concentrate instead on defeating Japan in the Pacific.[11]

Next morning, the Americans were woken by valets who helped them to dress. But Wedemeyer was not impressed by the hotel breakfast—"two slices of very stringy bacon, mushrooms which seemed tough, toast, and execrable coffee"—and pined for his usual orange juice, egg and "large cup of American coffee." At 10:30 a.m., Marshall briefed the BCOS Committee—Brooke, Mountbatten, first sea lord Admiral Sir Dudley Pound, and Air Chief Marshal Sir Charles Portal—in Whitehall. After he had spoken, the British chiefs responded in turn, each voicing reservations. It was a scenario that would, for Marshall and Wedemeyer, become wearingly familiar: the Americans arguing for "a decisive effort against the heartland of the enemy," while the British "kept returning to a concept of scatterization or periphery-pecking, with a view to wearing down the enemy, weakening him to a point which would permit almost unimpeded or undisputed invasion of Fortress Europe by our forces."

Of the four British chiefs of staff, by far the most "colorful" was

Mountbatten, the junior of the quartet. He was, noted Wedemeyer, "charming, tactful, a conscious gallant knight in shining armor, handsome, bemedaled, with a tremendous amount of self-assurance." He was still only 41, much younger even than Portal, and his views were not readily deferred to by the other chiefs. Yet they were careful to give him "a semblance of courteous attention," not least because he was a cousin of King George VI and a "great favorite" of Churchill's. Wedemeyer would come to respect Mountbatten as a "conscientious, energetic Allied commander."[12]

4

The Plough Project

Following his meeting with the British Chiefs of Staff, General Marshall was invited to the Combined Operations headquarters at 1a Richmond Terrace in Whitehall to hear about the various schemes that Admiral Mountbatten's organization had under consideration. But wary of being railroaded, Marshall said he needed to rest before meeting Churchill later, and sent Wedemeyer in his stead. "Whatever you do," Marshall told his deputy, "do not make any commitments."

At Richmond Terrace, Wedemeyer was given tea by Mountbatten and introduced to his "key men"—young admirals, generals and air marshals who all impressed him "favorably." After they departed, Mountbatten told Wedemeyer that he was anxious for him to meet a civilian inventor called Geoffrey Pyke who had come up with a "most important secret." Wedemeyer was surprised when a poorly dressed professorial type in wire-rimmed glasses—"tall, thin, cadaverous, with a neatly trimmed goatee"—shambled into the office and sat loosely on a chair. After the briefest of introductions, Pyke began to speak animatedly about his project, explaining that it was so hush-hush that only a very few people knew about it, and all their names had been entered into a book that was kept under lock and key. The book was then produced so that Wedemeyer could sign it. With the preliminaries over, Pyke got down to details.[1]

He had come to the conclusion that snow was in effect a fourth element—"a sea which flows over most of Europe each year and which usually tends to act as a brake on military operations." But what if the Allies were able to gain the same "mastery of the snows" as they had of the seas? Would that not provide the "opportunity of attaining certain strategic ends with an exceptionally low expenditure of production and military effort"? He felt that it would, and that the sooner the necessary preparations were made, the better. The key, he said, was to develop "a cross-country snow machine" that would make certain strategic snowbound regions—such as Norway and the Carpathians in Romania—accessible. It would enable the Allies to "move over snow at speeds greater than that of the enemy, and to go where he cannot follow." This, in turn, would open up the possibility of depriving the Germans—possibly by a single, coordinated blow delivered on one night—"of a very substantial proportion of his hydro-electric power and also of his natural oil resources."

Over the longer term, "mastery of the snows" would give the Allies a better chance of driving the Germans out of northern Norway and thus of protecting the northern sea supply route to Russia. It could do this by dropping or landing a force of British-based commandos and their "cross-country snow machines" into Norway so that, in concert with local resistance members, they could "help to prepare the country for a normal invasion from the sea." This would have the added benefit, said Pyke, of compelling the enemy "to pour in troops and materials to protect his railway and other communications." Norway would be turned into the "biggest internment camp for Nazi troops in Europe," thus relieving the pressure from other fronts. A similar force dropped on the southern slopes of the Alps might allow for the destruction of about "70 percent of Italian hydro-electric power," while a mission in the Carpathians could knock out "a large proportion of the enemy's natural oil output and refineries." It was, said Pyke, "impossible to exaggerate" either the "strategic importance" of such a weapon or its "positive political value in encouraging the populations of occupied Europe."

But first it had to be developed. Pyke was aware that snow-traversing machines for sport and commerce had already been built in the United States. But they were unable to move across all types of snow at speed, or up steep gradients; nor were they adapted, with their equipment and attachments, for war. However, said Pyke, such work—similar to that done in 1915 when the Holt tractor and the Diplock caterpillar were turned into the "tank"—could only be undertaken in countries where snow was available at high altitudes in summer months: countries like the United States and Canada where, in addition, there were the necessary "pure scientists and technicians" who could design and build such a vehicle.

He was, Pyke added, prepared to go to the United States or Canada to supervise the project, but only if it was given the necessary priority to enable it to "be put into effect during the winter of 1942/43." At the same time, the troops who would undertake the missions— including men "from the country being attacked"—needed to be raised and given cadre training in a suitable location in the United States, Canada or even Russia. Finally, it was necessary to appoint a suitable commander and a staff to deal with planning, research, development and intelligence. There were, in Pyke's estimation, just 270 days left until the mission needed to be carried out. An early decision on the whole scheme was, therefore, of "paramount importance."

Once Pyke had finished speaking, Mountbatten explained to Wedemeyer that the scheme had been thoroughly tested by various subcommittees. "I am now satisfied," declared Mountbatten, "that by no other means can we strike so crippling a blow at the enemy at so small cost in manpower and equipment." But the idea would be stillborn, added Mountbatten, unless it had the backing of either the United States or Canada to develop the snow vehicle and raise and train the strike force. So his question for Wedemeyer was: "Might the US Army provide assistance?"

Remembering his chief's warning, Wedemeyer's response was cautious. It *sounded* like an interesting idea, he said, but he would need to consult Marshall before making any commitment.

"Of course," said Mountbatten, "but just remember that the clock is ticking."[2]

Back at Claridge's hotel that evening, Marshall was "amused" to hear of Wedemeyer's meeting with Mountbatten and Pyke. Even so, he was prepared to invite the inventor "to discuss his weird [snow] contraption with our Inventors Council and with our people in production." That, at this stage, was as far as Marshall was prepared to go. What he did not realize—but would soon discover—was that Pyke's scheme was backed not only by Mountbatten but by the prime minister himself. That would change everything.

Churchill had invited the American delegation to spend the weekend with him at the prime minister's official residence at Chequers, a beautiful three-story Elizabethan manor house situated 40 miles from London at the foot of the Chiltern Hills. But as Wedemeyer had a full day of meetings on Friday, April 10, it was decided that Hopkins and Marshall would travel to Chequers that afternoon, and the colonel would join them the following day. Wedemeyer therefore missed the crucial meeting to consider Pyke's scheme that took place in the large oak-beamed drawing room at Chequers—its walls attractively adorned with "historic crests, flags and weapons"—during the morning of Saturday the 11th.[3]

Joining Churchill and his two American guests at the meeting were Lord Cherwell, the prime minister's chief scientific advisor; General Sir Archibald Nye, the vice chief of the Imperial General Staff; and Mountbatten. The other three members of the BCOS Committee—Brooke, Pound and Portal—were not present. But, having been told by Mountbatten that the conclusion of both his staff and the various subcommittees was that the scheme was both "practicable and desirable," they had authorized him to discuss it with General Marshall. Churchill, by this time, was another enthusiastic advocate. He was often drawn to grandiose schemes that promised great strategic advantages for relatively little military expenditure—insisting that, if Pyke's scheme came off, "never in the history of human conflict would so many have been immobilized by so few"—and what particularly attracted him to the Pyke project was the possibility that it would lead to an early liberation of Norway, an obsession of the prime minister's since his failed attempt to protect the country from German aggression when he was first lord of the Admiralty[*] in April 1940.[4]

As Pyke was not at Chequers, Mountbatten explained the scheme to Hopkins and Marshall and was fully endorsed by Churchill, Lord Cherwell—who two years earlier, as plain Frederick Lindemann, had condemned the first draft of Pyke's paper as "pretentious nonsense"[5]—and General Nye. Given that the British had already agreed in principle to the plans put forward by the Marshall Memorandum, it was perhaps inevitable that, as a quid pro quo, the Americans would support this lesser initiative. The result of the meeting, therefore, was that the "United States authorities" agreed to "develop and manufacture the necessary snow vehicles (to be known by some suitable 'cover' title, such as 'snow ploughs')." It was also decided that Pyke and one or two assistants would be flown to the United States "as soon as possible after General Marshall's return and work under his general direction." Overall responsibility for the scheme—which was earmarked for the winter of 1942—would rest with Mountbatten.[6]

After more meetings in London—including a "momentous" one on April 14 at which senior British politicians and military commanders accepted, in General Brooke's words, the American "proposals for offensive action in Europe in 1942 perhaps and in 1943 for

---

[*] A ministerial post equivalent to US Secretary of the Navy.

certain"[7]—the Modicum mission left for home on April 18, stopping briefly in Northern Ireland to inspect American troops stationed there. Two days later, after another long direct flight in the Pan American Clipper, they landed at La Guardia Airfield in New York, and continued on to Bolling Field near Washington, DC, in an air force plane.

Once he had spoken to Marshall and Hopkins, President Roosevelt cabled Churchill his conviction that the results of their agreement would be "very disheartening to Hitler" and "may well be the wedge by which we shall accomplish his downfall." Hopkins was a little more realistic, telling a friend that he was "greatly encouraged by everything," but that "the whole business is going to take a lot of doing."[8]

5

"Push ahead with all possible speed"

Shortly after his return from England, General Marshall briefed his senior staff on the Plough Project. A British civilian, he explained, had proposed the development of a "snow vehicle, armored, carrying adequate guns and a small crew" that could be used against certain key points in Europe, including the establishment of a "glacier base" in Norway "from which to operate against the critical hydroelectric [power] plants on which Germany depends." As the "civilian concerned" would soon arrive in the United States, it was necessary to designate an officer "to go into the matter."[1]

But no one had been assigned to the task by the time Pyke arrived in Washington in the evening of Sunday, April 26. He was accompanied by two British officers—Brigadier Nigel Duncan and Major E. A. M. "Sandy" Wedderburn—and carrying a letter from Mountbatten for Marshall. The letter explained that, since Modicum's departure, Mountbatten and Pyke had spoken to Ivan Maisky, the Russian ambassador to Britain; General Hansteen, the commander in chief of the Norwegian Army in exile; and General McNaughton, the senior Canadian officer in Europe. All had given their "full support" to

Pyke's scheme, as had Averell Harriman, Roosevelt's special envoy to Europe, who was based in London.[2]

Busy with other responsibilities, notably the planning for Bolero and the plight of the US forces in the Philippines, Marshall asked his able deputy, Lieutenant General Joseph T. McNarney, to meet with Pyke on April 28 at the War Department—situated in the huge three-story concrete-and-steel Munitions Building* on Constitution Avenue—and decide on how best to proceed. Also present were Major General Dwight D. Eisenhower, assistant chief of staff and head of the Operations Division; Brigadier General Raymond G. Moses, head of G-4 (the General Staff's Supply Branch); and a further 12 US Army generals and colonels. The outcome of the meeting was that McNarney considered "further examination was required" and gave the job to Moses of the Supply Branch. But already Pyke was sensing trouble, telling Mountbatten in a signal the following day that the US Army had "failed" to grasp the significance of his strategic concept and preferred "to concentrate on gadget problems."[3]

Nevertheless, the preliminary report by Colonel Earl S. Hoag of G-4 was that the project was "feasible," and he was ordered to "push ahead with all possible speed." With no suitable snow machine in existence, a "draft specification" was drawn up and given to Dr. Vannevar Bush, head of the US Office of Scientific Research and Development (OSRD), the new government agency tasked with co-ordinating war-related scientific research and industrial engineering. Bush, in turn, assigned two of his best men, Palmer Putnam and Hartley Rowe, to investigate the proposal. On May 1, accompanied by Major Wedderburn, the duo flew to the West Coast to inspect the performance of existing machines "as a basis for future development."[4] Two days later, Moses sent a memo to Eisenhower setting out their

---

* Built as temporary housing for the US military in 1918, the Munitions Building was given to the navy in January 1943 when the War Department moved into the newly completed Pentagon in nearby Arlington, Virginia.

respective areas of responsibility. The Supply Branch, wrote Moses, would "continue to develop all possibilities on equipment" and "look after the British representatives," while OPD considered "the worthiness of the project as a whole, the development of a plan, and the control of all operational activities." Moses thought it worth adding, however, that Pyke and his associates, the OSRD and G-4 were all agreed that "an acceptable plough will be developed and produced in time for the planned use."[5]

Dwight D. Eisenhower, the man in charge of OPD, would become the most famous Allied general of the Second World War and later the 34th president of the United States. But in the spring of 1942 he was still a relatively unknown, if highly regarded, staff officer. Descended from undistinguished Pennsylvania Dutch stock (his surname means "iron miner" in German), there was little in Eisenhower's upbringing to suggest he would scale such heights. His father, David, had once owned a general store in Kansas, but by the time Dwight was born in Denison, Texas, in October 1890—the third of seven boys—the business had failed and David was working as a laborer. He and his wife, Ida, moved back to Abilene, Kansas, where they eked out a modest living and invested all their frustrated hopes in their sons' careers. Both were religious fundamentalists—originally Mennonites, though Ida became a Jehovah's Witness—who stressed the simple virtues of "honesty, self-reliance, integrity, fear of God." They were fiercely ambitious for their sons and encouraged them to compete with each other and their contemporaries.

The young Eisenhower was a capable student, his favorite subjects mathematics and history, particularly military history. He was also a decent, if far from outstanding, athlete. His chief talent, however, was as a leader and organizer of sports and camping and hunting trips, an early sign of things to come. Persuaded by a friend to try the entrance examination for the service academies, he came second of eight candidates: not good enough for his first choice, the US Naval Academy at Annapolis, but sufficient for West Point. Once commissioned in the

US Army, he went from strength to strength. A temporary lieutenant colonel by the age of 28, Eisenhower was praised for his "unusual zeal, foresight, and marked administrative ability." He commanded the US Army's first tank school and, in 1925, passed out first of the Command and General Staff School at Fort Leavenworth. Earmarked as an officer of rare diligence and ability, he became a protégé of not one high-ranking general but two: Douglas MacArthur and George C. Marshall. He served as the former's chief of staff in the Philippines in the late 1930s, and in December 1941, a few days after Pearl Harbor, was assigned to the General Staff in Washington, DC. "I must have assistants," Marshall told him, "who will solve their own problems and tell me later what they have done."[6]

A broad-shouldered six-footer, Eisenhower could dominate any gathering by sheer force of personality. Now almost bald, he was still an exceedingly attractive man with his prominent forehead, broad, expressive face and toothy grin. His greatest asset was his limitless energy: he would go to bed late, rise early and work seven days a week, smoking incessantly. "The overriding impression he gave," wrote his biographer, "was one of vitality. Dwight Eisenhower was an intensely alive human being."[7]

He set himself the highest standards and expected others to match them. They rarely did. The first officer in OPD to consider the viability of the Plough Project as a whole—particularly the feasibility of Pyke's plans to destroy oil resources in Romania and hydroelectric power stations in Norway and the southern Alps, and to allow troops in northern Europe and Russia the same freedom of action in winter that they had in summer—was a Colonel Hull. On May 7, after just three days of study, Hull recommended equipping the US 87th Mountain Infantry, then in training, with 860 "ploughs" by "early fall, 1942, and that further consideration be given at that time to its employment."[8] This hasty and ill-thought-out response infuriated Eisenhower, who pointed out, quite rightly, that Hull had not answered the question as to the proposed use of the "plough." He was ordered, therefore, to reexamine the subject and report back as quickly as possible. If he felt Pyke's plans were "impracticable," he was to say so with supporting reasons, so that the report could be forwarded to Marshall.[9]

As Hull was having his knuckles rapped, the temperamental Pyke had already come to the conclusion that his project was being derailed by time-wasting and, as he saw it, the War Department's unwillingness to cooperate with either him or other civilians, particularly scientists. Pyke's other complaint was about Brigadier Duncan, a typical "brass hat" who, because their roles were not properly defined, had concluded that he was in America not only "to impress and persuade his military colleagues, but as the effective head of a mission and the arbiter of all policy and detail." He had, as a result, tried to obstruct and sideline Pyke at every turn—even going so far as to say he was off to inspect possible training grounds when, instead, he had joined Wedderburn, Hoag and the OSRD men on their hasty and inadequate examination of existing snow machines on the West Coast. The result of the West Coast visit was that Hoag had formally instructed OSRD to "design, develop, built and test" a "track-laying, airborne, amphibious snow vehicle" that could carry a load of 1,200 pounds up a 25-degree slope in deep snow and travel at 25 mph on level packed snow. Pyke, who preferred one of the other designs, was not consulted. For all these reasons, Pyke offered his resignation from both the mission and the project.[10]

On May 17, while Mountbatten was still trying to persuade Pyke to change his mind, Hull came back to Eisenhower with his assessment of future operations. Hurriedly produced, the new report lacked detail, insight and—though his chief had demanded them—solid conclusions. Instead Hull recommended further studies and, in the meantime, the development and procurement of "860 plough vehicles" by the early fall of 1942, with their allocation to either the 87th Mountain Infantry or another unit "to be decided at a later date."[11]

This was not much of an improvement on Hull's previous effort, and Eisenhower was furious. Five days later, he walked into the office of a young subordinate who was known for exhaustive and accurate staff work, and asked him to produce a new feasibility study of Pyke's proposal. "There's a sort of rush," added Ike, "to get it done."[12] Eisenhower was keen to get the problem off his hands because, at Marshall's request, he was due to fly the following day to Britain to speed up the planning for Operation Bolero. The trip would take about 10 days, he told the officer, and he would expect the report on his desk when he returned.

The man given the job was 35-year-old Lieutenant Colonel Robert T. "Bob" Frederick. Born in San Francisco when the city was still recovering from the devastation of the 1906 earthquake, the only son of a polymath medical doctor who specialized in ear, nose and throat but who also possessed a business degree from Harvard, a fluency in six languages and a rare talent as a violinist, young Bob was plagued by high parental expectations from the outset. By the age of nine, much to his fury, he was forced to learn German, Latin and the cello while his friends got "to play." He rebelled five years later by first joining a local National Guard unit and then, shortly after, getting a job as a brass polisher on a transpacific passenger ship.

Declaring on his return from sea that he wished to attend the nation's premier officer training facility at West Point, New York, Frederick had probably assumed his father would object. He did not—relieved, perhaps, that his errant son had chosen an honorable, if hardly intellectual, path of study. So after a stint at the Staunton Military Academy in Virginia's Shenandoah Valley, Frederick entered West Point—or, as he put it, "Hell-on-the-Hudson"—in the summer of 1924. Yet he thrived in the tough environment and, by the time he graduated in June 1928, was a company commander, on the fencing team and newspaper staff, an expert rifle and pistol shot, and in the top half of his year for academic performance. Respected by his fellow cadets, he was described in the academy yearbook as having an "inherent ability to make friends, command respect, and get things done." It predicted a "great career in the Army."[13]

Newly married to a gorgeous auburn-haired divorcée called Ruth Harloe, the daughter of an eminent Brooklyn surgeon, Frederick chose the relatively unglamorous Coast Artillery Corps as his branch of service because, as he told a friend, their bases "have the best housing." Postings followed in California, New York, Texas (where he flunked out of the Army Air Corps flight school) and Panama, and he spent time attached to the Civilian Conservation Corps in Oregon, where he was praised for his energy, initiative and "rare organizational skills." He then spent a year at the Coast Artillery School at Fort Monroe, Virginia, leaving in 1938 with the rating "Of highest value…Suitable for training for high command."

This gained him access to the Command and General Staff School at Fort Leavenworth, the first of his West Point class to attend. Having graduated in the summer of 1939, he was given command of a battery of coastal artillery in Hawaii and, within a year, was made director of Plans and Training for the islands. In February 1941, he warned an Army-Navy committee that Hawaii was woefully unprepared for a surprise Japanese attack by carrier-borne planes. His recommendations included: a ban on ships in Pearl Harbor (they could be refueled and supplied by barges); all antiaircraft batteries to be kept at minimum readiness level of five minutes, apart from an hour before and after daylight, when they would be ready to fire; all aircraft, apart from fighter planes ready to take to the air, to be widely dispersed; regular long-range sweeps of the sea approach to Hawaii by navy patrol planes; and barrage balloons at Pearl Harbor to hinder an air attack.

The response of the committee chairman was both blunt and short-sighted: "Major, we're not impressed with your ideas." Undeterred, Frederick sent his report to the War Plans Division (later OPD) in Washington, DC. It was never acted on—but it had been noticed by enough influential General Staff officers, including Albert C. Wedemeyer, to earn its author a transfer to that very same division of the War Department in September 1941.[14]

Frederick's first thought, on reading the title of Pyke's paper "Mastery of the Snows," was that it was "a wacky idea." But he approached the task with his usual thoroughness, arranging meetings with, among others, Brigadier General Moses and Colonel Hoag of G-4; Pyke, Duncan and Wedderburn of the British delegation; Colonels Kingenburg and Dahl of the Norwegian armed forces; and Colonel Wedemeyer of his own department who, according to Pyke, was "nowhere near as sold on the idea as was imagined in London."[15] This was probably because Wedemeyer now saw the Plough Project as part of a British conspiracy to delay Operations Sledgehammer and Roundup—which they feared would be unsuccessful—by promoting alternative campaigns in North Africa and Norway.[16]

Even so, Frederick was determined to do a thorough job. He read all of Pyke's papers and everything that had been prepared in the War Department. He also interviewed anyone who knew anything about Norway, arctic warfare and equipping cold-weather troops. Finally, after more than a week's exhaustive work, he typed up a 14-page report to go, like Hull's, "to the Chief of Staff over General Eisenhower's signature." It was not supportive of Pyke's idea. There were, said Frederick, no planes to transport the snow vehicles, and surprise would be lost in a seaborne landing; there was no proof that such a small number of men, scattered across Europe, would manage to engage and occupy any great number of the enemy; and there was no way to retrieve the crews of the sleds after their mission had been carried out (they would, as a result, be sacrificed). But his biggest objection was about available resources. If the project was carried out, concluded Frederick, "it would require diversion of personnel, equipment, aircraft and shipping from other definitely scheduled operations."

Frederick completed his report on June 1. As Eisenhower was not due back from his trip to Britain until the 3rd, the report was read first by his deputy, Brigadier General Robert W. Crawford, and his chief of plans (and successor), Brigadier General Thomas Handy. Both signed off on it, and Frederick assumed that was the end of the matter.[17]

6

"Frederick, you are now in charge"

On June 3, Bob Frederick was summoned to Eisenhower's office, where he found his irate chief holding a copy of his report. "I can't sign this!" roared Ike.

"Oh..." responded a shocked Frederick. "Why not, General?"

"Because in London I told them we were going ahead full speed with this. General Marshall said the same. So there's nothing to do but proceed in an energetic manner. Do you understand me?"

"Yes, sir."

"Good. Now bring me all the data you have on the development of the snow vehicles, the production rate, effect on other production, and any more details you've been given by G-4. I need to read it before the meeting this afternoon to discuss the vehicles with Admiral Mountbatten and the Russian ambassador. You're coming too."[1]

Having flown back with Eisenhower, Mountbatten had two main tasks: to convince the Americans that Operation Sledgehammer might "end in disaster" and should therefore be dropped in favor of a landing in North Africa (Gymnast) and/or Norway (Jupiter); and to rekindle enthusiasm for Project Plough. He made an immediate start on the second task by sacking Duncan and sending him home. Pyke was now in charge, with the newly promoted Lieutenant Colonel Wedderburn as his deputy.[2]

That day, at the meeting in the Russian Embassy attended by Mountbatten, Eisenhower and Frederick, the Soviets said they were "very interested" in the development of any vehicle that would perform well on snow, and would be keen to receive any for their own use. Mountbatten kept up the momentum the following day when he and Pyke addressed a conference of senior officers in Eisenhower's office in the Munitions Building. The outcome of the meeting, according to Frederick, was an agreement that the project would be "pursued with vigor" and Pyke's suggestions "would be further examined and, if feasible, complied with." During the conference, Mountbatten made it clear that, having spoken to Pyke, he was not entirely happy with the way the project had been handled thus far by either Brigadier Duncan or the War Department. Duncan had just been sacked for exercising "authority which had been vested in Mr. Pyke." From now on, he added, Pyke would be his personal representative in all matters relating to Plough.

When Eisenhower then asked Pyke what exactly the War Department had done wrong, the Englishman "was vague" and commented only that, in his view, several types of vehicles—including his own preference—should have been produced "as models for further experimentation" and not just one. Eisenhower's diplomatic response was that the problem would be "fully investigated" and Pyke's complaint given "full consideration." Henceforth, he added, an officer *not* in G-4 would be "put in charge of the project for the War Department," and this officer "would supervise all phases of the project for the future." He would not have any other responsibilities and would work "directly with Mr Pyke as a consultant."[3]

This was music to Pyke's ears, and he concluded that the project was gaining traction at last. The only fly in the ointment was the officer selected by Army Ground Forces to supervise the Plough Project in close cooperation with Pyke. On June 6 the initial choice, a major from the 87th Mountain Infantry, reported to the War Department for duty, but Eisenhower quickly decided that the officer had neither "sufficient background" nor "ability to handle a project of this type." So he was replaced by Colonel Howard R. "Skeets" Johnson, a tough, no-nonsense 39-year-old infantryman who had been recommended by Brigadier General Mark Clark, the Army Ground Forces' chief of staff. Johnson was given an office in the Operations Division so that he could begin "looking into the subject." He also spoke to Frederick, who handed over "all the information and material" he had on the project.

Three days later, Mountbatten spoke to Johnson and Frederick in the offices of the Combined Chiefs of Staff (CCS), quickly reviewing the project and Pyke's place in it. Johnson responded with "several remarks not entirely relevant," including the observation that "if the project was really going to amount to something and be carried out, he was willing to take part in it," but if it was "just another idea" that would not come to fruition, he was "anxious not to have anything to do with it." Mountbatten was not impressed. Later that evening, Frederick was rung at home by a British staff officer and told that, at Mountbatten's specific request, he was taking over from Johnson and would accompany the British chief of Combined Operations and Pyke to Montreal the following day to discuss Canada's possible involvement in the project.[4]

According to his biographer, Frederick was stunned by the news of his appointment and felt the wind had been "knocked out of him."[5] In fact, he could not have been as shocked as his biographer suggests, because only a day earlier he had actively lobbied to have Johnson sacked and himself named as his replacement. Pyke later told Mountbatten that Frederick had phoned him on June 8 and asked if they could speak in person and "off the record." The purpose of Frederick's visit was to inform Pyke of Johnson's "qualities" or, more strictly speaking, his lack of them. Intrigued, and not a little concerned,

Pyke asked his visitor to be more specific. Frederick's response was that Johnson's chief distinctions were of an "athletic kind." Frederick added: "I know him well and consider him to be 'scatter-brained.'"

When asked what he meant by that, Frederick replied: "When we had a tactical problem to solve, such as getting troops across a river, his attention every now and then seemed to wander. If I asked him what he was thinking about, he usually replied that he was thinking about his next hunting expedition."

Pyke was alarmed that Johnson might have been selected on his athletic prowess alone, and asked why that might be. "I don't know," responded Frederick. "But it may be telling that General Eisenhower was an enthusiastic athlete in his youth, and may still be now."

"Might there be any other reason for Johnson's selection?" asked Pyke. "His availability."

By now Pyke had the distinct impression that Frederick wanted Johnson's job for himself—his desire, as the Englishman put it, was "almost explicitly expressed." To test the young American, Pyke asked him more than once if it might "not prove embarrassing to suggest an alteration" if Johnson "had been appointed, or was even strongly recommended by the US military authorities." Frederick was adamant that "the C.C.O. [Mountbatten] had only to express a wish and General Marshall, General Eisenhower, etc. would grant it immediately without question of feeling."[6]

Pyke thanked Frederick for his candor and, following his afternoon meeting with Johnson, decided to inform Mountbatten in writing about Frederick's concerns. He almost certainly added his own verbal recommendation that Johnson[*] was unsuitable and should be re-

---

[*]   In late 1942, Johnson was given command of the newly raised 501st Parachute Infantry Regiment, which, as part of the US 101st Airborne Division, would fight with distinction in Normandy and Holland. Awarded the Distinguished Service Cross for extraordinary heroism during the D-Day landings, Johnson was KIA by an enemy shell near Driel, Holland, on October 6, 1944. His last words to his successor were: "Take care of my boys" (www.usairborne.be /Hall_of_honor/us_honor_johnson.htm).

placed by Frederick. So why did Pyke trust the supervision of the Plough Project, his brainchild, to an officer who, only a few days earlier, had argued against its feasibility as a military operation? Because, it seems, he was now convinced that Frederick had come around to his way of thinking. "I've captured or awakened the imaginations of some of their younger officers," he wrote to Mountbatten on June 7. "They are beginning to tell me of their troubles. That young Colonel [Frederick] at the Eisenhauer [sic] meeting who sat opposite you has begun to unbend. *He* is Operations. He was specially selected as a compliment [sic] to me to replace someone more innocent and less energetic. After another two meetings, I shall I think be able to begin to educate this nice young man."[7]

If Pyke's motivation is reasonably easy to discern, what about Frederick's? Why did he change his mind? Was it because he now knew more about the project than any other US officer and was less likely to underestimate the pitfalls? Was he genuinely concerned that an officer like Colonel Johnson was not up to the task? Did Pyke really convince him that the project was more than a pipe dream? Or did Frederick spot a once-in-a-lifetime career opportunity, a means by which a junior lieutenant colonel could carve out for himself a mini empire away from the cloying bureaucracy of Washington, and a chance to command elite troops in combat? It may even have been a combination of all four, but the last factor was probably dominant.

Events now moved at a dizzying pace. Frederick arrived in Montreal by train on the 11th and flew on to Ottawa with Mountbatten and Pyke to discuss the project with the governor-general, Lord Athlone, and senior Canadian politicians and military men, including the army chief of staff, Lieutenant-General Kenneth Stuart. They also spoke to members of Canada's National Research Council (NRC)—who said they would help to develop a suitable snow vehicle—and two officers with knowledge of winter warfare (one of whom, Captain Tom Gilday, would later join the Force as a battalion commander). On the 13th—by which time Mountbatten had set off back to England—Frederick spoke with Major-General John Carl Murchie, Stuart's deputy, who told him that Canada "was willing to enter the project 100 percent in cooperation with the United States." They were happy, they said, for the project to be based in the United States and for the US Army to carry out all planning and intelligence work. Meanwhile, the Canadian Army would provide officers and enlisted men while the NRC helped to develop "a suitable vehicle." Canada, in addition, was prepared to offer the use of any training area that might be desirable.[8]

Back in Washington, DC, on the 14th, Frederick was assigned to the office of Deputy Chief of Staff McNarney and told to prepare a directive on what he required for the project in terms of organization and cooperation. Once that had been achieved, and a force was in being, Frederick would take command. This, in effect, gave Frederick carte blanche to state exactly what he needed and from whom. Needless to say, he took full advantage. The directive was duly signed off by both Eisenhower and McNarney, and issued by the Adjutant General's Office with Marshall's signature on June 16. It stated, among other things, that Frederick was responsible for "all development and materiel and planning" for the "Plough Project," and for the "prosecution and organization of such forces as are necessary." Frederick was authorized "to communicate directly" with the representatives of foreign governments, and—crucially—all US military authorities were to "cooperate with and assist" him in "the vigorous and thorough accomplishment of this project."[9] This last point was hammered home in a separate instruction by Marshall to the four assistant chiefs of staff and the commanding generals of Army Ground Forces, Army Air Forces and Services of Supply. Frederick's needs, it stated, were to be accorded the "highest priority."[10]

Rarely, if ever, in the history of the US military has a midranking officer been granted such sweeping powers, and Frederick did not hold back. He began by appropriating five offices on the third floor of the Munitions Building and filling them with key staff officers such as Majors Ken Wickham, John Shinberger and Orval Baldwin and Captain Robert Burhans, who became, respectively, the heads of Administration and Personnel (S-1), Operations and Training (S-3), Supply (S-4) and Intelligence (S-2). He would soon add liaison officers from the Canadian and Norwegian armies, and, on Shinberger's advice, request two experienced Airborne officers from Fort Benning—Captain Harry "Tug" Wilson and Lieutenant Bob Ellis—to oversee parachute training. Hand-to-hand combat would be taught by Irishman Dermot "Pat" O'Neill, formerly of the Shanghai Municipal Police, who had been recommended by a colonel from the Office of Strategic Services (OSS, the forerunner to the CIA) as "one of the few really fine instructors for this work" available.

Informed by Colonel Hoag of G-4 that the Studebaker Corporation had been commissioned to build the snow vehicles, Frederick said he would need around 600 and that an amphibious capability was "not essential." The order for 600 nonamphibious vehicles with Studebaker engines—known officially as the "Cargo-carrier, light, T-15," or "Weasel" for short—was duly placed on June 21. Frederick was assured by Hoag that six prototypes would be ready for tests in mid-July, while the finished article would start to roll off the production line in early November at a rate of 15 per day, rising to 30 per day. Studebaker had guaranteed to deliver all 600 by December 31. Given that the type of snow vehicle suggested by the OSRD had only been approved by the War Department on May 13, this was astonishingly quick work by Studebaker and, according to Frederick, was a "record for the design, development, and production of a motor vehicle."[11]

Finding a suitable name for Frederick's new unit was considered a high priority, and various "fierce-sounding" suggestions were made by the War Department's Bureau of Public Relations. But Frederick eventually settled on the more prosaic First Special

Service Force *because* it was bland and would hide the true nature of the unit. The only drawback, as Frederick and his men would discover, was that the name was a little too similar to Special Services, the US Army's entertainment branch (whose World War Two performers included Burt Lancaster and Mickey Rooney), and this would cause some unfortunate mix-ups.[12]

In early July, Major Shinberger was sent to inspect possible training camps for the Force in North Dakota and Montana. On Shinberger's advice, Frederick went for the Montana option, Fort Harrison, near the state capital of Helena. It helped that it was "at the coldest point in the United States, and is close to mountainous country where snow will be available" for the rest of the year. Nearby there was plenty of flat land for building an airstrip and parachute training. The only drawback, in Frederick's eyes, was that the camp was "too close to the town." Yet overall it offered the "best general conditions for the training." Orders were therefore issued for work to start immediately on the "expansion and winterization of the camp to accommodate 2200 enlisted men, and about 180 officers." The first occupants would arrive on the 19th.[13]

The Force was formally activated at Fort Harrison on July 9, 1942. The activating document—issued four days earlier by the US secretary of war, Henry Stimson—stated that the Force would "operate directly under War Department control," not Army Ground Forces, thus removing another layer of bureaucracy. It would contain a maximum of 173 officers and 2,194 men (including a potential overstrength of 30 percent), but the initial Force would be 133 officers and 1,821 men strong, 546 of whom would form the noncombat Service Battalion, while the remainder—a headquarters and three regiments (each of 417 officers and men)—would be parachute-trained fighters. With limited time to train as "arctic-ski-demolition-paratroop-mountain climbing commandos," Frederick wanted his combat soldiers to be "free of K.P., guard, and supply duties."[14]

The Force HQ offices in the Munitions Building in Washington, DC, were a hive of activity in early July as the staff sought intelligence on possible targets in Norway and Romania, commissioned maps, drafted guidelines for recruiting men and officers in the United States and Canada, selected a wireless set for the Weasel and generally took care of the 101 other details that arise when creating an elite unit from scratch in just a few weeks. But the biggest call on Frederick's time was dealing with the eccentric and irascible Pyke, who had still not forgiven the OSRD for selecting the tracked Weasel over his own preference for a screw-propelled model.[15]

The matter came to a head on July 15 when Frederick, newly promoted to the rank of full or "bird" colonel,* was summoned to Marshall's office and asked if he thought that Pyke was still "essential to the project." His answer was no. "In that case," responded Marshall, "I shall request his return to England."

By now even Harry Hopkins, formerly sympathetic to Pyke's predicament, knew the disruptive Englishman had to go. He was eventually recalled by Mountbatten in early August, ostensibly to run the Plough Project from the UK. But on his return Pyke asked "to be released from any further participation," and Mountbatten granted him his wish. Pyke had ruffled more than a few feathers during his fractious three months' stay in Washington. But his fate was sealed when Frederick—the man he "thought he could educate"—decided that enough was enough. Like others before him, Pyke had underestimated the soft-spoken Californian who, beneath a mild-mannered exterior, possessed a keen sense of duty, a fierce ambition and a streak of ruthlessness.

By the time the first contingent of Canadian troops arrived at Fort Harrison on August 6, 1942, Frederick was in complete control of the

---

* So-called because the insignia of rank for a US colonel is a silver eagle; a lieutenant colonel is denoted by a silver oak leaf.

Plough Project, with responsibility for both planning its operations *and* executing them. With the 600 Weasels due to be delivered by the end of the year, he had just under five months to train his binational commandos to the necessary standard. It was, he knew, not nearly enough time. But he would give it his best shot.

7

1-2 Company

"We all got lined up in our parachutes," recalled Jack Callowhill, "put in the plane and told to sit down in order. Then the jumpmaster came along with buckets and put them down in front of us so we could be sick. Many were."[1]

Callowhill was one of 227 Canadian Forcemen making their first parachute jump at the makeshift airfield near Fort Harrison on Saturday, August 15. Jumping with him were Percy Crichlow, Joe Dauphinais and Don MacKinnon.[2] Only a couple of weeks earlier, to speed up the tempo of training, Colonel Frederick had ruled that his combat troops would qualify for their wings after just two parachute jumps instead of the usual six required by the US Army's parachute school at Fort Benning. He had previously ordered the construction engineer to level two 3,500-foot-long runways close to the fort so that his men would not have to travel to the nearest airport. They would jump from six C-47 Douglas Skytrain transport planes—known to the British as "Dakotas"—that Frederick had borrowed from the USAAF.[3]

At Fort Benning the five-week preparatory course included learning about the "design, function and packing of parachutes," jumping and landing techniques, and "strenuous physical conditioning" in the form of running and calisthenics. It also used several mock-up devices—including two 250-foot towers brought from the 1939 World's Fair in New York—to simulate exiting from aircraft and landing.[4] The Forcemen, by contrast, were put through a three-stage training program by Captains Wallace and Ellis that lasted between two and nine days, though most were ready to jump after five. The first stage was physical training, tumbling, hiking and jumping from a two-foot platform. The men then moved on to the four-foot platform, orientation flights, including a brief stop at nearby Butte Airport, and hanging in a suspended harness to learn control of the chute in the air. The final stage was exiting from the "mock-up," a box built to represent the cabin portion of a plane.[5]

Then came the actual jump. Before their own leaps, Callowhill and the others were forced to watch footage taken from a Piper Cub light aircraft. It showed a Forceman approaching the cargo door to the left rear of the C-47's fuselage. But instead of exiting, he turned, crouched down and grabbed on to the side of the door. "All you could see," remembered Callowhill, "was a jumpmaster's boot, *whack*, on his hands. He let go."

On another occasion a Forceman complained he couldn't get his hook on the static line. Coming down to investigate, the jumpmaster scolded: "Well, if you get up off your knees you might be able to."[6]

For the jumps on the 15th, the Canadians were counted off in 12-man sticks and loaded into the cargo hold of the C-47, where they sat on metal benches and fastened seat belts. The two-engined plane then took off and quickly circled back toward the drop zone. Having checked the location through the open door, the jumpmaster shouted, "Stand up and hook up!"

Burdened with their parachutes and tight harnesses, the men struggled to stand up before attaching the snap hook at the end of their static lines to the anchor cable that ran overhead the length of the cabin. They then moved toward the door, with the first man taking his position in the door. Beside him, kneeling, was the jumpmaster. When he was happy the plane was in position, he tapped the jumper and yelled "Go!"

Crossing his arms over his chest, the jumper was supposed to *step* out of the door, left foot first. On no account was he to leap.

The next man moved into position and the procedure was repeated. "The noise and the wind were overwhelming," recalled one parachutist, "as I grasped the door frame with my fingers wrapped around the edges and my toes over the sill so as to make a strong exit, all the while mustering my courage to go when the tap came, and it soon did. I pushed out as strongly as I could. I felt the static line pulling loose from its retaining bands as I gave the count aloud, then came the jarring opening shock. After that, peace and quiet. I was floating free in a most peaceful, quiet sky."[7]

One after another, the jumpers exited the plane. Percy Crichlow, the slightly built teacher from Barbados, was number one in his stick. He knew that it was impossible for him *not* to jump because the "big Texan" behind him was so anxious to get out that "he seemed to be ready to push me ahead of him if necessary." He leapt.[8]

So too did Callowhill, but in the process his knee came up and struck his nose, causing blood to stream down his face as he floated to earth at a speed of 18 to 20 miles per hour. It took the men less than a minute to descend from their altitude of 1,200 feet.[9] The only danger now was the landing. At the last moment it seemed as if the ground was rushing toward them. They had been taught to pull on the risers just before contact and to roll in the direction of the parachute's drift. But not everyone got it right. Of the 257 Canadian officers and men who jumped on the 15th, 11 were injured on landing (4.3 percent) and 6 refused to jump. The casualty percentage was, however, lower than that suffered by American Forceman a day or two earlier when 34 of 381 jumpers (8.9 percent) were hospitalized.[10]

Among the US injured was 1-2 Company's Ray Holbrook, the former lumberjack from Washington State, who sprained his right knee on landing. "It is still a little stiff today," he wrote to his 16-year-old sister, Gladys, "but I hope to jump again tomorrow or Tuesday. I was sure scared stiff when I made my first jump but I made it and I am determined to make the second one, too. They say after the second jump it isn't so hard to step out of a plane. A man has to be a little bit barmy to step out the first time."[11]

One soldier obviously thought so, because he froze in the door and would not move. Eventually the jumpmaster grabbed him and threw him to the back of the plane, where he remained, hands and feet still spread apart, "petrified in that position." Next in line was 31-year-old Private Walter "Pop" Lewis—a mining engineer and graduate of Washington State College from Butte, Montana—who had the sense "not to look down" before he was tapped. He "went out, did a beautiful turn, and the chute opened as pretty as can be."[12]

The men had been instructed to count to three, and if at that point their main canopy had not opened, they were to use their reserve chutes. So Joe Dauphinais, the former miner from Manitoba, did just that: "Thousand one, thousand two, thousand three." Nothing. But instead of deploying the reserve, he wasted precious seconds by craning his head up to see what was happening. As he did so, the main canopy popped out and almost tore his head off. Badly shaken, he could feel the parachute oscillating as he swung from side to side. He knew he was descending too fast and tried to control the chute by yanking on the risers, but this caused the swing to worsen, and the parachute eventually struck the ground first, followed by Dauphinais. "*Bam!*" he recalled. "Holy shit, was that ever a tough landing." Fortunately nothing was broken and, after a stern talking-to, Dauphinais was allowed to jump a second time—this time without incident.[13]

Jack Callowhill's second leap was even more painful than the first. Caught by a gust of wind, he landed on his shoulder and was taken to the hospital on the base with a suspected dislocation. After a brief examination, the medical officer asked him: "Okay, you had enough?"

The young Canadian was flummoxed. "What do you mean, enough?"

"Well, you got hurt. So is that it?"

"No. I'm fine. I want to stay."

They let him. But an officer who was brought in at the same time was not so lucky. He was in "real agony," having failed to buckle his parachute tightly enough, and when they took his clothes off, Callowhill could see "every stitch in the cotton and the belts" imprinted on his body. "I don't remember his name," said Callowhill, "but that was the last of him. If you can't follow instructions, you're gone."[14]

By the end of the month, more than 1,200 Forcemen had completed the two jumps necessary for parachute qualification. But many others had been returned to their units for refusing two chances to jump. The Canadian total, alone, was 176 rejects* (including one officer), the majority of whom had lost their nerve. "It is," reported Lieutenant-Colonel McQueen, "imperative that such personnel leave this Force immediately in the interest of the morale of the remainder of the troops."[15]

The successful jumpers included Lorin Waling, a 20-year-old private from the Peace Country of northern Alberta. The eldest of four children, Waling was just 15 when his blacksmith father left home and he became, by default, the family's main breadwinner. He got work as a manual laborer and, in his spare time, drank excessively and hung out with the "wrong sort of people." It was almost a relief for his mother when he enlisted in 1940. By the summer of 1942, however, he was bored with garrison life in Petawawa, Ontario, and tried to join the US Army in Detroit. But he was turned back at the border and visited a nearby girlfriend instead.[16] On returning to his unit, he was

---

* By the end of November 1942, a total of 9 officers and 326 Canadian servicemen had been rejected by the Force: 193 were "afraid to jump"; 70 were "injured"; 42 left for "medical reasons"; 26 were "undesirables"; 3 were "deserters"; and 1 was "under age."

given a month in the jug for being absent without leave (AWOL).*
Three weeks in, he told his family: "I have learned my lesson...Never
again in here for me."[17]

Waling was as good as his word. But he was still keen to go overseas
and "couldn't volunteer fast enough" when he heard about the Force.
They were looking for hunters and outdoorsmen, and this is what he
had done as a kid: "fished, hunted, trapped, and shot squirrels during the Depression." It was an ideal fit, but his chief motivation was
"to get the hell out of Petawawa."[18] Once through jump training, he
wrote to his mother:

> I have done it safely and I sure am proud...Yesterday we
> had a big parade and received our wings. There were over a
> thousand of us who had qualified and the colonel went to
> each man, pinned his badge or wings on, shook hands and
> congratulated him. Just imagine shaking hands with over 1000
> persons in a period of three hours. I sure wish I could send
> you a pair of wings but we are only given one set and can't get
> another as yet anyway. It sure is an honour to be able to wear
> one. They are made of sterling silver and have a pair of wings
> with a chute in the middle.[19]

Even before jump training ended, the Forcemen had been formally
organized into companies of 70 or so men. Second Lieutenant Bill
Rothlin, the former metalworker from Berkeley, California, was given
1-2 Company, one of three in Captain Tom MacWilliam's 1/2nd
Battalion. MacWilliam's immediate boss as commander of the 2nd
Regiment was Don Williamson, promoted lieutenant-colonel after
McQueen broke his leg and now the senior Canadian in the combat
echelon. A 35-year-old married father of two, Williamson had owned

---

* "Jug" is North American slang for military prison; in the British Army it is
  known as the "glasshouse" or "choky."

and managed a laundry in his native Brantford, Ontario, before the war. But he had always maintained an interest in the military, first as a cadet, then a militiaman and, from 1940, a member of the Dufferin and Haldimand Rifles. A promising officer with a good command of administrative detail, Williamson was originally selected to act as a liaison officer between Force HQ in Washington, DC, and the Canadian military. But when the latter realized that good Canadian officers were needed to help train the fledgling Force, Williamson was added to its strength. Tall and well built, with dark hair and brown eyes, he certainly cut a commanding figure. However, even from the earliest days, some of his colleagues harbored doubts about his temperament. After his leg break, McQueen considered Major Robert Keane more levelheaded than Williamson and better suited to become the senior Canadian. But when Keane also injured himself parachuting, Williamson got the job. Soon after, McQueen informed Ottawa that his replacement had a "great amount of drive and energy in his duties…and is doing a satisfactory job." He felt, moreover, that Williamson's judgment was "sound" and that his impulsive tendencies would be curbed by the "added responsibility and experience."[20]

Williamson's 2nd Regiment was made up of two battalions, the 1st and 2nd, which in turn were subdivided into three companies (six in total). The companies were numbered 1-2, 2-2, 3-2 (1st Battalion), 4-2, 5-2 and 6-2 (2nd Battalion). All companies had three platoons, each commanded by a junior officer. The odd one out in Rothlin's 1-2 Company was Lieutenant Tom Gordon of 2nd Platoon, who was for a while senior in rank to his company commander. This had come about because Gordon, though just 22 years old, had been commissioned for longer than Rothlin and the other two platoon leaders. Born in St. Catharines, a small city close to Niagara Falls in southern Ontario, Gordon had soldiering in the blood: his accountant father had been injured in the First World War battle of Vimy Ridge, and young Tom had accompanied him to France for the unveiling of a memorial to mark this famous Canadian victory in 1936. A year later, during a period of turbulence in his parents' marriage, he was sent to St. Andrew's College, a prestigious university-preparatory (or "prep") school north of Toronto, where he excelled at rugby and won the J. L. Wright Cup for the Best Upper School Cadet. He went on to Queen's University in Kingston, Ontario, and, like MacWilliam, joined the COTC. He had only recently been promoted to First Lieutenant when he volunteered for the Force. A gifted athlete and sportsman who loved the outdoors, he was keen to get into action "sooner rather than later."[21]

Interestingly, only one officer in Gordon's chain of command up to regimental commander—his company commander, Bill Rothlin— was an American. But Canadians were not so well represented among the senior enlisted men of 1-2 Company: just the first sergeant and one of the six section commanders were from Canada; the rest were American (though this would change). As throughout the Force, 1-2 Company's platoons contained a mixture of both nationalities. Assigned to 1st Platoon were Sergeant Percy Crichlow and Private Ken Betts, 32, an itinerant orphan from Derry, Pennsylvania, who had volunteered for the extra jump pay.[22] "They were," thought Crichlow, "a mixed crowd, but good soldiers—every single one of them—and I was as happy in that platoon as I have been anywhere."[23] Young Bob Davis from North Carolina, Jack Callowhill and his American tentmate Clyde Spofford were in Gordon's 2nd Platoon, while the 3rd Platoon included Canadians Don MacKinnon, Lorin Waling and Joe Dauphinais, and Americans Ray Holbrook, Howard Van Ausdale and Walter "Pop" Lewis. All had qualified as parachutists, an achievement that, according to the company history, contributed more than anything else to "moulding the men together."[24]

A typical day for Rothlin's men began with the sounding of reveille at sunrise. Soon after, Tom Gordon expected the men of his 2nd Platoon to be on parade for roll call. But according to Jack Callowhill, the attendance at platoon roll call was poor: "There was no one there, or hardly anyone. A few guys were there with blankets round them.

But everyone else was in their huts." Eventually Gordon gave up and allowed roll call to be taken in the huts. It was the job of section commander Staff Sergeant Art Schumm, who slept by the door, to do this. "In the morning," recalled Callowhill, "he would reach over, grab the roll and call your name. You'd say: 'Here.' When he'd finished, we'd all roll over and go back to sleep."[25]

But not for long, because by 6:30 a.m. the whole company had breakfasted, cleaned their quarters and were "bending at calisthenics." By 8:00 a.m. the men had gone through a circuit of the mile-and-a-quarter obstacle course "on the run." Then training began in earnest—both physical and in the use of weapons—breaking for lunch at noon and continuing from 1:00 p.m. to 5:00 p.m. On four nights a week there were lectures.[26]

The need for urgency and precision was drilled into the men. All marching was done at 140 steps a minute—as opposed to the US Army standard of 120—and movement from one drill or training field to the next was always at the double. The reason for putting the men through such a brutal physical training program was to produce a level of general fitness and stamina that would enable them to withstand even the severest demands made upon them by the "fatigue of combat, unfavorable terrain or adverse weather." It consisted chiefly of "crawling, rope climbing, boxing, push-ups, games, much doubling and running."[27]

The men of 1-2 Company ran everywhere, including up "Muscle Mountain," the steep-sided hill that flanked Mount Helena to the southeast of the camp. It was a grueling one-and-a-half-hour ordeal, but many of the men chose to scale it in their spare time. Just as "deadly," particularly to the older Forcemen like Howard Van Ausdale, "Pop" Lewis and Percy Crichlow, were the forced marches of up to 30 miles under full combat loads. "When it came to running," noted Lewis, "that thirty-one years told on me."[28] The aim was to get every officer and enlisted man running a mile in under ten minutes. Soon most could do it in seven, while a few dipped under five and a half minutes. The idea for an obstacle course, not generally used by the US Army, had come from the Canadians. It contained the usual "hand-over-hand, rope climbing and eight-foot walls," and took at least an hour and a half to complete. It was, stated the Canadians' monthly report, the "Grand-Daddy" of all obstacle courses.[29]

8

"Everybody fought somebody"

Toward the end of August 1942, 1-2 Company began weapon training. This involved stripping and firing a host of American and German weapons. The original plan was to issue every Forceman with the brand-new .30-caliber semiautomatic Winchester M1 carbine, effective at 300 yards and weighing just over five pounds. "I fired the new US caliber 30 carbine yesterday," wrote Ray Holbrook to his sister Gladys on August 23, "and it is a sweet little gun. It fires and feels like a .22 but has the punch of a military weapon. I hadn't seen the gun before except in pictures."[1]

But the decision was quickly made to replace the carbine as the Forceman's main weapon with the heavier gas-operated .30 M1 Garand, the first standard-issue semiautomatic military rifle, because the latter was "much superior in range, hitting power and proven ability to 'take it.'" It also used the same cartridge as a number of other US weapons—which the carbine did not—and therefore simplified the ammunition supply. Weighing nine and a half pounds, the Garand could rapidly fire a clip of eight bullets, one after the other, by repeated pulls on the trigger. Once the last bullet had been fired, the clip would drop out and the bolt lock open, ready to be reloaded. This gave it a much higher rate of fire than the bolt-action weapons still in use by British, Canadian and German armies. For this reason most of the Canadian Forcemen welcomed the M1, though it was slightly heavier than the Lee-Enfield. Its one slight defect, according to Jack Callowhill, was that "in the cold you had to keep the sliding action well lubricated or it would stick." That aside, it was a fine weapon, one of the best small arms of the conflict: well constructed, durable and easy to operate and maintain. All Forcemen became expert in its use, with and without its 16-inch (later 10-inch) bayonet, though the officers would continue to carry the M1 carbine.[2]

The Forcemen also became familiar with the .45 Thompson sub-machine gun (the "tommy gun"), weighing 11 pounds and fed by detachable 20- and 30-round magazines. The favored weapon of gangsters in the 1930s, the tommy gun was an excellent close-quarter weapon because of its heavy slug and high rate of fire — 700 rounds a minute. It could be fired in semi- and fully automatic modes and had a shoulder stock and hand grip to improve its accuracy. Yet because it was relatively heavy, expensive and ineffective at long range, it was only carried by section commanders.

Other weapons included the tripod-mounted and belt-fed .30 M1919 Browning medium machine gun, weighing 45 pounds (with the tripod) and firing up to 600 rounds a minute. This was an air-cooled mobile support weapon, issued one per section and crewed by two Forcemen — one to fire and one to load — while other men helped to carry extra ammunition. One 3rd Platoon man who needed no instruction in the Browning was 27-year-old Private Ray Kushi from Pittsfield in rural western Massachusetts. Dark haired and well built, Kushi was one of 11 children born to a Pittsfield factory worker and his stay-at-home wife. From the age of six, Kushi had worked in a grocery store to help supplement the family income. A natural entre-preneur with a high IQ, Kushi did well at school before continuing on to a local business college to learn accounting. At 17 he started his own oil delivery company—Ray's Oil—carrying 50-pound buckets of oil from his van to the customer's tanks. This combination of "physical strength, mental discipline and intelligence, and fearless attitude" made him a perfect fit for the Force, as did the excellent record he had compiled as a machine-gun instructor and sharpshooter at Camp Edwards, Massachusetts.

Kushi also had experience using the much lighter .30 M1918 Browning Automatic Rifle (BAR). Designed to be carried by infantrymen during an assault, it could fire at 600 rounds a minute from either the shoulder or the hip. Yet its 20-round box magazine meant it needed constant replenishment, and the Canadians complained that its bipod legs collapsed and its long barrel got caught in brush. One dubbed it "worse than useless to a unit like the Force." What was "really needed," he thought, was the Czech-designed Bren light machine gun, then standard issue in Commonwealth armies. The BAR would eventually be supplemented in the Force by a lighter, more versatile weapon developed for the US Marines: the Johnson light machine gun (the "Johnny" gun).[3]

Unusually for the US military, each Forceman would carry, in addition to his rifle, a .45 semiautomatic M1911 pistol. Based on a pre–World War One design, it weighed less than two and a half pounds and was recoil operated, firing repeated single shots from a seven-round detachable magazine. The Forceman's other close-quarter weapon was a fighting knife, the V-42, that Frederick and his staff had helped to design. Sent three prototypes by different cutlery companies, Frederick chose the one made by W. R. Case & Sons of Bradford, Pennsylvania, and promptly ordered 1,750. He also requested a leather sheath that would "hang low on the leg" and be accessible below a winter parka. The sheath was later lined with metal after "countless" Forcemen were injured when the needlelike tip penetrated both the leather and their flesh during training.[4] Similar to the Fairbairn-Sykes knife used by British commandos, the V-42 featured a seven-inch double-edged stiletto blade, made of high-carbon

steel, and a leather-bound handle with a pointed skull-crushing pom-
mel (the latter suggested by Major Orval Baldwin, the supply officer).
A vicious cutting and thrusting weapon that could easily penetrate
leather, heavy clothing and even thin metal, the V-42's only drawback
was that its tip would sometimes get stuck in human bone, making it
difficult to withdraw.

The men of 1-2 Company also learned to strip and operate the
principal weapons of the German Wehrmacht, including the 9mm
MP 40 Schmeisser machine pistol, the 7.92mm Mauser bolt-action
rifle (effective to 800 yards), the PzB 39 anti-tank rifle, and the versatile belt- or drum-fed 7.92 MG 34 all-purpose machine gun, light
enough to be carried by one man but which could fire a blistering
900 rounds per minute and was effective at distances of up to 2,000
yards.[5] Their familiarity with these weapons would be extremely useful when the Forcemen eventually saw action.

Other weapons they learned to use later in the autumn included
the new M1A1 anti-tank rocket launcher known as the bazooka,
weighing just 13 pounds and firing a 2.36-inch high-explosive M6
projectile that could penetrate two inches of armor plate; the M2
60mm light mortar, weighing 42 pounds, operated by a three-man
team and firing three-pound high-explosive smoke and illumination
rounds over a distance of a mile; and the M1 portable flamethrower,
capable of shooting burning napalm (thickened fuel) from a five-
gallon tank at a short range of just 16 yards. It was almost certainly the
heavy 72-pound M1 flamethrower, as yet unused in combat,[*] that Ray
Holbrook was referring to when he told his sister they were due to fire
another "secret weapon."[6]

Joe Dauphinais was amazed by the Force's spendthrift attitude toward ammunition. In Canada he had fired "about five shots a year"
from a .22 Enfield or a .303 Ross rifle. In the Force there was "no

---

[*]   The M1 flamethrower was first used in combat against the Japanese in the
      Pacific in December 1942.

limit." The instructors would, he recalled, "let you take the guns out and shoot the hell out of them any time you wanted." If you did not have money to spend in town, you could "pick up a rifle and a few hundred rounds and go up in the mountains to shoot."[7]

Frederick and his HQ staff were constantly on the lookout for new weapons. They even considered using poisonous darts. By enabling the Forcemen to kill silently and from a distance, wrote Robert Burhans, the dart would be a "symbol of our new superiority over the deadly German craft, even as much as our operation surpasses in conception anything the Germans have ever conjured up."[8] Evidently, Frederick did not agree, because the dart idea was never taken up.

As well as learning about weapons, the men of 1-2 Company were taught armed and unarmed combat by former Shanghai policeman Dermot "Pat" O'Neill, the man recommended to Frederick by the OSS. Born in County Cork, Ireland, in 1905, the son of a police inspector, O'Neill had crewed a steamer before jumping ship at Shanghai, where his brother worked for a bank in the International Settlement. There, at the age of 20, he joined the Shanghai Municipal Police (SMP), quickly rising to sergeant and then subinspector in the Special Branch. He became a protégé of William E. Fairbairn,* the former British Royal Marine who as a Shanghai patrolman had learned the Japanese martial arts of jujitsu and judo before developing his own method of close-quarter combat known as Defendu. O'Neill also became expert in Eastern martial arts and was handpicked by Fairbairn to train the SMP's anti-riot "Reserve Unit." He later moved to Tokyo for a three-year stint as the British Legation's head of security and left shortly before the attack on Pearl Harbor. He

---

* Having retired from the Shanghai Municipal Police in 1940 with the rank of assistant commissioner, Fairbairn taught close-combat, pistol-shooting and knife-fighting techniques to British commandos and OSS operatives. "There's no fair play," he declared, "no rules except one: *kill or be killed*." With fellow close-combat instructor Eric Sykes, he designed the Fairbairn-Sykes fighting knife used by British commandos.

was teaching unarmed combat to OSS operatives at a training base in Ontario, Canada, when Frederick asked for his services. Keen to instruct larger groups, he jumped at the chance.[9]

Tall and broad-shouldered, his roguishly handsome face only slightly disfigured by a broken nose, O'Neill was a master of what one Forceman described as "the 'kick and poke' school of mayhem": the use of vicious kicks, gouges and punches into the vulnerable points of the body—particularly the groin, eyes, nose and throat—to disable an opponent. "I am not here to teach you how to hurt," he would tell each new class of Forcemen. "I'm here to teach you how to kill!"[10] That included instruction with a garotte, a wire with a toggle at each end, and the V-42 knife. The trick with the latter was to use the thumbprint on the top of the blade to keep it flat so it could slide between the ribs and reach the heart. Otherwise it could get stuck in the ribs. When reversing the knife and using the skull crusher, the most vulnerable target, said O'Neill, was either temple. A separate technique, to be used on sentries, was "coming up behind a guy, grabbing his helmet, pulling his head back, and using the knife to cut his throat."[11]

To make the training as lifelike as possible, O'Neill got the men to practice knife and bayonet fighting with real blades. Even Colonel Frederick took part, once nicking his executive officer and former West Point classmate, Lieutenant Colonel Paul D. Adams, in the neck. Frederick "was tough," noted Adams.[12] By the end of O'Neill's training, the men knew "how to kill easily using our hands, our feet, and utilizing the knife."[13] Lorin Waling told his mother: "We don't take jujitsu but learn how to counter it and believe me it's not what you call clean fighting."[14]

The cumulative effect of all this intensive training was that the men of 1-2 Company got leaner, fitter and stronger. "I am solid muscle and must weigh 165 pounds now," Waling informed his family at the end of August.[15] Joe Dauphinais had arrived as a 165-pound "butterball," but the fat soon turned to muscle. He was eating as well as he ever had, with huge breakfasts of bacon, eggs, toast and cereal, and "three or four different kinds of meat" for lunch and dinner. "You could pig out at every meal," he recalled, "but when they saw you stuffing your face like that, they would give you a couple of hours of physical training." That cured the gluttons, who thereafter took only what they needed.[16]

To let off steam, Forcemen drank beer at ten cents a bottle at the camp canteen known as the post exchange (or PX). It was, noted Lorin Waling, cheaper than in Canada "but the bottles are smaller and the beer is only 1/3 as strong."[17] On weekends, they headed for the many bars and whorehouses on Helena's main street, Last Chance Gulch, where the first gold had been prospected in 1864. In the early days, before they were all issued with the same uniform, the Canadian and American Forcemen would swap hats and tunics in an attempt to fool MPs into thinking they were beyond their jurisdiction. "It was somewhat unsettling," recalled a Canadian Forceman, "to hear a Tennessee or Texas accent coming from under a tam-o'-shanter, or a French-Canadian accent from a soldier wearing a cavalry patch."[18]

A favorite watering hole was the Gold Bar, where Forcemen mixed with local cowboys, lumberjacks and miners. Inevitably fights broke out, and not just between Forcemen and locals. "Everybody fought somebody," remembered Ken Betts. "Americans fought Canadians, Canadians fought Americans, we all fought civilians." Hyped up from their training, and keen to test out their hand-to-hand combat skills, the Forcemen enjoyed "getting into a real good fight without any trouble."[19] Sometimes these barroom brawls got out of hand and windows were broken. After it had happened a third time, the Force's provost marshal promised the owner of the Gold Bar that he would find the men responsible and make them pay damages. The owner laughed. "Hey, I sell whiskey in this place and your men come in here, and whiskey tends to excite some people. So I just figure a broken window is part of my overhead."[20]

Occasionally the Forcemen took the bus as far as Butte, a tough copper-mining town 60 miles south of Helena, where there were no MPs to break up the fights. "We looked for them," remembered Lorin Waling, "and they looked for us, just to test our fighting abilities." According to Jack Callowhill, it was only the copper miners of Butte who got the better of the Forcemen in a scrap: "The guys never went back."[21]

Not that the men of 1-2 Company always had to leave camp to release their aggression. One afternoon, Canadian Joe Dauphinais was approaching the door to his hut* when his way was barred by Johnny Walter, a "real cowboy type" from Ekalaka, Montana, who was in the same section. "I don't like your face!" exclaimed Walter.

"Well then…change it!"

The pair set to, though Dauphinais was slightly disadvantaged by the fact that he was wearing his dress uniform—which he had just picked up from the cleaners—while Walter was in coveralls. When the fight was over, it looked like Dauphinais had "tangled with a bloody bear." Walter's injuries were almost as bad. But there were no hard feelings. "It was just having fun," recalled Dauphinais, "trying out our unarmed combat on one another."[22]

When they were not drinking and fighting, the Forcemen chased women—or were themselves pursued by some of the more brazen local girls who, deprived of the town's young men (most of whom had joined the 163rd Infantry), were delighted by the sudden influx of new blood. Dauphinais was sitting in a bar with a colleague when two beers arrived, quickly followed by the girls who had paid for them. The Forcemen were wearing their new dress uniform of smart buttoned-up tunic worn over a shirt and tie, with a striking red, white and blue lanyard, or shoulder rope, that was looped through the left

---

* The Forcemen moved from their four-man tents to huts with stoves that could accommodate 12, or a whole section, in late September.

epaulet and under the arm.[*] On the right shoulder was the unit patch: a red spearhead surcharged with a white USA running horizontally and, below it, a vertical CANADA, also in white. The prized parachute pin was on the left breast, above the pocket, while on each lapel was a gold button. The one on the left was superimposed with crossed arrows, the insignia of the old Indian Scouts; the one on the right denoted the soldier's nationality, either US or CANADA. It was toward this button on Dauphinais's lapel that one of the girls pointed. "What's that Canada thing?" she asked.

"Oh, I'm from Canada."

"But you speak English!"

"So?"

"But you're all French up there!"

"That's news to me!"

Later, Dauphinais and his pal met in the bathroom and switched buttons, causing the perplexed girls to exclaim: "Who the hell are you?"[23]

For those Forcemen happy to pay for sex, Ida's Rooms on Last Chance Gulch was a favored hangout. One of 2nd Platoon's regulars was Californian Paul Barnhizer, recruited like a number of other 1-2 Company men from the 15th Infantry at Fort Ord. A professional gambler before the war, Barnhizer "played everything and made a lot of money," which is probably why he could afford to spend so much time in a brothel—that and the fact that he and Ida eventually became an item. Even after the Force had left town, Ida would write to Barnhizer—and enclosed in each letter was a $100 bill.[24] One Forceman not missed by Ida was a member of 1st Platoon who was thrown out for "pissing in the potted plant in the reception room."[25] On a sep-

---

[*] Frederick had introduced this lanyard to replace the many shoulder ropes in different colors that the Canadians were used to wearing. The men were charged 90 cents per lanyard, and when one complained, Frederick responded that he could not *make* the men buy them, but that "nobody leaves this post unless he is wearing one" (Hicks, pp. 73–74).

arate occasion, another 1st Platoon man called Lew Weldon ("a kind of Canadian Buster Keaton in appearance") caused "a bit of a stir" by standing outside a restaurant and loudly announcing "that all steaks served that night were on the house." Only when the restaurant was full of people ordering steaks did Weldon clear off "before the truth became known and the numerous arguments started." The cerebral Percy Crichlow preferred the more sedate pleasures of the movie theater, though even he spent a few evenings in the Club Lounge, the Gold Bar and the Placer Hotel with "friends from the platoon and a few student nurses."[26]

A few of the married officers were joined at Helena by their wives. They included Tom MacWilliam, who taught his wife, Bobby, to use a pistol so that she could shoot a rattlesnake if she encountered one. "It really was," commented her son, "the Wild West." All officers were made honorary members of the well-appointed Montana Club, an imposing five-story triangular-shaped building on Helena's Sixth Avenue that contained a library, a bar and a dining room. "I often had Saturday-night dinner there," noted one officer, "and my usual order, a large T-bone steak." The one oddity about the club was that the tiles on the floor of its entrance hall were decorated with swastika-like symbols. But unlike the clockwise Aryan symbol adopted by the Nazis, these were counterclockwise and derived from Native American designs that were said to represent friendship and well-being.[27]

9

Waling and Glass

One of many young Forcemen adopted by local families was Lorin Waling. He and fellow 3rd Platoon man Walter Wolf from Millington, New Jersey, were invited to the ranch of a young couple and given a slap-up dinner. "They cooked us each a chicken," Waling told his mother, "and we ate them along with about ten cobs of corn. All in all we had a swell time." Invited back, Waling fell for his host's cousin, who was "a lot of fun." They arranged to meet at the Casino Bar in East Helena, a tiny smelter settlement of fewer than 1,200 souls.

Arriving first, Waling noticed a cute brunette with a broad smile sitting with a blonde friend and a dark-haired corporal from the Force. Intrigued, he sat down beside the girl and discovered that her name was Steffie Broderick. Next to her was her best friend, Dorothy "Dot" Strainer. They were both in their late teens and worked at Eddy's Bakery. Dot had met the corporal, Joe Glass, in the Casino Bar a week earlier, and they were on their first date. Which meant, Waling realized, that Steffie was not spoken for. He was delighted. His only problem now was what to do with his own date: he solved it by palming her off on a sergeant from his platoon who was also in the bar.[1]

After that first meeting with Steffie, Waling was smitten, and all thoughts of other women, including the girlfriend he had left behind in Grand Prairie (the sister of a fellow Forceman), were banished from his mind. He and Glass spent every evening they could with the girls, and they soon became best pals. At six feet one inch tall, Waling was a forehead taller than Glass but not so heavily built and two years younger. They came, moreover, from very different backgrounds. Waling was the son of a drifter and sometime mechanic who had grown up on the prairies of Alberta. Glass's upbringing was more conventional and less hand-to-mouth. Born in the small city of Sarnia, Ontario, at the southern tip of Lake Huron, he was descended from a long line of Great Lakes shipmasters, and the sea was in his blood. As a young scout he "learned to handle canoes, outboard motor boats, sailing and the outdoor skills of hunting, fishing, camping, hiking and everything that goes with conquering the great outdoors." Strong and fit, he also tried boxing, but a broken nose soon convinced him that being a lover "was much more pleasant."

Not that Glass shied away from danger. One of three boys, he was forever getting into dangerous scrapes, such as the time he and a friend were crossing the ice bridge between Point Edward and Port Huron, Michigan, when the section they were on broke away and they were saved from drowning by the last ferry of the night. The one dark cloud on his childhood horizon was the gradual realization that his family was poor. "The depression years were bad," he remembered. "Dad lost any money he'd managed to invest and all his property." It got so bad that the family moved in with their Glass grandparents and, to help out, young Joe would scrounge for coal that had fallen from passing trains.

For all his love of the outdoors, Glass also enjoyed school and was forever nose-deep in a book. But economic necessity forced him to drop out of high school and find work, first as a butcher's assistant

and then an ice cutter. In 1936, at the age of 16, he joined the crew
of a Buffalo-based ore freighter, quickly rising to the rank of junior
officer. When war broke out three years later, he "couldn't wait to
get in" and tried to join the navy. Stymied by color blindness, it was
not until late 1940 that he was accepted into the Kent Regiment.
Keen to see action, Glass was frustrated by a series of postings across
Canada and then, in 1942, a job as a bayonet instructor at Lansdowne
Barracks, Ottawa. He was, however, in just the right place when the
call went out for volunteers to join a special parachute unit. He put
his name forward because he knew it would get him into combat "a
little quicker." Even the offer of a commission could not get him to
change his mind. He had "had enough of waiting to get into the big
show."[2]

What Glass and Waling had in common, as well as a thirst to
see action, was an insatiable appetite for training—particularly the
physical aspect. Now, having fallen for two best friends, they spent
most of their leisure time together as well.[3] They met up with Dot
and Steffie not only on weekends but also on weeknights, when
they would sneak over the wire at the back of camp and head for
the airstrip where the girls were waiting in a car they had borrowed
from Steffie's sister. They then drove to East Helena and danced
the night away in the Casino Bar or Tivoli Tavern to songs by
Glenn Miller and Tommy Dorsey. Joe and Dot's personal favorite
was "For Me and My Gal" by Judy Garland and Gene Kelly, the
title song of a popular musical film released that year. The boys
usually drank a Coke Highball (whiskey and Coke) or Whiskey
Ditch (whiskey and water); the girls stuck to soft drinks. At 1:00
a.m. Steffie and Dot went home and the boys grabbed a few hours'
rest in the town jail, courtesy of the local sheriff, before getting an
early morning lift to the base in the back of a milk truck. It was
never checked at the gate.

Eventually Bill Rothlin got to hear of these unauthorized excur-
sions and, in an attempt to put a stop to them, moved Waling to a

different hut and often checked up on Glass after lights-out. Poking his head in the hut, he would say: "You still here, Glass?"

"Yes, sir."

"Good night, Glass."

"Good night, sir."

Minutes later, Glass would be up and on his way to meet Waling.[4] The Albertan had endured a tough childhood, forced to take responsibility for his family when he was still a boy. Despite this, he was an open and affectionate character who preferred to look forward rather than back. He was even prepared to build bridges with his feckless father, then living in Washington State. "I am going to fly to Seattle," he wrote to his mother in late August, "and see 'Dad' if I get leave that is too short to get home on."

It only costs around $40 or $50 to Seattle and back. Boy I sure would like to see him and I imagine he would sure like to see me too. I am sorry to hear he has been sick again…Say by the way, does Dad write anymore often than he used to and when he is working does he send money? I'm not trying to pry into your affairs but I done my best to induce him to do better. I will also try and persuade him to go home if you want me to. I sure hope I can get to see him before I go over or into action.[5]

September 1942 saw the arrival at Fort Harrison of two officers who would play a central role in the Force story: Lieutenant Ed Thomas and Second Lieutenant Larry Piette. Thomas, 23, was the first to arrive. A native of South Carolina, he had attended Alabama Polytechnic Institute (later Auburn University) and Georgia Tech, graduating from the latter with an engineering degree and an army reserve commission a few months before his call-up in January 1941. While training at the Fort Benning Infantry School, Thomas heard about the recently formed Parachute Test Platoon and applied to join. Accepted in July, he was enrolled in Class 5 of the parachute school.

He qualified in August, after a five-week course and six jumps, and was assigned to the 503rd Parachute Battalion, commanded by Major Robert Sink (who, as Colonel Sink, would lead the 506th Parachute Infantry Regiment in northwest Europe, the legendary unit featured in Stephen E. Ambrose's *Band of Brothers*). For a time his company commander was Captain James M. Gavin,* "a fine leader" who taught Thomas "much in the short time we were together."

Thomas had only recently been appointed a company commander of the new 505th Parachute Infantry Regiment, raised by Gavin, when he received orders from the War Department to report to the First Special Service Force, "a strange unit" he had never heard of. He became, therefore, one of only a very few members of the Force who did not volunteer. He attributed his posting to Lieutenant Colonel Shinberger, whom he knew from Fort Benning. Arriving at Fort Harrison by taxi in early September, Thomas felt a sense of "anticipation and apprehension" as he was deposited outside the headquarters building, which was marked by two flags: the Stars and Stripes and the Union Flag (then serving as the Dominion colors of Canada). With Frederick absent in Washington, DC, he was introduced to Shinberger, who gave him a "hearty welcome," and the adjutant Wickham, who told him of his assignment: executive officer (XO) of the 2nd Regiment's 2nd Battalion (2/2nd). As an XO was senior to a company commander, a position Thomas had held for only a few weeks, he felt more than a little disoriented by his sudden elevation. "My cultural shock was beginning," he recorded, "and there was much more to come."

Chief among the many differences that Thomas noticed between the Force and any other unit he had served in was "Colonel Frederick's power to get equipment, even specialized equipment,

---

* In August 1944, at the age of 37, Gavin was promoted major general and given command of the 82nd Airborne Division. He was the US Army's youngest two-star general of World War II; Robert T. Frederick was the second youngest.

quickly and in plenteous quantity." This included a brand-new explosive, Ryan's Special (known as RS), that was "more powerful than dynamite," silk underwear to ward off the cold—an item that Thomas had not seen in the army before and "never saw again"—and eiderdown-filled sleeping bags.[6]

A week or so after Thomas's arrival, nine newly commissioned second lieutenants flew in to Helena from the Engineer Officer Candidate School at Fort Belvoir, Virginia, to replace officers sent back to their units. Top of the OCS "Final Selection" list was 25-year-old Larry Piette from Appleton, Wisconsin, a small city on the Fox River known for its paper mills and as the site of the nation's first hydroelectric power station. Larry was one of seven children—four boys and three girls—born to Charles and Josephine Piette, both Roman Catholics of French descent. Charles came from blue-collar stock: he worked as a millwright for the Fox Paper Company for 30 years and, until Larry, no member of the Piette family had ever graduated from high school, let alone college. Larry Piette did both and, according to his son, "he did so over his family's strong objections." The youngest by far of seven siblings—the next youngest, Madeleine, was eight when he was born—Piette was effectively brought up by his eldest sister, Mary. His brothers, the owners of a grocery store, wanted him "to stay at home and be productive for the family." But he chose to go to Lawrence University in Appleton, where he majored in psychology and graduated summa cum laude.[*]

In early 1941, Piette was earning a postgraduate degree in chemistry while still living at home and working part-time in his brothers' store, when he realized that his country's involvement in the war was inevitable sooner or later. So he abandoned his studies and joined the US Army Corps of Engineers as a private, receiving specialized training as a medic. His 72-year-old father had died in May 1940;

---

[*] Latin for "with the highest distinction." Today the equivalent would be a GPA of 3.9 or higher.

his mother went to the grave as he was training in July 1941, leaving Piette an orphan at the age of 24. En route to her funeral, Piette was introduced by Roman Catholic nuns to a "17-year-old beauty who was being raised on a sugar plantation" in St. Mary Parish, Louisiana. Her name was Marin deGravelles, one of eight children. She had large, green, widely spaced eyes, dark shoulder-length hair and even white teeth. Piette was instantly smitten and asked if he could write to her. She said yes, and they exchanged addresses. Piette himself was quite a catch: tall and broad-shouldered—six feet one and 175 pounds— he was all-American handsome with short dark hair, green eyes and a square jaw. Apart from long, slightly pointy ears, he was an impressive physical specimen, intelligent and serious-minded, and Marin was flattered by his attention.

In 1942, the army identified Piette's potential—recognizing in him "leadership, intelligence, wisdom, strength"—and sent him to OCS at Fort Belvoir. It was during this accelerated two-month training program that he saw the notice asking for people who could ski and were "used to cold temperatures" to volunteer for a new parachute unit. He did so because he thought it would be an "adventure" and because, despite his regular letters to Marin, he still thought of himself as unattached. He had "no parents," was unmarried and had no immediate plans to get hitched. "It sounded good," he recalled. "We were going to be a select group."[7]

On reaching Fort Harrison, Piette was assigned to 1-2 Company. But before he could take over his own platoon, he had to qualify as a parachutist and catch up with weapons and combat training. It was a hectic few weeks, but in the rare moments he had to himself, he wrote to the young plantation belle in Louisiana.

10

"Suspend effort on present line"

At 8:55 a.m. on Tuesday, September 15, 1942, a huge Sikorsky VS-44 four-engined flying boat took off from the seaport at La Guardia Field, New York City, and set a course for Newfoundland. One of three seaplanes owned by American Export Airlines that had recently been requisitioned for military use, the VS-44 could carry 11 crew and 40 passengers in cruise-ship standards of luxury that included full-length beds, dressing rooms, a galley, snack bar and lounge. Among the 12 pampered passengers on this trip to Ireland, via Canada, was Colonel Robert T. Frederick, traveling in civilian clothes and under an assumed name.

Frederick's destination was London, and his mission, as he explained it to General McNarney the day before, was to gauge "the attitude" of General Eisenhower, commanding the US Army's new European Theater of Operations (ETOUSA), and General Hansteen, the commander in chief of the Norwegian Army in exile, "towards the [Plough] project," now refined to an assault on multiple Norwegian hydroelectric power plants and industrial targets; to determine whether the British were going to cooperate fully by providing the intelligence that the Force needed; and to discuss "progress and planning" with Admiral Mountbatten. It was, responded McNarney, vital that Frederick's proposed mission had the support of both the UK and US military authorities in Britain because, once there, the Force would operate under Eisenhower's orders.

After a brief stop to refuel in Newfoundland, the plane flew on to Foynes on the west coast of Ireland, a 12-hour journey that was broken up by dinner and, for Frederick, a few hours' sleep in a "very comfortable" lower berth. The plane splashed down at 9:30 a.m. local time (4:30 Eastern War Time) on the 16th, and after breakfast in a local restaurant, the passengers were taken 40 miles by bus to Shannon Airport, where they boarded a BOAC plane, its windows blackened to avoid detection, for the short flight to Bristol Airport. Frederick finished his marathon 28½-hour journey to London by bus and train, arriving at Paddington Station at 6:30 in the evening. There he was allocated a "simple room" in Bailey's Hotel on Gloucester Road, Kensington.

Next morning, after an unsatisfactory breakfast of "oatmeal without sugar, milk or cream, a sausage and potatoes, a small roll and some poor coffee," Frederick went to see Eisenhower at his headquarters at 20 Grosvenor Square, an imposing redbrick mansion in the heart of Mayfair. He explained the purpose of his trip and the progress they were making back in the United States. But while Eisenhower seemed "interested," he could not see how "the project was within his province." Preoccupied as he was with the planning for Operation Torch—the forthcoming Allied invasion of Vichy territory in North Africa that had superseded the earlier Operation Gymnast—Eisenhower can be excused for not giving the project his full attention. But his lukewarm response was not a good sign, and the omens would not improve.

Frederick's next stop was the Combined Operations HQ at 1a Richmond Terrace, where he met Brigadier Wildman-Lushington, Mountbatten's "extremely pleasant" and helpful chief of staff, and then the boss himself. Mountbatten was supportive until Frederick asked about the availability of RAF aircraft to transport his men and vehicles to Norway.

"I don't know what you mean," responded the admiral, frowning. "When the project was first proposed to General Marshall, it was agreed that it would be American in its entirety. Moreover, Marshall gave the impression that there would be ample US aircraft in the British Isles to carry out the mission. It is, therefore, the responsibility of the US to provide the aircraft, and I don't see why an adequate number of the new C-54 Skymasters can't be allocated."

After lunching with Mountbatten and his wife, Edwina, Frederick went to General Hansteen's office, where Brigadier Colin Gubbins, the head of Britain's Special Operations Executive (SOE), was also waiting to meet him. For two hours they discussed the proposed mission and the list of possible targets. Hansteen came across as "a competent, intelligent officer" but one who was "naturally attempting to get all advantages at minimum cost to Norway." He agreed to examine the list and get back to Frederick. But he was noncommittal and "declined to promise" that the Force would be assisted by members of the Norwegian resistance. Gubbins was even less cooperative and insisted that his organization "would take care of all the worthwhile objectives" on the list.

The following day, Frederick appeared before the British Chiefs of Staff—Pound, Portal, Nye (standing in for Brooke) and Mountbatten—to present a paper on the Plough scheme. As Mountbatten had predicted, the response was unfavorable. Pound "said nothing," while the others questioned the American "in detail about C-54 production," suggesting that he ask the War Department "to increase the production rate" and make 50 to 100 planes available to the Force "for training and rehearsal." They were "friendly and pleasant," noted Frederick, "but obviously antagonistic to the project and particularly to the use of British aircraft." Portal's one concession was that he wanted to study Frederick's Norway plan in detail before he would even consider authorizing the diversion of British planes. But it was said in such a "supercilious" tone that Frederick held out little hope that any authorization would be forthcoming. Portal's final request—to be sent a dummy of the Weasel for "aerodynamic tests in British planes"—was almost an afterthought.[1]

Frederick's next appointment was with Major-General Andrew McNaughton, commanding Canadian troops in the UK, at his Surrey headquarters, Headley Manor, an hour's drive from London. McNaughton seemed "keen and interested" in the Plough Project and asked many questions about training and equipment. But he also urged Frederick to read his own plan for the capture of northern Norway that winter: Operation Jupiter. It was, he explained, an "extremely hazardous" mission that could either produce "quick and decisive local successes" or result in a "military disaster of the first magnitude." A lot would depend on luck. If it were to be authorized, he added, it would make sense to include the Force in its order of battle and land its "ploughs" by sea. Whatever was decided, he would "ask Ottawa to speed action on all matters pertaining to the Force."[2]

Frederick set off for home on September 19, but bad weather delayed him in Ireland and he returned to London on the 25th. There he received written confirmation from both Gubbins and Hansteen that the Force's proposed mission to Norway was neither necessary nor desirable. Gubbins's letter—addressed to Brigadier Wildman-Lushington, who passed it on to Frederick—backed up Hansteen's by pointing out that the eight most important targets on Frederick's list were already the subject of SOE planning. Of the remaining 14, most were, in Gubbins's opinion, "of relatively little importance."[3]

Frederick would later accuse Gubbins of killing the Plough Project stone dead, and not without cause. Clearly this was a turf war in which the chief of SOE felt that the Force was trying to appropriate missions that his own organization could carry out much more effectively. Gubbins later denied acting out of professional jealousy, saying he simply gave an honest commentary on the target list. But the effect of his letter, when read in conjunction with Hansteen's, was to make Frederick's plan redundant. The latter's fury was at least partly fueled by the realization that he had personally spent $8 million on a project that would never come to fruition. As Major Wedderburn later put it to Gubbins, "Frederick had to blame someone in order to save himself, as so much money had been spent, apparently uselessly, on the project."[4] There was also the issue of promotion, with one British liaison officer in Washington, DC, suggesting that "a promise to be made Brigadier [General] to command the force when the scheme takes place has probably added" to Frederick's "annoyance at the delay."[5]

Determined to salvage some kind of role for the Force, Frederick met Mountbatten on September 27 and agreed to shift the focus of the Force's planning from attacking power stations to spearheading a possible amphibious invasion of northern Norway (Operation Jupiter). Mountbatten confirmed this switch at a meeting of the BCOS Committee the following day when he proposed to his fellow chiefs that "the idea of dropping 'ploughs' by air in 1942 should now be abandoned owing to the lack of aircraft," and that Frederick "should investigate operations [in the North of Norway] by sea early in 1943 and by sea or air late in 1943." They agreed.[6]

Meanwhile, Frederick had cabled his intelligence chief, Robert Burhans, in Washington, DC:

Suspend effort on present line... New plan may be radically different and not concerned with hydroelectric or other industrial installations... Inform Adams at Helena to... stress general tactical training to include attack of fortifications, pill boxes, barracks, and troop concentrations. Change in weapons may be necessary to provide greater firepower.[7]

Frederick finally arrived back in Washington, via Prestwick in Scotland, on October 5. A day later he informed an incredulous General McNarney that, chiefly thanks to Gubbins and the attitude

of the British Chiefs of Staff, the Plough Project was hanging by
a thread. The only viable alternative—the one suggested to him
by McNaughton and Mountbatten—was for the Force to spearhead
the invasion of northern Norway as part of Operation Jupiter. This
was quickly scotched by McNarney, who told Frederick in no uncertain terms that General Marshall regarded Jupiter as a pointless
sideshow that was unlikely to go ahead. Marshall was still smarting
from Roosevelt's decision to back British plans to invade North Africa
(Operation Gymnast, later Torch) instead of landing in France
(Sledgehammer), and he regarded Jupiter as a further distraction from
the main aim of defeating Germany on the Continent.

McNarney's message to Marshall was brief. The attitude of the
British Chiefs of Staff to Frederick's mission had been "quite unsym-
pathetic," and he saw only three options: "continue the force on its
present mission"; "disband the force" and give its equipment to Army
Ground Forces; "prepare the force for operation in another theater."[8]

Marshall—who must have been, in Wedderburn's words, "extremely angry that a scheme which the British proposed they should
take up was destroyed (after six months and 17 million dollars had
been spent on it) by the British"[9]—chose the third option. The Force
had, he told his deputy, "received considerable publicity," and to disband it would impact unfavorably "on the Canadian public." Nor did
he feel that such a unit, "composed of picked fighters of high morale,"
and on whom "much effort and considerable funds" had been expended, should "be allowed to go to waste." It could either be sent to
the South Pacific—where American troops were engaged in a bitter
campaign at Guadalcanal that would last into the New Year—or to
the British Isles to await deployment in Europe. He preferred the latter option.[10]

A few days later, influenced by the German drive toward the oil
fields of the Caucasus in southern Russia, Marshall changed his mind
and instructed McNarney to tell Frederick (via the commanding general of the US Ground Forces, who now had overall responsibility)

that the Force would "continue Arctic Training, as originally planned, at its present location, with a view to its possible employment in the Caucasus early in 1943."[11] Marshall also informed the Canadian authorities about the change of mission, adding:

> Force training policy has been and will continue to be the readying of troops to endure hardships in Arctic and mountainous regions; to operate as saboteurs against vital industrial installations; to train personnel in the use of skis and snowshoes, and in parachute operations; and to develop special equipment which could be transported either by air or ship, and which could negotiate terrain covered by snow and ice.

Was the Canadian government happy for its troops to participate in this new Caucasus mission? asked Marshall.[12] The answer was yes. Other options were considered, such as disbanding the Canadian contingent, amalgamating it with the 1st Canadian Parachute Battalion and retaining it as a separate formation. But all were ultimately rejected by the Canadians because they would have resulted in "unwelcome publicity."[13]

Another possible area of deployment for the Force that was being considered by the OPD at this time was Kiska in the Aleutian Islands, the only part of US territory occupied by Japanese troops (since June 1942). The possibilities were endless. But all that really mattered to Frederick, after the shock of his trip to the UK, was the knowledge that the Force had survived, that it would continue to train for winter warfare, and that, before too long, he would have the opportunity to lead his men into battle.

11

"They blew up bridges, culverts and everything"

"There was much conjecture," noted new arrival Lieutenant Ed Thomas, "about what our mission might be. It obviously involved demolition of power plants, because a plywood mock-up was built near the barracks area."[1] Sergeant Percy Crichlow thought the same, and pinpointed the destination as probably Scandinavia after a "one-armed Commando officer" spoke to the Forcemen about his own mission to Norway a year earlier.[2]

Of course, unbeknownst to Thomas, Crichlow and all but a handful of the most senior Forcemen at Fort Harrison, the original plan had changed, and power plants in Norway were no longer the target. But the intensive training of the men would continue as planned. The program included instruction in small arms, demolition, small and large unit tactics, skiing, rock climbing, surviving in cold climates, operation and maintenance of the Weasel (the first samples of which arrived in Montana in late October) and a constant preoccupation with physical endurance.[3]

The demolition training was conducted by engineers from Fort Belvoir who instructed every Forcemen in the use of various types of explosives, including TNT (the standard US Army issue in a half-pound package), nitrostarch ("not quite as stable as TNT") and dynamite "of an equivalent strength."[4] But by far the most effective explosive was the new RS, sticks linked by Primacord and bundled into a 30-pound pack. Its chief value, recalled Joe Dauphinais, was that it was "a dry explosive and really safe to handle; it would not go off until you pulverized it." To prove its stability, the engineers fired into the sticks of RS "and it never did explode." It required Primacord and a detonator to set it off.

Dynamite was much less safe, although that did not stop the former miners like Walter Lewis from "playing a game of chicken." They would form a circle and throw a lit stick of dynamite to one another. Only when the fuse was almost burnt would the "chicken" throw the stick away, causing the others to "run like hell." They had, remembered Dauphinais, "some close calls," none closer than the time a block of three sticks of dynamite with a lit fuse was brought back by a dog. All but one man, braver than the rest, ran for cover. He coolly grabbed the dynamite and threw it as hard as he could. It exploded in midair. "If the fuse had been a little shorter," admitted Joe Glass, "that damned dog would have blown us all to hell."[5]

According to Bill Becket, commanding the 1/1st Battalion, the demolition training "provided the men, perhaps unfortunately, with the opportunity to wreak a little havoc locally." After one demolition exercise by his battalion, he was summoned by his regimental commander, Lieutenant-Colonel "Cookie" Marshall, and asked what had happened. Becket said he did not know because his XO had been in charge. "You are lucky, Bill," replied his grinning boss. "Your boys just blew up the private weekend camp of one of Helena's more distinguished businessmen, which he kept for his own weekend maneuvers. Apparently he went out there this evening with one of his attractive lady companions only to find that the camp had disappeared."[6]

In early October, a group of 50 officers was chosen for an advanced

demolition course run by First Lieutenant Ryan of the US Engineering Board and Major Harvey of the Royal Engineers, in the hope that
they, in turn, could act as instructors. The plan was to use real structures in the community that needed to be demolished, including a
450-foot steel-and-timber railway bridge, the mill of an abandoned silver mine and a large brick smokestack. Unfortunately the students'
enthusiasm got the better of them, and so much explosive was used
to blow up the railway bridge near Libby, 300 miles northwest of Helena, that it damaged nearby houses and shattered windows in the
town. As for the mill near Marysville, the owner was hoping to sell
the metal machinery for scrap. But it was blasted into unusable tiny
pieces by excessive quantities of RS, the surrounding building was destroyed and the resultant flames caused a forest fire. This prompted
the first of several compensation claims.[7] "They blew up bridges, cul-
verts, and everything around Helena, Montana," said Walter Lewis.
"Good God! I had never seen anything like it."[8]

While the officers rearranged the Montana landscape, the men
were sent on a series of exhausting forced marches with full packs.
On October 7, Bill Rothlin led his company at the head of the 2nd
Regiment to Marysville and back, a total distance of more than 36
miles. Four days later, the regiment was trucked to Adel, a town to
the northeast, and told to navigate back to the base on foot across 45
miles of the most rugged terrain imaginable, including rivers, peaks
and forests. Once again, Rothlin's company led the way. But freezing rain and low cloud hampered their progress, and at the top of
one mountain range, at an elevation of 8,200 feet, they encountered
snow. They were scheduled to camp the second night near the town
of Nelson, roughly halfway to their destination. But as their clothing
and blankets were soaked through, it was decided to return them to
Fort Harrison by truck. "A very tired bunch of men arrived back in
camp," noted the Canadians' war diary, "at 0100 hours."[9]

The strain was beginning to tell on less athletic soldiers like Percy
Crichlow, who, as he acknowledged, was small by Force standards

and "not very strong." It was a constant struggle for him "to keep up with the training," and one not unnoticed by the PT instructor, "Tarzan" Coombes, who called him Mustache and constantly bellowed that "the door swung open to let us out as easily as it swung open to let us in."[10] The men soon got the message. "If you fell out of a march," recalled Jack Callowhill, "you were gone the next day. Everybody knew that."[11]

There was fierce competition between the different regiments, companies, platoons and even sections as to who could outdo the others in training. More often than not the 2nd Regiment came out on top. In late September, for example, it easily outscored the other regiments 7 points to 2 in a weeklong series of training tests. But occasionally the rivalry got out of hand, as it did when an American Forceman was accidentally shot through the head and mortally wounded—the Force's first fatality—during a combat exercise between two sections on, of all days, October 13.[12]

A less serious accident involved the two sections of 1-2 Company's 3rd Platoon. According to Percy Crichlow, who was later posted to the 3rd Platoon as a section commander, the accident happened when "one part of the platoon...tried to kill the other half in a live-round training exercise at Helena and there had actually been one man injured—but not seriously." Crichlow did not name the wounded soldier or explain the reason for the bad blood between the 5th and 6th Sections. But it may not have been a coincidence that 5th Section contained an unusually high proportion of Canadians, including the section commander, Sergeant William Kotenko, Lorin Waling, Joe Glass, Don MacKinnon, "Herby" Forester from Edmonton and Syd Gath, a friend of MacKinnon's from Winnipeg.

The 6th Section, on the other hand, had only two Canadians—Joe Dauphinais and Tommy Fenton, a former miner from Quebec who, like Crichlow, had served with the Victoria Rifles. The others were all American. They included Don Fisher, Ray Holbrook, Howard Van Ausdale, Walter "Pop" Lewis, Johnny Walter, Harry Deyette and

Clarence DeCamp. The 31-year-old Deyette—5 feet 11 inches tall and 161 pounds—hailed from Grays Harbor, Washington, and had quit high school after one year to help support his family. Prior to enlisting in the days following Pearl Harbor, he had worked as a rigging man in a logging camp.[13] DeCamp also had experience in the lumber business, having been briefly employed in his father's sawmill near San Francisco. But so outraged was he by the surprise Japanese attack on Pearl Harbor that he enlisted the following day. Over six feet two inches tall and immensely strong, the 23-year-old DeCamp—known to his friends as "D"—was an ideal fit for the Force. "He was very much into the outdoors," remembered his daughter. "He was also a risk taker. He had no qualms. Joining the Force was probably a challenge to him. No matter what, he was going to do his job."[14]

Deyette and DeCamp were similar to the other Americans in their section: all tough former miners, loggers and trappers from wilderness states like Oregon, Washington and Montana. Walter had already come to blows with Dauphinais, and it may have been national rivalry—Canadians versus Americans—that had caused the bad blood between the 5th and 6th Sections. Whatever the reason, the 3rd Platoon as a whole was rapidly acquiring a reputation for ill discipline and unruliness. "That platoon," noted Crichlow, "didn't have a good name...There were always a lot of A.W.O.L. and difficult boys." To solve the problem, Bill Rothlin would eventually be forced to transfer not only the platoon leader but also both section leaders. But at this relatively early stage in the training program, he simply warned the men that there would be serious consequences if their fractious behavior continued.[15]

One possible cause of ill feeling between American and Canadian Forcemen was that, since qualifying as parachutists, the former had been getting jump pay of $50 a month ($100 for officers, all back-dated to the time they were taken on the Force's strength), while the latter had not received a cent. Even without jump pay the Americans' basic salary was more than the Canadians received. Conscious of the harmful effect this must be having on Canadian morale—"it is obviously difficult," Lieutenant-Colonel Don Williamson reported, "with men completely mixed as they are, to have the lad in front of him jump out of a plane…and know he is getting $50.00 per month extra for doing it, while you are not getting anything and don't even know what or when you will be paid for taking a similar risk"—Williamson had urged his government to authorize "equivalent rates of pay" and at "the earliest possible moment."[16]

But as no decision had been made by the end of September, and the discontent was growing, Williamson spoke to all the Canadians in the theater on the afternoon of Wednesday the 30th in an attempt to defuse the situation. Assuming that Williamson had good news for them, the Canadians arrived at the theater "singing and laughing." Their mood quickly altered when Williamson explained that he was doing everything he could, but that no extra pay had yet been authorized. While he understood their disappointment, he also reminded them of the terms of the form they had signed before joining the Force: that they would accept Canadian rates of pay. "I will do my best for you," he concluded, "but I can make no promises as to what, if any, additional pay will be authorized or when."

Though only a few voiced their anger, the Canadian Forcemen left the theater a "sullen and sober bunch." It was obvious that their morale had been shaken and that the pay issue needed to be settled. "The Lord help us," noted the Canadians' war diary, "if the situation is not cleared up before the mid-month pay."[17] The fact that the Canadians were paid twice a month, and their American colleagues only once, meant that in a few cases the Americans were forced to borrow money until payday from their poorer northern cousins. But this was little consolation to the Canadians when their next payday on October 15 brought no word of extra money. "The men took their pay without saying a word," recorded the war diary, "but it is quite evident that they are really mad and a few paraded to their Company

Commanders wishing to be returned to Canada...[This] situation cannot go on much longer."

Finally, on October 30, word arrived at Fort Harrison that the Canadian paymaster general had approved parachute pay at the same rate as flying pay, which meant only an extra 75 cents a day for the men and $2 for the officers. It was, noted the war diary, "a very great disappointment," as the men would be getting "less than half" their American comrades' parachute pay. There would now be Canadian staff sergeants "drawing less than the American privates under them."[18]

12

"A very special Force"

The gripes felt by the Canadian Forcemen with regard to pay were just one issue of discipline and morale giving Colonel Frederick cause for concern. Another, and potentially more serious, was the lax attitude to rules and regulations shown by a number of the Force's officers and men. The problem had first been brought to Frederick's attention by an inspecting officer sent by Ground Forces HQ in late September who, having observed the training program, made a number of recommendations: to increase the collective tactical training at all levels; to test soldiers more regularly; and to develop an officer leadership program. This last recommendation was a tacit acknowledgment that not all the officers knew their role and were, perhaps, a little too close to their men.[1]

To address the problem, Frederick spoke to all the officers in the theater on October 21, the day the first snowfalls were reported on nearby hills. He began by praising the Canadians for adjusting so quickly to the "American way," especially as they had had to adopt more American customs than vice versa. Yet, he added, discipline was not up to the required standard, and the "onus of correction" was placed squarely on the shoulders of the platoon leaders. He then pointed out the "essential qualities required in good officers," which included a willingness to take responsibility and lead from the front, to gain the men's respect but not to become their friend. They were to impress on their men that they all belonged to a "very special Force, the only one of its kind in the world," that they were all "either volunteers or specially selected" and were "now taking part in a training program more extensive, thorough and difficult than any attempted."[2]

Frederick's serious tone was briefly interrupted by a moment of farce as a cat appeared beside the Force commander on the stage and was instantly attacked by Lieutenant Colonel Shinberger's two black Labrador pups, Cain and Abel, who executed a textbook tactical maneuver by racing simultaneously from opposite sides of the stage. The attack, however, was not successful. "The cat was rescued," noted the Canadians' war diary, "the dogs expelled, and the address continued."[3]

In his concluding comments, Frederick insisted that he had tried to be "reasonable and considerate" when placing demands upon his junior officers, many of whom lacked experience. In the future, however, more would be expected of them and it was their responsibility "to make good." They had been placed in positions of responsibility by the government, and in return were expected to do their duty "properly, thoroughly and wholeheartedly."[4]

Not all the officers present that evening were convinced by Frederick's oratory. Just three days later, a young 1st Regiment platoon leader from Saint Paul, Minnesota, put in a request for a transfer to Military Intelligence. His name was Second Lieutenant John H. Richardson, a graduate of Harvard Law School, where he had ranked in the top 20 percent of his class, "served on the Legal Aid Bureau, and won the law school moot court competition." Having joined the Force direct from the Engineer OCS at Fort Belvoir in late July 1942, this "legal eagle" had since come to the conclusion that his civilian background and education made him a better fit for Military Intelligence.[5]

That, however, was not how a furious Frederick saw it when the Adjutant General's Office informed him of Richardson's transfer request. "Not favorably considered," was the Force commander's pithy response, before explaining why. Richardson had been selected by personal interview after "volunteering for hazardous duty involving parachute jumping in cold climates." The candidate had insisted he was suitable for such an assignment "because of his knowledge of skiing and other winter sports, his college background of mathematics, and his wide practical experience in navigation." After he was selected, his graduation and commission were "requested and granted prior to the normal graduation of his class at the Engineer School." Since then, wrote Frederick, Richardson had been given all the advantages of special training and possessed the "necessary intelligence" for his position. Yet he had "shown an increasing tendency to shirk the more hazardous phases of the training," with his actions making his intent "immediately obvious to his troops and brother officers." In Frederick's view, it was "chiefly to obtain relief from dangerous duty" that Richardson had put in for a transfer.

Having effectively accused the young officer of cowardice, Frederick insisted that his reassignment to the Intelligence Corps—"where the conditions of service will be ideal, from his standpoint"—was not in the interests of the Service because of the "detrimental effect" such a move would have on the other junior officers. Presumably Frederick feared that it might encourage other young lieutenants to throw in the towel when the going got tough and seek a more comfortable billet. To prevent that, he wanted Richardson to be assigned for duty "in the nearest Engineer Replacement Training Center" as a warning that the Force could not be used as a temporary stepping-stone for career advancement.[6]

Frederick's response could be seen as harsh, even vindictive. But in his eyes, Richardson was exactly the type of self-serving officer that he did not want in the Force. It was important, therefore, for Richardson to be humiliated as a lesson to others. In any event, only part of Frederick's wish was granted: Richardson was not allowed to join Military Intelligence, nor was he sent back to the Engineers. Instead, some sort of compromise was reached whereby Richardson remained in the Force as a platoon leader in 5-1 Company. It cannot have been easy for him. He had declared his intention to leave, and it had been denied by Frederick on the grounds that he was simply trying to avoid dangerous duty. Was this true? It is impossible to know for certain. But Frederick was of that opinion and, as his letter to the adjutant general implies, so too were Richardson's fellow officers and soldiers. Henceforth, Richardson was someone his superiors would keep a very close eye on, and he would need to work doubly hard to gain their acceptance.

In Washington, DC, and London, meanwhile, the best use of the Force was still being discussed by the politicians and senior commanders. On October 23,* having spoken to George C. Marshall, the US Army chief of staff, Field Marshal Sir John Dill cabled London that the Force was training for a "possible employment in Caucasus Area early in 1943." Dill was convinced that Marshall was being urged to use the Force "somewhere," and that the Caucasus was the "only place that seemed possible." However, he was doubtful that the idea had been "seriously considered."[7]

Having read Dill's telegram, Winston Churchill concluded that only an urgent appeal to President Roosevelt could save the Force and its snow machines for possible use in Operation Jupiter in the winter of 1943/44.[8] "Although I understand from Mountbatten," wrote Churchill on October 30, "that the Plough Scheme as originally con-

---

* The day General Sir Bernard Montgomery's Eighth Army launched a huge offensive against Erwin Rommel's Axis forces at El Alamein in Egypt. After twelve days of bitter fighting, Rommel withdrew and the tide had turned in favor of the Allies in North Africa.

ceived is not a practicable proposition this winter, I do think that it is of the utmost importance that the development and production of the vehicle should not be delayed."[9]

Roosevelt finally replied on December 2, assuring Churchill that the "vehicle will be produced on schedule and the special service force will have the vehicles for use this winter."[10] But by then much had changed. The same day that Churchill's telegram was dispatched from London, Colonel Frederick told General McNarney in Washington, DC, that the Caucasus mission could not go ahead because the terrain and tactical situation were unsuitable. Instead they discussed possible operations in Kiska, New Guinea and Northwest Africa. A day later, at a conference at Army Ground Forces HQ, Frederick still "seemed to be in a state of confusion" as to where his men would be sent, but he thought they might need amphibious training.[11]

Frederick's hunch was correct. By mid-November, with the Allies safely ashore at Algiers, Oran and Casablanca in North Africa (Operation Torch), the latest thinking in the US General Staff was that the Force should be used as a Ranger assault unit for probable follow-up operations in the Mediterranean against Sardinia, Italy or Sicily.[12] Dill was horrified. "Apart from question of suitability and waste of snow training already given," he cabled the chiefs of staff in London, "this proposal may entail no properly trained force being ready for Plough project next winter or other operations in snow." His proposal, therefore, was to press for the retention of the Force, "or at least for the replacement of the men taken to the Mediterranean by others," so that there would be a Plough Force available in the winter of 1943/44 "should it be required."[13]

When Dill's telegram was discussed at a BCOS meeting in London on November 17, Mountbatten told his fellow chiefs that the reason for the "sudden change in policy" was the "disappointing performance" of the Weasel in recent snowfield tests in the United States.

He had learned this from a British representative of the Ministry of Aircraft Production who was present at the tests and who thought Studebaker would need another year to repair the defects (which included a tendency to overturn on steep slopes). In the meantime, said Mountbatten, it was vital that the Plough force was retained.[14] The other chiefs agreed, as did Churchill, and the following reply was cabled to Dill:

> We agree that you should press for retention of snow warfare force, and that this force should have the best equipment of all kinds that is available...We think it very unwise to disperse a unit whose personnel have been specially picked for snow warfare, and urge that it should continue its specialized training throughout this winter.[15]

Dill forwarded the text of the cable to McNarney, who replied on November 20 that he had obviously not made himself clear about future plans. The intention was still for the Force to continue its special snow warfare training and to get its "special vehicles," the development and improvement of which would be ongoing. No final decision had been made to deploy the Force in the Mediterranean area, but possible operations were being considered. It was for this reason that the Force would move on to amphibious training after it had completed its winter program. McNarney ended his letter with the assurance that "there will be no abandonment of the project as a whole even though the 1st Special Service Force as now organized is diverted to other objectives."[16]

This response satisfied Dill, who regarded the US General Staff's plans for the Force as "entirely sound."[17] But when Churchill was informed, he objected strongly to the likelihood that the Force would be used for "other objectives." Mountbatten was told to draft a reply to Dill in the prime minister's name. Approved by both Churchill and the chiefs, and sent on November 26, it expressed the prime minister's belief that the Force would play a "vital role in possible ultimate re-conquest of Norway," and that it needed to be retained for this role. The target date for planning "should be October 1943."[18]

There the matter rested until Colonel Frederick, at the end of his tether, went to speak to Dill in the latter's office in the Munitions Building on December 15. In an extraordinarily candid—some might say ill-advised—conversation, Frederick said he was satisfied with the Force's training and morale but was "groping in the dark" as to the "right tactical doctrine to inculcate." This was because he still did not know where and when the Force would be deployed. It would, in his view, be ready for action by the end of January 1943. But thereafter it would "quickly get stale" if not actively employed, and he viewed "with horror any idea of remaining idle till another winter comes round." His men were thirsting for action, and it would be impossible to keep them inactive *and* contented. He was anxious, in any case, to try out under active service conditions the tactical ideas they had been practicing. Frederick's preference, he told Dill, was to fight in the snow. But if that was impossible, he was prepared to try out his force in other conditions and adapt his tactical training accordingly.

Dill knew from recent comments made by both McNarney and Roosevelt that an imminent use of the Force was likely. Therefore, if—as was probable—the Americans were determined "to blow the gaff this winter," would it not, he asked the British Chiefs of Staff, "be well to consider blowing it in our direction against some objective in Norway," where the British could exert some control over the security of the operation. A raid with a limited number of snow vehicles would, he believed, "satisfy the strong demand for action."[19]

After consulting Churchill, the chiefs of staff urged Dill to resist *any* pressure to use the Force prematurely. To deploy the snow machines "in small numbers, imperfectly developed and against unimportant objectives would merely lead," they said, to revealing the secret of the surprise weapon to the enemy without reaping the full benefits. Dill agreed to do as asked, but foresaw much difficulty in preventing the use of the Force for another year. "They certainly will want to blood the men," he wrote, with great prescience, "but we may be able to prevent the use of the vehicles."[20]

13

"The battle of the slabs"

Monday, November 23, 1942, dawned bright and cold at Fort Harrison. The first proper snow—four inches—had fallen a few days earlier, and with more forecast, it was time to begin the winter phase of the Force's training, which included survival in cold climates, rock climbing, skiing and driving and maintaining the Weasel.[1] The survival training began on the 28th when 36 officers, including all the company commanders, were trucked 15 miles west of the base to MacDonald Pass on the Continental Divide, an altitude of 6,300 feet. Weighed down by their packs, they trudged through knee-deep snow to a wooded area about a quarter of a mile from the road, where they split up into groups of four and built shelters and fires. Well sheltered from the wind, the officers spent a fairly comfortable night in their down sleeping bags and returned to their base at 2:00 p.m. the following day, "all having benefited from their experience" and able to pass on their knowledge to their men.[2]

A couple of days later, all the Force's officers listened to a lecture on "Living in Frigid Weather" by Second Lieutenant Lincoln Washburn of the Army Specialist Corps, a well-known Arctic expert who had spent years exploring the wild expanse of northern Canada and Alaska for the National Geographic Society. Washburn's talk covered everything from the securing, preparing and cooking of food and drink to methods for erecting shelter and how to prevent frostbite. It was, noted the Canadians' war diary, "most interesting" and gave many "helpful hints." A second lecture to the officers by Washburn, the following day, covered travel in winter conditions.[3]

As temperatures dropped to 10 below, the Forcemen were taught the rudiments of mountain climbing, particularly rock-face technique. It was not a skill that came easily to Bill Becket, who froze for a full five minutes on his first ascent, clinging grimly to the rock with his fingernails and the toes of his parachute boots. "I had," he recalled, "nowhere to go—neither up, across or down—and I was roped to the men above and below me." Eventually persuaded to move, he made it up the face. Coming down was more to his liking. They used the technique known as rappelling, where the climber descends a fixed rope by pushing out from the rock face in a series of controlled drops. It was fast and exciting, and Becket thought the reason he was good at it was because he "wanted desperately to get off that mountain."[4]

Ski training was scheduled to begin at the start of December, but the lack of both snow and equipment forced a postponement. With time moving on, it was decided to give each regiment a week's instruction at Blossburg Mountain, a small ski resort with a single tow rope, not far from MacDonald Pass on the Continental Divide. The 1st Regiment went first on December 9, followed by the 3rd Regiment a week later. Then there was a pause for Christmas, which many Forcemen enjoyed at home, courtesy of nine days' furlough.[5] Those still at Helena were congratulated by Frederick for the "outstanding manner" in which they had undertaken the "fastest and most strenuous training program of any unit in the Western Hemisphere." He added: "Keep up the good work, and regardless of what the New Year brings I feel sure that the First Special Service Force will be prepared for its task and will come out of the battle the victors."[6]

A few days later, back from leave, the 2nd Regiment was trucked to Blossburg, where the men were quartered in railway freight cars. "There was," remembered Ed Thomas, "no heat in the cars and at night temperatures dropped below zero. Chow lines were set up outside near the cars. An epidemic of the 'GIs' (diarrhea) struck, allegedly due to failure of mess personnel to get utensils completely clear of soap. The entire experience was cold and unpleasant."[7] There were, however, some lighter moments for the men of Rothlin's 1-2 Company, particularly the unruly 3rd Platoon, whose former commander had been moved for his own good to 2-2 Company and replaced by the tall and imposing Larry Piette. But even Piette—described by Percy Crichlow, who would later serve under him, as "soft-spoken, clever and courageous...as good an officer as I was to see anywhere among the Americans"— would need time to stamp his personality on such a group of forceful individuals.[8]

Ski instruction was given by experts from the Royal Norwegian Army under a Captain Kiil. They quickly divided the men into four groups: three groups of beginners who practiced simple snowplow turns on shallow slopes and took short route marches; and an advanced group of about 120 men, all with skiing experience, who executed "Christie" turns and were sent on much longer treks in bitterly cold temperatures that could reach minus 50. The best skiers were assigned as "trailbreakers" and stationed at the front of the column. They would make fresh tracks in the soft snow, covering as much ground as they could before falling back and letting the next man take over. "It was," noted one Forceman, "surprising how fast we could move through poor terrain in this way."[9]

Both experienced skiers, Tom MacWilliam and Larry Piette were in the advanced group. Piette remembered one march in their fur-lined parkas, encumbered with pack and rifle, that covered a hundred miles in just 24 hours. A couple of men broke a binding on this trip and "failed to show up." So Piette and the rest went to look for them, "making concentric circles until we found the guys." They had built a fire and were "perfectly okay."[10]

The best skiers were typically Canadians from the French provinces and the Maritimes and Americans from the mountain states. They would laugh at Forcemen who had never seen snow or, if they had, were uncomfortable on skis—men like Jimmy Flack of 3rd Platoon, a vertically challenged prewar serviceman from Renton, Washington, who was heard saying: "Who would want to run around the country with them blasted things tied to your feet!"[11] Percy Crichlow felt much the same. "My ability on skis," he noted, "was very limited, and one wag said of me that for a whole winter he had seen me either falling down, down, or getting up."[12] Americans from the South described ski training as "the battle of the slabs." But eventually, noted Joe Dauphinais, "everyone could navigate on the damned things."[13] According to Captain Kiil's final report—submitted in February 1943 after all three combat regiments had completed two weeks' training at Blossburg—99 percent of the Forcemen had become competent skiers by Norwegian Army standards.[14] Ironically, one of the odd men out was Frederick himself, a self-proclaimed disaster on skis who spent most of his time on his backside.[15]

When not on skis, the men of 1-2 Company amused themselves with juvenile practical jokes—like the time they carried a bed, containing a sleeping Forceman called Benny Bernstein, outside the boxcar and left it in "about ten inches of snow"—and drinking illicit liquor. On New Year's Eve, for example, the 1st Platoon gave a party with huge quantities of smuggled liquor, which they had hidden under the boxcar. The party was in full swing when in walked the company commander, Lieutenant Rothlin. "For one stunned moment," recalled Percy Crichlow, "there was silence. But somehow a quick thinker put a glass in his hand, and another, and another, until it was safe for one or two of the boys to take

[Rothlin] quietly back to the Officers' Mess and leave him blissfully seated in the can."

By getting drunk with his men, Rothlin had taken Frederick's advice to lead from the front quite literally. But this spontaneous act also helped to break down the invisible barriers that often existed between officers and men, building a sense of camaraderie and shared endeavor in 1-2 Company that would stand it in good stead for the challenges to come.

The party finally ended when Lew Weldon, the Buster Keaton lookalike prankster from Manitoba, went outside to relieve himself, "ran into the coal box cover, got up and attacked it for hitting him as it fell and eventually had to be restrained and brought back inside."[16]

On New Year's Day, hangover or no, the men were expected to train. Only the sick were exempt. They included two 3rd Platoon men, Joe Glass and Lorin Waling, who had gone AWOL the night before to spend New Year's Eve with their girlfriends Dot and Steffie. Their plan had been to sneak away after training, ski to Blossburg station and take the next train to Helena, returning in time for duty on New Year's Day with no one the wiser. It did not work out like that. They got to East Helena in time to join their surprised but delighted girlfriends at a big party in Union Hall where they welcomed in the New Year in style, drinking and dancing the night away. But they got even drunker on the return journey, sharing a bottle of whiskey with a man headed for Seattle, and arrived back after their platoon had left on an exercise. Their only hope was to jump into their sleeping bags and pretend to be sick—which they were, from alcohol. When they were questioned soon after by their platoon leader, Larry Piette, who wanted to know why they had not gone on the exercise, the obvious answer was that they were ill. Befuddled by drink, however, Joe Glass told the truth. "I was in town last night, sir."

Asked the same question, Waling answered: "I was with Glass, sir."

Piette—an occasional drinker who insisted on high standards of discipline and morality—was disgusted. "You're both under arrest."

In truth, this meant little until they returned to Fort Harrison a couple of days later and were hauled up in front of Tom MacWilliam, the battalion commander. Despite his sharp intellect and cool demeanor, MacWilliam had an "affable, small-town look about him that to some was reminiscent of the actor Jimmy Stewart." He preferred to reason with miscreants rather than bawl them out, to make them feel ashamed of what they had done rather than put the fear of God in them. Another member of the 1st Battalion who, like Glass and Waling, was sent to MacWilliam after going AWOL, recalled: "That's one experience I'd never want to go through again. He didn't yell or even raise his voice. He made me feel the damn'est heel that ever walked. He made it like a personal offence to him when you messed up."[17]

It was the same for Glass and Waling. What you did, MacWilliam told them, was unforgivable. By going AWOL during ski training, you missed a whole day of instruction. And for what? A night of revelry. He turned to Glass. "You're too intelligent to do these things. What's the matter with you?"

Glass, sensibly, said nothing. MacWilliam sighed. He knew from Rothlin and Piette that both men were promising soldiers who regularly topped the fitness tests. He decided to give them a second chance. "We don't want to lose you," he said at last, "but something has to change."

That something was demotion for Glass from corporal to private. Already a private, Waling was punished by being separated from his buddy—and partner in crime—by a move to 1st Platoon. Knowing how close they had come to being thrown out of the Force, they both breathed a sigh of relief and vowed to stay out of trouble.[18]

Tom MacWilliam's rejigging of his command was simplified by the fact that, in mid-December, the Force had grown by more than 340 men (as part of its 30 percent overstrength) to a total of 2,200.[19] The extra 100 or so Canadians were all volunteers from the 1st

Canadian Parachute Battalion, still in training at Fort Benning. "A good-looking group of boys," noted the Canadians' war diary, "and really looked smart marching through camp. All but one are qualified parachutists." Most, in fact, had received a much higher standard of airborne training—including mass jumps—than the original Forcemen. What they lacked were the Force's other areas of expertise—particularly the winter training—and it was to bring them rapidly up to speed that they were grouped together with the 230 or so new American volunteers in a temporary training battalion.

Many of the Americans required jump training at Fort Helena. But a few were qualified, including 21-year-old Richard "Dick" Daigle, who had been transferred from Colonel Sink's 506th Parachute Infantry Regiment (506th PIR) at Fort Benning. Daigle was from the US shoe capital of Lynn, Massachusetts, a small town located a few miles north of the state capital, Boston. The fourth of six children born to a shoe patternmaker of French-Canadian descent and his American wife, he was brought up in a staunchly Roman Catholic neighborhood in Lynn and regularly attended services at the nearby St. Jean Baptiste Church. When he was still a toddler, his father bought a steep plot of land and built his own timber-framed house, complete with red oak floors. But money was always scarce—particularly during the depression, when his father was often out of work and breakfast was invariably oatmeal—and the lack of it was the cause of many domestic arguments that often turned violent. As a young teen, Daigle's eldest sibling, Doris, would stand between her parents so they could not hit each other.

Daigle's youthful anger issues may not be unconnected to his parents' fights. He worked them out by first learning to box and then using his pugilistic skill against bigger and stronger opponents. One memorable fight against a much taller bully left the latter nursing a broken nose and two black eyes. Daigle was unmarked. He made less impression on his teachers and, a mediocre student, he left school after 11th grade to earn money to support his family. With his mechanical aptitude—he loved repairing his neighbors' 1929 Model A roadster—he should have enrolled in the Lynn Trade School. Instead he got a job in the local garage, earning just 50 cents an hour (later raised to a dollar).[20]

He finally enlisted in the summer of 1942 and, once basic training was over, selected Airborne as his specialty. He was assigned to the 506th PIR at Camp Toccoa. In early December, the 506th left Toccoa to complete its jump training at Fort Benning. Two of its battalions took the train; the other—Daigle's 2nd—was selected by Sink to march the 118 miles with full packs and rifles over mostly unpaved roads made treacherous by freezing rain. They covered the distance in a scarcely believable 75 hours, at a marching average of four miles an hour. Only 12 of the 586 officers and men fell out en route.[21] Daigle was not one of them. He completed his first jump at Benning on December 14 and his fifth and last on the 20th, his 21st birthday.

A couple of days later, the fully fledged paratrooper went home on leave, proudly sporting the prized silver wings and parachute pin on his left breast. When he reached the Daigle residence at 71 Fays Avenue, Lynn, on Christmas Eve, light snow was falling and the house was lit up with Christmas decorations. In one front window sparkled three blue stars, one for each member of the family serving in the US armed forces:* two brothers, Bill and Don, in the navy and Dick in the army. Almost all of Dick's family was present: his parents, both brothers, elder sister Doris and her husband, and younger sister Phyllis, a high school sophomore. They all marveled at Dick's teak-tough, Airborne-conditioned physique. He was barely five feet seven inches tall, and less than 140 pounds, but looked and felt as if he could go 12 rounds with anyone.

The only sibling missing was Irene, the second eldest, who was living with her husband, Arthur, a chief engineman in the US Coast

---

* This was the custom across the United States. A gold star represented a family member who had made the ultimate sacrifice.

Guard, and young son, Ken, at Mobile on the coast of Alabama. To mark the occasion of Dick's 21st birthday, Irene had sent him a charming picture of young Ken wearing white dungaree shorts and his dad's outsized Coast Guard cap. Looming behind the cute toddler is the trunk of the family car, a '37 Chevrolet. Irene had written in pen on the back of the photo: "December 20, 1942, Mobile, Alabama. Almost 21 months old Kenneth Paul Beaton." Dick loved the picture of his tiny nephew and, hoping it would bring him luck, decided to keep it in the lining of his helmet so that it would always be near him.

The holidays were enjoyed by the whole family until, all too soon, a Western Union telegram arrived for Dick with the unexpected news that he had been posted to the First Special Service Force, a unit he had never heard of. It was not a move he had asked for or wanted. He was happy in the 506th. But orders were orders. Told to report to his new unit by January 11, 1943, he took the train from Lynn— via Chicago, Wisconsin, Minnesota and North Dakota—and arrived at Fort Harrison a day early. He reported to his new company commander, Lieutenant Rothlin, who told him he had been assigned to the 6th Section, part of Larry Piette's 3rd Platoon. His bunkmate was Harry Deyette, the former lumberjack from rural Washington. Apart from their French surnames and brief stints in high school, they had little in common. Yet they "became instant friends and more." Their minds "were on the same wavelength." On night maneuvers, one knew instinctively where the other was located. In barroom fights they had each other's back.[22]

The intense bond of friendship between Daigle and Deyette was not unusual. All across the Force, small close-knit groups of buddies were forming. They were often from the same 12-man section, but there were exceptions. Despite the bad feeling between Piette's 5th and 6th Sections, the former's Glenn Surprise and Melvin Hinkle (both from Oregon) and the latter's Clarence DeCamp (the gangly Californian) had all served together in the 15th Infantry and were now inseparable. So too were Joe Glass and Lorin Waling, though they were now in different platoons. Such close ties are typical of all elite military units. A US paratrooper wrote of the small groups that made up his squad: "They would literally insist on going hungry for one another, freezing for one another, dying for one another."

It was the same for the Forcemen. But there was something else. By early 1943, noted the Force's intelligence chief, the two nationalities had been successfully melded into a single entity that was "neither Canadian nor US, but just plain Special Service Force." The original selection of "rugged individualists" and "highly aggressive, capable officers" had produced a singular unit made up of "the leaders of gangs." Each soldier had "resourcefulness, mental and physical toughness, and an initiative that surmounted all obstacles."[23] Desperate to prove themselves, they yearned for action. But still the War Department procrastinated.

14

"Their chance will come"

The Forcemen spent much of January 1943 completing their cold-weather training, which included driving and maintaining the T-15 Weasels, 160 of which had been delivered by Studebaker to Fort Harrison. The general opinion of the two-man tracked vehicle, with a top speed of 40 mph over snow, was favorable. They were, noted Joe Dauphinais, "pretty good machines" with "very few flaws." Don MacKinnon remembered having "a great time running them all around Fort Harrison and the nearby hills."[1] Each Weasel had two gears: one for normal terrain and one for heavy. They were steered with the brakes, like a tank, and had a plastic windshield and a canvas cover that went over the top. The ski rack was on the side, and there was room to carry supplies, including a jerrican for gas.[2]

The Weasel's main weakness was a tendency to throw a track on tight turns and to flip over while crossing, rather than climbing, a steep slope. Yet overall, Frederick was satisfied with the Weasel's performance, telling Captain J. N. Knox, Mountbatten's liaison officer in Washington, that it could negotiate snow slopes of 25 degrees with full loads and had "proved better than the tests had indicated."

Frederick's main gripe was that they were "very awkward" to get in and out of and to fire weapons from. Frederick had gone to see Knox in the Pentagon,[*] the War Department's huge, newly completed headquarters in Arlington, Virginia, to fish for information on the likely deployment of the Force.[3]

But even as Frederick was meeting Knox in Washington, a much higher-level conference was taking place at Casablanca on the Atlantic coast of Morocco. Attended by Churchill, Roosevelt and the Combined Chiefs of Staff, its main point of discussion was what to do *after* the Axis forces had been cleared out of North Africa. As before, General Marshall and the other US Joint Chiefs wanted to suspend operations in the Mediterranean so that Operation Roundup, the cross-Channel invasion of France, could be launched later in the year to assist the Russians. Churchill and the British chiefs, meanwhile, preferred to attack Sicily next (Operation Husky) and not commit to Roundup until sufficient landing craft were available and, more important, German morale and resources had been more seriously eroded. The capture of Sicily would safeguard Mediterranean shipping, tie up German troops, provide airfields to bomb targets in occupied Europe, and threaten mainland Italy, possibly driving Hitler's Axis partner out of the war.

Roosevelt saw the sense of this argument and, much to the fury of Marshall and his other senior commanders, again sided with the British. The chief outcome of the conference, therefore, was that an "attack against Sicily would be launched in 1943 with the target date as the period of the favorable July moon."[4] The operation would be directed by General Eisenhower, the supreme commander in the

---

[*]   Arlington, just across the Potomac from Washington, DC, had been chosen as the site for a new building to house the scattered and ever-growing number of War Department employees because there was not enough room in the nation's capital. Work had begun on the Pentagon-shaped structure on September 11, 1941, and was finished 16 months later. The three-story, concrete-reinforced building covered six million square feet and had room for 40,000 people. Its build cost was $75 million, more than double the original estimate.

Mediterranean, from his headquarters in Algiers. No final decision was made on Roundup beyond a general commitment to launch it when it was thought likely to succeed. Elsewhere, the Allies would attempt to recapture Burma and make advances against the Japanese in the Pacific (where Guadalcanal in the Solomon Islands had just fallen to US forces after a brutal five-month campaign on land and sea)—but only if such operations did not compromise the Germany First strategy.[5]

Barely a week after the conference at Casablanca had ended, General Eisenhower was asked by the General Staff in Washington, DC, if he needed the Force for the forthcoming invasion of Sicily. He replied on February 2 that he did, and that if the Force was allotted to him it should cease its winter training and begin an intensive course in amphibious operations. It should also keep up its parachute proficiency and "be shipped with organizational equipment required for beach landing and mountain warfare in semi tropics only."[6]

But when the OPD looked into the matter in more detail, it realized that it might take too long to complete the Force's amphibious training and ship it to North Africa in time for the Sicily invasion. So instead General Marshall offered the Force to the British Chiefs of Staff "for operations now being planned" in the north European theater.[7] Their response, on February 12, was that they were not contemplating the use of the Force in the "near future"; yet they strongly urged that the Force "should be held available and training continued" with a "view to employment in Norway or similar terrain where its services would be essential to success." To use it in the Mediterranean would be a "grave mistake" because another similar force "could not be fully prepared for service before spring 1944."[8]

Marshall's terse reply was that the Force was "growing stale" and, according to its commander, it would be better to disband it if it did not see service soon. His recommendation, therefore, was either to send the Force to the UK "for possible use by Mountbatten this summer or for Minute Jupiter [Norway], or it should go to Africa for

Husky as desired by Eisenhower."[9] This prompted Mountbatten to consult Churchill, who repeated the chiefs' earlier request to allow the Force to continue its training in snow warfare so that it would be ready for any future operation in Norway.[10] Fine, said Marshall, but what would be the nature of its mission, and were the British prepared to provide planes to transport both the Force and its snow vehicles? He wanted to know, he added, because no US aircraft would be available.[11]

It was, replied Mountbatten, impossible to know the exact nature of the Force's future mission, but "operations with plough type vehicles, either seaborne or airborne, are envisaged." As for aircraft, only the British Lancaster and the American C-54 were suitable, and neither would be allocated "unless and until an operation of overriding importance justifies this diversion of air effort."[12] On the same day that Mountbatten cabled his reply, February 27, Eisenhower repeated his request for the Force to be sent to the Mediterranean on the grounds that it had been included in his plans, and the only other similar type of assault unit was a single Ranger battalion, whereas he required four.[13] Taking both signals into account, Marshall and the other US chiefs were minded to grant Eisenhower's request. "The idea," Dill informed the British chiefs, "is that this force, which is reported to have finished its snow training, should be used in North Africa without its special vehicles, where it would get battle experience." Only after that, said Dill, would the Force reassemble in England with its Weasels so that it was available for Jupiter. It was a proposal that Dill strongly supported.[14]

Churchill, however, did not. "On no account dissipate PLOUGH force," he cabled Dill on March 5. "Their chance will come and may alter the whole strategic position of the war, whereas to break them up now is to blot out large strategic possibilities in the future." Unless Dill was able to assure him that all was well, he would appeal directly to President Roosevelt, "who has always been the patron and protector of this idea."[15] The prime minister's message was backed up by another from the chiefs of staff, who argued that to send the Force to the Mediterranean would waste both shipping and men "specialized in snow warfare," and that it was "unsound militarily" to "yield to impatience."[16]

Faced with such united British opposition, the US chief of staff changed his mind. "Marshall has deferred to your request," Dill informed Churchill on March 6. "Plough force will remain here and intact. Eisenhower will be informed."[17]

Britain's premier was delighted. "Tell General Marshall," he replied, "I am deeply grateful."[18]

At Fort Harrison, meanwhile, Lieutenant Colonel Don Williamson was worried that "morale is not too good, owing to the fact that these men, all selected volunteers, are impatient for action and consequently exhibiting considerable restlessness."[19]

Unaware of the disagreements in Washington, DC, and London, the Forcemen were desperate to hear word of imminent combat, the reason most of them had volunteered in the first place. There were, recalled Jack Callowhill, "a heck of a lot of guys" who thought they could get into action "faster with this outfit."[20]

While most Forcemen waited anxiously for news of their deployment, winter training gave way to refresher courses on weapons, hand-to-hand combat, tactical problems and field exercises. Individual platoons practiced battle drill, a training procedure that the British had picked up from captured German manuals and adapted for their Commonwealth colleagues. It taught, wrote Canadian Sergeant Bill Story, "the basics of any form of attack: frontal right flanking, left flanking pincer, house-to-house fighting, and so on." The chief principle was fire and movement: identifying a target, then getting some men to lay down suppressing fire while the others maneuvered toward it. "It was," noted Story, "far superior to anything that Forcemen saw in standard infantry US training manuals of the time. It enabled a platoon leader, for example, to scout out a position to be attacked, decide on the mode, and then simply tell his troops 'left flanking.' Each soldier knew his assigned position and responsibilities. It would save a lot of lives in the Force, and would make attacks more effective."[21]

Tens of thousands of rounds were expended on the firing ranges, and the Forcemen's fitness regime was as tough as ever. "Friday," wrote Private Sam Byrne, a new arrival in 2-2 Company, to his father, "we went on an eighteen mile hike with about eighty pounds in our rucksacks. Boy we sure got tired. It was uphill most of the way and we had to walk." Despite wading through snow that was more than a foot deep in places, they covered the distance in just seven and a half hours.[22] Before March was out, all three regiments had easily surpassed Frederick's benchmark of 50 miles in 24 hours, with most men taking only 17 hours, a US Army marching record.[23]

Apart from training accidents, the most persistent threat to the men's health came from venereal disease, typically caught off Helena's prostitutes. To help alleviate the problem, the post commander of Fort Harrison had asked the city authorities to close all suspected brothels and apprehend the most flagrant whores so they could be treated for VD. But this had not been done, the post commander complained on February 18. Instead, known prostitutes were allowed to "solicit publicly and operate in new locations." Moreover, Ida's Rooms, the most notorious whorehouse, was still "selling liquor after hours" and "engaging less openly in prostitution." In a letter sent jointly to the county commissioners, the governor of Montana and the mayor of Helena, he demanded immediate action to stamp out the scourge.[24]

The fullest response was provided by the city's police judge, who insisted that they had been doing their bit by arresting a number of women on mere suspicion, and if on further investigation they were found to have been guilty of prostitution, either professional or nonprofessional, they were prosecuted. Moreover, said the judge, the police warning to the camp authorities that two known prostitutes were going to marry Forcemen had not been acted upon. So that when the women were given "floater sentences" to leave Helena, they had simply gone to the fort, where without hindrance, they met up with their "soldier boys" and married them, and were now "pretending to live the life of respectable people." He ended the letter by pointing out that before the Force came to Helena the incidence of VD in the male population was 1.2 percent, "as low as any place in the United States." Soon after their arrival it had jumped to 8 percent. "It looks to me," concluded the judge, "like your problem, but we are doing everything we can to help you."[25]

An obvious way to avoid VD was to find a respectable girlfriend in the Helena area, as a number of Forcemen had done. What Frederick and his senior officers did not want, of course, was for girlfriends to become wives, believing as they did that unattached young men made better, more daring soldiers. But with a foreign posting in the offing, that is exactly what happened. Officers were among the first to tie the knot: four Canadian lieutenants married local girls in the space of a week in early February 1943.[26] A few weeks later, Joe Glass of 1-2 Company followed suit. He had fallen in love with both Dot and the area, but a more pressing reason might have been the fact that she was pregnant with his child.* First he needed a ring, and to buy one he borrowed $10 from his platoon leader, Larry Piette, who seems to have forgiven him for the AWOL incident at Blossburg. It may have helped that Glass was one of Piette's keenest soldiers and had recently scored 198 out of 200 in a test of fitness and ability over the camp's obstacle course, the top score by an enlisted man, matched by only one officer.[27]

Dot accepted Joe's proposal. She loved him, had recently turned 18 and was ready for marriage. Unsure how her reserved Austrian-

---

* Joe and Dot were married on March 6, 1943. Their son Chuck was born on October 17, just over seven months later, so she was probably at least six weeks pregnant when he proposed. Another 3rd Platoon man who tied the knot for similar reasons was Sergeant Harry Deyette. He married 24-year-old Ida Spencer on February 28th, and their daughter Henrietta was born in July.

born parents would react to the news, however, she decided not to tell them until after the ceremony on Saturday, March 6. As she was leaving home that afternoon, wearing makeup and her best dress, her mother suspected something was up. "You aren't going to do something silly like getting married, are you?" The wedding was a small affair in Helena's justice of the peace office: just Dot and Joe, with their best friends, Steffie and Lorin, as witnesses. Pronounced man and wife by the judge, they celebrated with drinks and dancing. Only later did they return to Dot's home in East Helena to tell her parents, the shock only partly relieved by Joe's gift of a bottle of whiskey.[28]

Joe Glass and the four Canadian officers were among more than 200 Forcemen who married local girls in the spring of 1943.[29] Most got hitched in a hurry after it was finally announced, in early April, that the Force would soon be on the move: its destination was Camp Bradford, the Naval Operations Base near Norfolk, Virginia, where the men would receive amphibious training prior to their deployment on active service. The news provided a noticeable boost to morale.[30]

The last few days at Fort Harrison passed in a blur of forced marches, tactical exercises and hurried packing. "We are going to be awfully busy this coming week," wrote Ray Holbrook to his sister Gladys, "as we have two night problems and one big problem in the day time. I am a machine gunner now. I fired the machine gun last week and made expert. I am quite proud of myself (109 out of a possible 128)." He and his 3rd Platoon colleagues were, he added, handing in their ski equipment, so he knew that if they went into action in the spring it wouldn't be on skis. He ended by mentioning a 24-mile hike that had left most of the platoon "all pooped out" with sore feet. But it had not deterred him from a visit to town to "see the girl friend." She was a local girl called Dorothy who, from the start, had told Holbrook that she was in love with another serviceman, a sergeant serving in Africa. As long as he was okay with that, she was happy to go out with him. He had said he was, secretly hoping that she would eventually prefer him.[31]

15

"We had a crazy bunch of guys"

To say a proper goodbye to the city that had welcomed them so warmly, all 2,300 men of the Force paraded through downtown Helena on Army Day, Tuesday, April 6. Marching in column in their smart dress uniforms (Class A), parachute boots and steel helmets, and led by the Force's band, they made quite an impression on the thousands of cheering residents who lined the streets of the business district. The salute was taken on a raised platform in Main Street by Colonel Frederick and Brigadier F. G. Weeks, the deputy chief of Canada's General Staff. Also in attendance were state governor Sam C. Ford and Helena's mayor, Jack Haytin. The parade ended at Hill Park, where the public was able to view and even handle some of the Force's weapons and equipment. That evening, having replaced their steel helmets with caps, the Forcemen returned to Helena to celebrate their imminent departure.[1]

Next day, Haytin wrote Frederick a letter of thanks for the "glorious show" his men had put on. Helena was, he said, "just as proud of the First Special Service Force as you are, and it was an inspiring thing to see this exceptional group of men who obviously are highly trained and in the finest possible condition." There had been, said Haytin in a nod to the burst of recent marriages, "many close friendships established" and the whole community would "follow the Force with most intense interest and the most fervent prayers."[2]

Five passenger trains and one freight were needed to transport the Force's men and equipment from Helena to Norfolk, Virginia. Bill Rothlin's 1-2 Company was in the third train to leave in the early evening of Sunday, April 11. As it chugged slowly away from the siding near Fort Harrison, the men hung from the windows and waved to girlfriends and wives, some of whom, like pregnant Dot Glass and Steffie Broderick, followed the train for as long as they could in cars.

After a long and circuitous rail journey, they arrived at Camp Bradford, the US Navy's Amphibious Training Center, on April 15 and were met by the Force's advance party, including Larry Piette. Located in a large fir wood, the camp was 12 miles from Virginia Beach on Chesapeake Bay. Its living quarters and office buildings had been painted a dull green for camouflage, and the whole area was under tight security and blacked out at night. As at Fort Harrison, the men were housed 12 to a hut; officers' quarters were almost as crowded. "The meals are good," noted the Canadians' war diary. "Everyone is eating in the Navy mess or galley as we must now learn to call it."[3]

The training began the following day in damp and chilly conditions, a contrast to the dry, thin air of Montana. It was designed to prepare the Force for ship-to-shore or shore-to-shore landings with its winter equipment and vehicles, and included learning how to scramble up and down nets from landing craft to ships and vice versa, swim with weapons, use rubber boats, land secretly at night on beaches and rocks, embark from beaches, carry out battalion, regimental and Force landing maneuvers, and scale steep rocky slopes.

It was a lot to learn in just a few weeks, but the men were both supremely fit and highly competitive. They sensed, wrote their intelligence chief, "they were being judged against every outfit that had been through this amphibious mill." So they set to each task with a will. "Harking back to the daily runs over the arduous obstacle course at Harrison, with its long stretches of overhead rope walks, the regiments swarmed like monkeys over the rope ladders at the training field."[4] It helped that the Force was now at sea level, whereas all its previous training had been at 4,000 feet or higher. "One morning," recalled Jack Callowhill, "we were a little late, and they said we'd have to double-time to get to the beach. This is the BS [bullshit] starting. So we double-timed and left the Marine instructor behind. He couldn't keep up...With us training in the thin air, we could run for miles down there."[5]

On April 24, the Forcemen were paraded for the first time in front of their colors: the Stars and Stripes, the Union Flag and the newly designed Force flag, comprising a spread eagle on a scarlet background, surmounted by a white shield with a V-42 knife slanting across it. The eagle symbolizes war and peace: clutched in one set of talons is a bundle of arrows, in the other an olive branch. Unable to decide on a motto, Frederick had ordered the scroll in the eagle's beak to be left blank until something suitable came to him. It never did. Yet the simple ceremony seemed significant, "like the last brick in a well-built edifice."[6]

The following day—a "perfect Easter Sunday, bright and warm, the best day we have had yet"—the Forcemen were embarked on three troopships to practice combat landings along the Chesapeake coast. The 2nd Regiment was assigned to the USS *Neville*. For the first two days the Forcemen raced down scramble nets from the deck to the landing craft beneath, a distance of at least 35 feet, with full combat loads. Then they did it at night. Until then, the record for loading a platoon in the dark was a minute for the army and 52 seconds for the Marines. The fastest Force platoon—from 3rd Regiment—managed the feat in an astonishing 33 seconds.[7] The trick, according to Ken Betts of 1-2 Company, was to let go of the ropes and nets at the top and catch them again at the bottom. "We had a crazy bunch of guys, I'm telling you," he recalled. "That is how we were doing it."[8]

The Forcemen's performance in landing on the coast at night by both rubber boat and landing craft was almost as impressive. Each assault by landing craft was made simultaneously at six points, reported the training officer, yet the troops "deployed well on reaching the beach" and discipline was "generally high." The same officer had recently observed a battalion of the Marines and men of the 9th Division make a similar assault by landing craft and, in his opinion, the Forcemen did as well as either, yet they had trained for a much shorter time.[9]

Like the rest of the Force, the men of 1-2 Company went through amphibious training with "flying colors."[10] Percy Crichlow, recently appointed supply sergeant at company HQ, was proud that they were able to carry out any of the training drills "as fast and as expeditiously as any unit that had been there before us." He mostly enjoyed his time at Camp Bradford, where the food was excellent. But two incidents were not to his liking. The first was when the newly promoted Captain Rothlin made the company double to the beach for an evening exercise after a hurried meal, causing Crichlow and a few others to fall out with stomach cramps. "I was bitterly annoyed," commented Crichlow, "because I was made to break my good record and fall out." Far more worrying, however, was Rothlin's request that he move to Piette's 3rd Platoon as a section leader. Crichlow was all too aware of the platoon's unruly reputation and the fact that its sections did not get on. That bad blood had already caused the transfer of the platoon officer and one of the section leaders. Now Crichlow was to replace the other. It was not an appointment he relished. "I told the captain flatly that I just didn't want the job even if it did carry promotion to S/Sgt [staff sergeant]."

But Rothlin was adamant that Crichlow *would* take over 6th Section, and he eventually got his way. Crichlow felt, he wrote later, "like a lamb going into a lion's den." Yet for all his misgivings, the move was a good one. A cerebral man who had not done a day's physical labor in his life, Crichlow could not have been more different from the tough former loggers and trappers who dominated his section. Yet he would lead them by quiet and determined example, and they appreciated that. It helped that his platoon leader, Larry Piette, was "as good an officer as I was to see anywhere among the Americans"; and that the other section leader, Staff Sergeant Hugh McGinty from Oregon—a larger-than-life "former miner, logger and soldier—a good shot, very skilled with a mortar, a first-class purveyor of 'bull,' possessed of a colorful vocabulary, and a collector of VD"—took no nonsense from his men.[11] There had been, in any case, one or two recent additions to Crichlow's 6th Section who were not quite as rough-hewn as the originals. East Coast men like Dick Daigle, the former Airborne soldier from Lynn, Massachusetts, and Phil Clark from Kearny, New Jersey. Daigle, in particular, had settled in well to the section, helped by his instant friendship with bunkmate Harry Deyette.

Meanwhile, some of the 5th Section originals were still giving Rothlin a headache. The trouble started when Syd Gath, 28, an old sweat who had been in uniform since the start of the war, objected to a dressing-down by his company commander. When Joe Glass tried to intervene, he was asked by Rothlin if he agreed with Gath. "Yes, sir," said Glass. "I guess I do." For their insubordination, they were both given seven days' pack drill, a punishment that required them to exercise in full uniform with a heavy pack on their backs. "We did it," recalled Glass. "We were tough little buggers. We marched to a helluva tune. I don't think Rothlin trusted me. But he knew I was a good scout."[12]

16

"The objective now was perfection"

The original plan for the Force, once it had completed its amphibious training at Camp Bradford, was to move down to Fort Pierce in Florida for scout and raider training. But this was changed in early May when word reached Frederick that the Force would shortly be deployed overseas, probably to the United Kingdom. So instead of going south, the Force went north—via Washington, Baltimore and Philadelphia—to Fort Ethan Allen near Burlington, Vermont, where it would be within easy striking distance of Boston, the most likely port of embarkation.[1] The fort—a picturesque former cavalry post named after the popular leader of the Green Mountain Boys who captured Fort Ticonderoga from the British in 1775—was four miles from Burlington, a sleepy city of 28,000 souls, and three from Lake Champlain. It comprised a number of whitewashed timber-framed buildings: single-story for the mess and office buildings, and two stories for the soldiers' quarters. The main difference from Camp Bradford, and Fort Harrison for that matter, was that the men were housed on bunks in huge halls, while the officers were two to a room.[2]

The training was less intense than before—"the objective now was perfection."[3] Yet it still felt strenuous enough as the Forcemen were put through a series of forced marches, night demolition raids, weapon firing, living under field conditions and amphibious exercises on Lake Champlain to prepare them for combat. "We are working night and day," wrote a corporal in 2-2 Company to his mother on June 9. "This last week I got about forty-eight hours sleep. I think something is going to happen but I don't know when."[4] The frustration of not knowing when they would see combat caused fights to break out. Corporal Sam Boroditsky of 1st Regiment was set upon by four men from another company after a long drinking session in Burlington. Objecting to "some remarks" made earlier by one of his friends, the group had jumped Boroditsky as he made his way back to camp alone in the dark. He took a savage beating—two black eyes and a broken nose—and had to spend a couple of days recovering at the hospital. Most of the punishment was administered, the corporal learned later, by the former light-heavyweight boxing champion of Texas. "I wasn't the only one," he noted ruefully, "he did that to."[5]

When they were not fighting among themselves, the Forcemen were learning how to use a new weapon that had just been issued to each section: the M1941 Johnson light machine gun. Weighing just 14 pounds with its loaded magazine, the Johnny gun had first been procured for Marine paratroopers. Fed by a curved, side-fitting 20-shot magazine, and with a rate of fire that could be adjusted from 200 to 600 rounds per minute, it packed as much punch as the 23-pound Browning Automatic Rifle. But it was much lighter and could be broken down into three pieces, making it an ideal weapon for airborne troops. The only source of supply, however, was the Marine Corps. So Frederick's S-4, Orval Baldwin, had to horse-trade by offering a quantity of RS explosives for 125 Johnny guns. The Marine Corps accepted, but it was not until June 1943 that the first guns arrived, giving the Forcemen only limited time to get used to the new weapon. In Crichlow's section, the pair assigned to the Johnny gun team were good pals Harry Deyette and Dick Daigle.[6]

Off duty, Daigle met and dated a student from Burlington's Fanny Allen School of Nursing, named after the sister of Ethan who had tended soldiers in Montreal during the War of 1812. Daigle's girl was Rachel "Rae" Bourgeois, a 20-year-old French-Canadian from Bennington, Vermont.[7] Others hooked up with "Bell Aircraft Girls, popularly known as Bags," who were employed by the firm that made the famous P-38 Lightning fighter-bomber.[8]

With a foreign posting imminent, Colonel Frederick allowed the married Forcemen to be joined at Burlington by their wives. Among those who traveled up from Helena were Bobby MacWilliam and the pregnant Dot Glass. Bobby's husband, Tom, now a major, had recently changed his will so that his wife, rather than his parents, was his sole beneficiary.[9]

Shortly after the Force reached Fort Ethan Allen, Colonel Frederick was informed by the OPD that his men would embark for the United Kingdom on or around July 25. Winston Churchill had set the ball rolling on April 18 when he sent his chiefs of staff a minute on "Future Strategy." As a German collapse that year was "extremely unlikely," and neither American reinforcements nor landing craft were available, he did not feel that an invasion of France was possible in 1943. To keep up the pressure on Germany, therefore, he insisted that Operation Jupiter—the invasion of Norway—had to be considered "as a possibility for January 1944, or whatever is the best winter month." That, in turn, would require the deployment of "the snowplough force and [its] equipment." Churchill wrote: "How is this getting on?"[10]

The requested progress report was compiled by Mountbatten's deputy, Brigadier Wildman-Lushington, who stated that the Force was continuing its training in the United States and was ready to come over to the United Kingdom as soon as any suitable operation, such as Jupiter, was on the cards. As for its snow vehicle, a new and improved version (known as the T24)—more reliable and with "10 percent better performance"—had been ordered by the US Army and would be ready by mid-October.[11]

Yet by the start of the high-level Trident Conference in Washington, DC, on May 12—attended by Roosevelt, Churchill and their Combined Chiefs of Staff—Mountbatten's representatives* had come around to the idea that it would be good to give the Force some combat experience before it was sent to the UK for use in Operation Jupiter. A possible loss of 20 to 25 percent casualties would, they told Brigadier General Wedemeyer, be justified because it would make the Force "100 percent more effective in future operations."[12] Wedemeyer passed on this welcome news to General Marshall, adding:

> The troops are superior in physical condition, able to negotiate difficult terrain and move rapidly on foot. They are well trained in demolitions, hand-to-hand combat and operations at night. A period of amphibious training, landing by both landing craft and rubber boats, has been completed and the force has been declared highly proficient by instructors and observers. Training has included dropping personnel and equipment by parachute.[13]

The final decision to blood the Force before "its proper role in the winter" was made at a meeting by Roosevelt, Churchill and the Combined Chiefs of Staff in the White House on May 25, 1943. It was, General Marshall told the meeting, "the firm opinion" of all relevant US and British officers that the Force "should be given battle experience as soon as possible," with likely destinations to include the

---

* Mountbatten caught pneumonia in April 1943 and was forced to miss the Trident Conference, which agreed among other things to postpone the invasion of France until May 1, 1944. As for the Mediterranean, Eisenhower was left to decide what operations after the invasion of Sicily seemed "best calculated to eliminate Italy from the war and to contain the maximum number of German forces" (Atkinson, p. 21).

Aleutian Islands, post-"Husky" operations in the Mediterranean, or commando raids from the UK or even in the Azores. All those present were in agreement. But Churchill was still determined that the Force would carry out its original role, and so he suggested it be sent to the UK, where it would be "quite easy to create an opportunity for its employment," possibly in a raid on the coast of Norway. It would be up to the British Chiefs of Staff to make a specific proposal.[14]

This all changed in early June, however, when General John L. DeWitt, commanding the US Fourth Army, requested more men for the task of recapturing the Japanese-occupied island of Kiska in the Aleutians, a chain of more than 300 volcanic islands off the southern coast of Alaska. His troops had just ousted a smaller Japanese garrison from Attu, another of the islands, at a cost of more than 3,500 casualties, and DeWitt anticipated an even bloodier struggle on Kiska. Marshall's response was to offer him the Force, and DeWitt, having consulted his subordinate commanders, was quick to accept.[15]

All that remained was for Marshall to get the go-ahead from the British Chiefs of Staff. He wired on June 8:

> An operation against Kiska is to be undertaken about 15 August 1943. It will involve a difficult landing and probably bitter fighting with a Japanese force of from six to ten thousand. Under the circumstances it is desired to utilize the PLOUGH force, to be relieved immediately following completion of the operation. It will gain valuable experience prior to transfer to the United Kingdom.[16]

On reading the cable, Churchill replied: "Surely we should say 'Yes.'"[17] His chiefs thought so too, not least because they had already agreed in principle that the Force be given operational experience if the opportunity arose. The Kiska battle would, they thought, be an "excellent" opportunity.[18] They cabled their agreement on June 9,[19] the same day that Frederick was told by telephone of this latest change of plan. He was delighted. A posting direct to the UK might have resulted in another long wait while Mountbatten made up his mind how best to use the Force. Morale would have plummeted. Kiska meant combat, and soon.[20]

Frederick flew to San Francisco to be briefed on the Force's role in the attack — code-named Operation Cottage — by General DeWitt. The Force, explained DeWitt, would be part of Major General Charles H. Corlett's Amphibious Task Force 9. Its job would be to land at night ahead of the main body of troops and secure the beaches before moving inland. To prepare for the operation, Frederick's men would be quarantined on Angel Island in San Francisco Bay before taking ships to the Pacific island of Adak, their jumping-off point. Their departure from Fort Ethan Allen was scheduled for the end of June.[21]

For reasons of operational security, Frederick could only share the plan with his four senior staff officers. All he would tell the men, when he returned to Burlington, was that "in the place where they were going, there was a girl behind every tree." It was, he noted wryly, not a lie. At their base camp in the Aleutians, "there was no vegetation taller than eight inches."[22]

Commencing on June 15, each one of the Force's 18 companies was put through a series of rigorous tests to see that it had reached the standards of training, equipment and physical fitness set by Army Ground Forces for troops heading into combat. First each company had to complete a four-mile march route with pack and rifle in less than an hour, with marks deducted for stragglers and late arrivals. Further tests included proficiency in map reading, maintenance of weapons, tactical problems, calisthenics and foot races. Every company easily surpassed the benchmark of 75 percent. Their average mark was 125 percent, and on some tests they rated as high as 200 percent, forcing the inspectors to admit that the US Army's rating structure was inadequate for a unit as well trained as the Force. "The result," recalled Jack Callowhill, "and I'm not kidding, is that they scratched their heads and said, 'We want nothing to do with these guys. They just don't fit any of our scores.' We were off the chart."[23] The inspectors were particularly impressed by the loads the men were able to carry without difficulty and the complete confidence each man seemed to have in himself and his comrades. The Force, they reported back, "was ready for any job that had to be done."[24]

The Forcemen spent their last few days at Fort Ethan Allen being issued new weapons and equipment—including their winter parkas—packing up and saying goodbye to wives and sweethearts. It was an emotional time and, with their futures uncertain, many shed tears. Even new couples like Rae Bourgeois and Dick Daigle found it painful to part. To remind him of her, and to keep him safe, Rae gave Dick a Buck folding knife engraved with her name, a Winooski Park money belt and a Fanny Allen Hospital coin for good luck.[25]

Finally, in the early hours of Monday, June 29, the first train moved out of the siding at Fort Ethan Allen for "destination unknown" with 1-2 Company and the rest of the 2nd Regiment on board. Another four followed. Assuming they were headed for the East Coast, the cry went up: "Boston, here we come. Look out, Kraut!"[26] But when the trains turned west and not east at Albany, it slowly dawned on Rothlin and his men that their likely foes were not Germans but "Japs."[27]

17

"We want to take as many prisoners as possible"

At noon on Saturday, July 3, after a long and uncomfortable four-day journey across the United States, 1-2 Company's train pulled into a siding at San Francisco's Pier 41. The sky was overcast, the temperature cold and the air damp. Transferred to a ferry, the men and their equipment were taken across the bay, past the rocky outcrop topped by the Alcatraz Federal Penitentiary, to the much larger Angel Island, where they would spend the next week in quarantine. For security, they had removed all unit insignia, and until they left for their mission, no one would leave the island.[1]

They were quartered in Fort McDowell, a comfortable if slightly overcrowded camp on the east of the island with good views of the San Francisco and Golden Gate Bridges. The first full day—July 4, Independence Day for the Americans—was spent sorting out equipment and being issued with new items—lightweight arctic sleeping bags, wool-lined jackets, rain suits and thick socks—that indicated their likely destination was cold and wet. Most people's money, by this stage, was on the Aleutian Islands. The officers and senior NCOs received confirmation that evening when they were addressed by

General Charles H. Corlett, the task force commander, "a small grey-blond, pockmarked soldier with a humorous glint in his eyes." He did not go into specific details but said the Force would be part of a much larger formation, designated Amphibious Task Force 9, and would operate under the navy in northern waters. The area in question, he added, was "not as cold as you might expect at this time of year" and included over "fifty varieties of wild flowers." The last time they fought the Japanese on Attu, said Corlett, they took just 31 prisoners from a garrison of 2,300. "This time, we want to take as many prisoners as possible and see if we can't put an opening wedge into their Samurai code."

Corlett ended his talk by telling the Forcemen that the expedition would include a brigade of Canadians, which pleased their fellow countrymen. He seemed to be "energetic, frank and generally a good head," which boded well for the operation.[2]

Embarkation began during the evening of July 9. The plan—known to only a few staff officers at this point—was to ship the Force to the Aleutian island of Adak, where they would prepare for the assault on Kiska in mid-August. Warned of their departure, the men of 1-2 Company got last-minute haircuts and spent their remaining pay in the PX, which was soon out of candy, toilet articles and stationery. At 9:00 p.m., after a cursory medical examination, they shouldered their weapons and bulky rucksacks and filed aboard a ferry for the return trip to San Francisco docks. As they did so, a watching US officer commented: "These are the heaviest packs I've seen, and the first troops that didn't stoop under their load. They look like real soldiers."[3]

At the docks they and the rest of the 2nd Regiment were loaded on the Liberty troop carrier SS *John B. Floyd*. They were joined by the Supply Battalion and Force HQ (minus Colonel Frederick, who had flown ahead to Adak). The other two regiments were in a second Liberty ship, the SS *Nathaniel Wyeth*. Crewed by merchant seamen, the Liberty ships were mass-produced to a simple design to augment the US Navy in wartime. They had not been built for either comfort or speed, as the Forcemen would soon find out.

July 10 was spent at the pier as landing craft were loaded onto the ships, a laborious process that convinced the Canadians' war diarist that the navy and longshoremen were competing "to see who could take more time." The cramped quarters included "hammock like bunks, one on top of the other, in the cleaned up cargo hold" for the men, while the junior officers were stowed 18 to a large cabin on rows of triple bunks. Only the senior officers, including Colonel Paul Adams, Lieutenant-Colonel Don Williamson and Major Tom MacWilliam, had the relative comfort of sharing smaller staterooms. Meals were served from hatches, but as no names were taken, there was no way to prevent men from going up twice, a problem only partially solved when Rothlin and the other company commanders were told to take their men through in groups.

Next morning the ships moved to an anchorage near the San Francisco–Oakland Bay Bridge to await the rest of the convoy of seven transports and four escorting destroyers. Finally, at 5:30 p.m. on the 11th, the ships weighed anchor and headed for the open sea. "As we sailed under the bridge," noted Captain Ed Thomas, "we made plans for the great return party we'd have in San Francisco, at least by those of us who survived the operation."[4]

But such happy thoughts were soon dispelled by the rolling of the ships as they entered the open sea and turned north into a stretch of very rough water known as the "potato patch." Thomas recalled:

Our boat began to pitch and heave and the seasickness started. The rough seas lasted a couple of days, not a very pleasant experience on a troop ship, with bunks in 8-high tiers in the hold. Our food service was provided by our unit cooks but for those two days there was little incentive or desire…The cooks were as sick as the rest of the men. By some miracle, I was spared. I think there was only one other Force member who was not sick.[5]

There were, in fact, a few—and two of them were in Crichlow's 6th Section: "Pop" Lewis and Joe Dauphinais, both recently promoted to sergeant. On the second morning, Lewis went to the galley to get something to eat and was told the cooks were ill. So he made his own breakfast from powdered eggs and some bread, using a huge two-feet-square frying pan, and was delighted with the result.

Dauphinais managed to find a cook well enough to make him a pork sandwich. He was still eating it as he took his turn on watch, causing his "Indian buddy" Howard Van Ausdale ("Van" to his friends) to ask: "How can you eat? What in hell do you have there?"

"A big fat pork sandwich," replied the Canadian.

"That's cruel. I haven't eaten for two days!" said Van Ausdale, turning on his heel. He had spent most of his life in the wilderness of Oregon and "just couldn't take ships at all."[6]

So bad did the rolling of the *John B. Floyd* become that some of the equipment on deck was lost overboard. It was a miracle that no one was injured when a few of the landing craft broke their cables and slid around the deck before finally, and at great risk to the sailors, they were resecured. Down below, the heavy sea caused more than a hundred bunks to come crashing to the ground, some with men in them, though no one was seriously injured.[7]

One morning, with the weather improving, Colonel Adams warned Rothlin and the other officers that they were losing control of their men. Discipline, said Adams, was "very bad" and needed to be reestablished. At the very least, the men needed to shave once a day and get up on deck whether they were sick or not. By now the officers and men had been told they were part of a 32,000-strong amphibious task force whose mission was to storm the Aleutian island of Kiska and capture it from the Japanese. The news was a total surprise to Sergeant "Pop" Lewis. He had been expecting a mission that involved a parachute drop "behind the lines" in an Arctic region. That, after all, is what the Force had been raised and trained for. "I just figured," he recalled, "it would have been someplace special, but the Aleutians? That simply amazed me."[8]

Finally, as the sun was setting on Friday, July 23, the first fine weather of the Forcemen's tedious 12-day voyage, the pronounced silhouette of Adak Island's high peaks came into view. Soon after, the convoy slipped past the submarine nets and into the spacious bay that served the military base on the northeast of the island. But instead of disembarking, the men on the *John B. Floyd* were joined by their commander, Colonel Frederick, who had flown ahead to inspect the Force's bivouac area. What he found was a soggy tundra with a poor supply system and inadequate shelter tents. So he requested, and received, permission to divert the Force to the island of Amchitka, just 50 miles from Kiska (whereas Adak was 180 miles) and with a slightly less waterlogged terrain.[9]

Leaving behind his intelligence chief, Lieutenant Colonel Robert Burhans, to liaise with General Corlett, Frederick sailed with the two Liberty ships for Amchitka the following morning. They arrived on July 25 as a bright, warm sun was burning through the morning mist to reveal a long, thin island—40 miles long but only two to four miles wide—with a few mountains at its center but the rest lowlying, barren and boggy. The ships docked at the wooden pier and the men, carrying weapons and heavy rucksacks, disembarked down steep wooden planks before forming into companies.

With Rothlin at its head, 1-2 Company was the first to begin the five-mile march to the bivouac area up the island's only road. "To everyone," noted the company diary, "unaccustomed as they were to Aleutian weather, it was a perfect day. Bright sunlight, lush green vegetation—not a bad spot at all. They learned quickly just what a hell-hole they were in. Only too soon did the sun disappear, the fog and rain roll in and within two hours the Company was wading, knee deep, through that lush green vegetation."[10]

Two tents were provided for each section, but they had to be dug in to a depth of four feet to reach solid, dry ground and to provide a shelter wall against possible bomb splinters. Even then, many Force-men used wood and packing cases to construct a dry platform for their sleeping bags. This was taken to extremes when one supply officer, ig-norant of the danger, floored his tent with mortar shells still in their cardboard packing tubes.[11]

With Amchitka's average of six days of sunshine a year, the weather on the Force's first day was an anomaly. Thereafter the climate re-verted to type: damp and chilly, with shifting fog. So poor was the visibility on one battalion route march that Ed Thomas, leading the column, noticed other soldiers in the distance and assumed the train-ing area had been "invaded." The closer he got, the more familiar the soldiers appeared, until he realized he had led his column in a circle and was looking at its tail.[12]

A lot of the training involved launching rubber boats off landing craft, then paddling a thousand yards in to the shore. "Biceps and backs were strained to the utmost," recorded 1-2 Company's diary, "in trying to reach some rocky cove or other prior to an assault on some pre-designated objective."[13]

The island of Kiska was 21 miles long and seven wide, with the harbor and main Japanese base protected by the island of Little Kiska off its east coast. Its steep, hilly terrain favored the defender, as did the profu-sion of valleys, caves, streams and swamps. Kiska's vegetation was, like Amchitka's, chiefly muskeg and long grass, while the climate was just as harsh. The overall plan of invasion—agreed between Corlett and the Navy commander, Admiral T. C. Kincaid—was for a naval diver-sion and simulated landing on the south side of Kiska while the actual assault was carried out in two locations on the northwest or Bering Sea coast.

Each attack would be spearheaded by a regiment of the Force "whose task it was to precede the main bodies, land in rubber boats and move rapidly inland to neutralize enemy installations." The 1st Regiment would land in the more southerly of the two sectors in the early hours of D-Day, August 15, before seizing and holding the high ground that overlooked one of the main enemy positions at Gertrude Cove. Three hours later, the main infantry force would land in support. An identical mission in the northern sector was assigned to the 3rd Regiment for the following day. The 2nd Regiment, meanwhile, would be on standby at the airfield at Amchitka, ready to "land by parachute at any point on Kiska...in order to relieve or exploit an emergency situation."[14]

When Ed Thomas heard about the 2nd Regiment's assignment, he was shocked. Most Forcemen, he knew, had made only two parachute jumps and "there had never been any training in tactical jumps, nor in the most important element of a parachute operation, assembly on the ground." What he was able to change, however, was the plan to drop all weapons, including rifles, in bundles. He did this by arranging a demonstration jump with a rifle holster known as the Griswold container or "violin case," which allowed the parachutist to keep his weapon and not waste time searching for a bundle. Designed by a Major George Griswold of the 501st Parachute Infantry Regiment, the container was made from canvas padded with horsehair felt or jute, rectangular in shape, and could carry an M1 rifle that had been dismantled into four parts. It was closed with a heavy-duty zip and attached to the parachute harness by a V-ring and snap hook on the back.

To show how easy it was to use, Thomas chose a drop zone between two lakes, not far from his bivouac area, and went up with two others in a C-47 to do the jump on August 13. To make the demonstration more spectacular, he asked the pilot to come in "on the deck," a technique he had watched a couple of times at Fort Bragg. "The first two attempts," he recalled, "to hit the DZ at the right altitude missed the mark. On the third approach, [the pilot] missed the mark again and was climbing when we were over it, so I led our group out anyway at about 250 feet. We all landed with no problem. Muskeg is a great cushion on which to make a parachute jump."[15]

Next morning, just a few hours before the 1st Regiment was due to be embarked on a landing ship, Bill Becket was summoned to a meeting with Colonel Frederick in the large tent that housed Force HQ. Handing Becket an aerial photograph, Frederick looked him in the eye and asked: "That's your beach, isn't it, Bill?"

Becket studied the photograph. It was indeed his primary objective, Quisling Cove, code-named Blue Beach—a stretch of coast barely 100 yards in length. But as Becket looked more closely he could see something that looked like a machine-gun nest on slightly higher ground to the left of the beach. It had a clear field of fire both along the beach and out to sea, and would cut his men to pieces unless it was knocked out.

"Yes, sir," answered Becket.

"This photo was taken by one of our observation planes *this morning*, Bill. What do you think you ought to do about it?"

"Well, sir," said Becket, after a pause, "subject to Colonel Marshall's orders, I could put one rubber boat in about 15 or 20 minutes ahead of time with one section headed by the platoon officer, and I'd put it in the rocks to the left of the beach. Then he'd take the machine gun position from behind and above."

Frederick grinned his assent. "Sounds okay to me. I'll speak to Marshall. But don't talk about this to anyone except Cookie and the company and platoon leaders involved. And tell them *no* talking, not even to the men in the section going in ahead. I don't want any panic."

"I understand, sir. I'll make sure there's no leak."[16]

18

Kiska

In the early hours of August 15, as the landing ship pitched and rolled in a lively sea, Bill Becket and his men, weighed down with 100 pounds of equipment and ammunition, struggled one by one from the lowered ramp into the large rubber boats. When everyone was loaded, they began to paddle for Kiska and the waiting Japanese, one boat behind the other. It was pitch black, and no sign of the island, neither mountain nor shore, was visible. After a short distance, Becket checked his compass and realized their heading was 90 degrees out. He had a serious decision to make. "If I was going to trust my compass," he wrote later, "and I should have to once the ship was lost in the darkness, I had better trust it now. It was one of the most difficult decisions of my life—the success of a mission and the lives of hundreds of men were involved, and there could be no delay. So I made it and I swung those twelve rubber boats some ninety degrees to the east."

Luck was with them as, within minutes, the clouds parted to reveal a full moon. "The sea lit up," noted Becket, "and suddenly we had amazing visibility—enough to show me the volcanic peaks of my mountain objectives and moments later our tiny beach. I knew then that we were on the right course." Becket and his men also knew that the bright moonlight made it easy for any alert Japanese sentry to see the approaching boats. They were tense and nervous as they neared the shore. Becket had sent a single boat ahead to take out the machine-gun nest, but had his men succeeded? They would soon find out.

The remaining rubber boats hit the shore at almost exactly the same time. Becket jumped into ankle-deep water and had just reached dry sand when the platoon leader, who had been sent ahead, came running up. "There was nobody there, sir!" he yelled. "Nobody there, all clear!"

Becket nodded his relief, then watched his battalion landing as he had hoped it would, "with no fuss nor fury, quickly, quietly and in fighting order." He could not have been prouder. Turning to his XO, Ed Pearce, he said: "We are going up that hill there, right now. You see that the companies go up one after the other—1st Company leading—and you come up in the rear when you are satisfied they are all on the way. I'll see you up there when you've got them all up."

It was a tough climb in the dark, and Becket and his men took more than half an hour to reach their objective, Larry Hill, where they set up defensive positions. "It puzzled me a bit," Becket recalled, "that there was no fire ahead nor on either flank nor farther over to our left where [Lieutenant-Colonel Jack] Akehurst would be taking his 2nd Battalion."[1]

Back on Amchitka, meanwhile, Rothlin and his men were anxiously waiting with the rest of the 2nd Regiment beside C-47s on the improvised airfield for the word to take off and parachute into Kiska in support of their comrades. Woken at 2:00 a.m., they had drawn parachutes from nearby sheds before being trucked to the airfield, where they identified their assigned aircraft by their tail numbers. Percy Crichlow, commanding Rothlin's 6th Section, was so laden with weapons, equipment and Mae West life vest that he felt like a "trussed chicken, hardly able to move." He envied the Alaskan Scout—one of 20 "hard-bitten, motley-uniformed" men accompanying the Force—who kept most of his possessions in the back of his blouse. This envy became even more pronounced when he realized he "had to have a crap." He recalled: "It was a major operation to get off all the top layers, starting with the Mae West and the parachute until some time later I was able to get down to my trousers and underwear. God knows what would have happened if we had got the order just then to go into the planes."

The plan, once they were over the target, was for platoon leader Larry Piette to throw out the equipment and jump first. The men of 6th Section would follow, and Crichlow had been given an extra pistol to use on anyone who froze in the door. Once they were all out, he was to drop the pistol and jump himself.[2] As the minutes ticked by, the men chain-smoked to calm their nerves and eventually "broke out cards and dice, and the games began." Finally, in mid-morning, Colonel Williamson received a radio message from Frederick on Kiska: "Baby needs a new pair of shoes."[3]

It was code for "abort the mission": the 2nd Regiment would not be needed that day. The reaction was mixed. Desperate to see action, some of the men were disappointed. They were pumped full of adrenaline and inevitably felt a psychological letdown when the mission was canceled. The Japanese must have "heard we were on our way," commented the fire-eating Larry Piette. Why else would they have left? Others, like Ed Thomas, were relieved. "We were," he noted, "ill trained and unprepared for such an operation." Jack Callowhill was somewhere in between: "Personally, it didn't seem to bother me one way or the other."[4]

Returned by truck to their bivouac area, the 2nd Regiment men caught up on their sleep. All but Ed Thomas, who had something he needed to do first. The night before, anticipating his death, he had written a "rather sentimental" letter to a young lady he was sweet on. But in the "cold, gray light of that morning," as he thought about the letter and the fact that he was not even going into combat, he decided it had been a mistake to write it. So he sought out the mail clerk and persuaded him, against regulations, to return the letter. The clerk found the whole situation very funny.[5]

Colonel Frederick had had an eventful morning. Transported in the same landing ship as Becket and his men, he had waited for the 1st Regiment to move off before following with four members of his staff, radiomen and Alaska Scouts in two six-man rubber boats (instead of the larger twelve-man version). Lieutenant Finn Roll, his assistant intelligence chief, had persuaded him that a smaller boat would be easier to maneuver. But Roll reckoned without the extra weight of radios, batteries and flags—and a strong current. In the end, only the boat with Frederick, two staff members (including Roll) and two scouts made landfall—and it had taken two hours longer than planned. The other one, containing Major Emil Eschenberg, Dermot O'Neill (acting as Frederick's bodyguard), and the radio operators, shipped so much water it could not make progress and was eventually spotted and rescued by a US Navy minelayer. Paralyzed by cold, the men could not use their legs and had to be picked up in a landing net and dumped humiliatingly on the minelayer's deck.

A disgruntled Frederick, meanwhile, was tramping through the hills above the landing beaches, looking for the advanced units of his 1st Regiment. He was "madder than hell" at Roll for suggesting they use the small boats, and refused to speak to him. He eventually linked up with Marshall and heard that not a single Japanese had been encountered by his men. Instead they had found meals hastily abandoned in caves and huts, and in one instance a warm stove with live coals in the grate. But no enemy. Had they withdrawn to a stronghold in the north? It was impossible to know until the island had been searched from top to bottom. In the meantime, the invasion continued as planned, with the first infantry coming ashore in daylight at 6:30 a.m. They came "wading in, arms at high port, blood in their eyes." Ignoring warnings by Forcemen to "take it easy," they raced inland "looking for prey."[6]

Becket was alerted to their arrival by the sound of gunfire. Had the Japanese been found? he wondered. He received his answer when he saw, through his field glasses, that the 87th Mountain Infantry was climbing the ridge behind them, and that more than one of them was firing his weapon at an imaginary foe.[7]

By mid-morning the whole southern sector, from Lief Cove to Gertrude Cove, had been searched and no enemy discovered, prompting Frederick to stand down the 2nd Regiment. That evening, he sent a second message to his Amchitka base. It read: "Marshall's outfit reached objective without meeting a single enemy or exchanging a shot. Hills terrific. Fog dense. Wind and tide raised hell with rubber boat movement... No yellow bastards in sight. Hoping for better hunting."[8]

Frederick would be disappointed. His 3rd Regiment preceded the landings in the northern sector on D + 1, August 16 — daubed in yellow-and-green camouflage paint and with sprigs of dry tundra covering their helmets[9] — and again no opposition was encountered. Scouts from both sectors entered the main Japanese naval base at Kiska Harbor at 10:00 a.m. and found bomb craters, damaged buildings and abandoned equipment. They also discovered fresh footsteps on a path leading down to Beach Cove. There the sand bore signs of a recent, hasty withdrawal. In fact, under the cover of a severe fog, the bulk of the Japanese garrison had been evacuated by its navy as long ago as July 28. There had been a number of clues: a bombing run on August 5 had received only scattered rifle and machine-gun bullets and no antiaircraft fire; Japanese radar signals disappeared altogether the following day; and air reconnaissance revealed a demolished radar screen, motor trucks lined up on the harbor's west beach (normally they were dispersed) and the disappearance of houses and other structures in the main camp area. But all had been ignored or given alternative explanations.[10]

The unopposed landings would still cost the US and Canadian troops more than 200 casualties from trench foot, booby traps and friendly-fire accidents (including two lightly wounded Forcemen); a further 70 US sailors were killed and 47 wounded when the destroyer USS *Abner Read* hit a mine.[11] Of the land casualties, 14 were killed and 13 wounded in the southern sector by the morning of August 18, most because of mistaken identity. "In the uncertainty that prevailed during the first thirty-six hours of the landings," read one report, "the almost total lack of visibility on some of the fog-covered ridges made it impossible to distinguish friend from potential foe."[12]

During the evening of the 18th, by which time it was obvious that the Japanese had gone, Frederick boarded the headquarters ship USS *U. S. Grant* in Kiska Harbor and was handed a terse message from Admiral Chester W. Nimitz, commanding the US Pacific Fleet, in Hawaii: "Highest authority directs you return the Special Service Force to San Francisco without delay."

Frederick was amused. "They don't want us running around up here," he told his staff. "I'll bet Churchill asked General Marshall, 'Where's the SSF?' and when he said 'Kiska,' the prime minister probably said, 'What are they doing up there? We need them in Europe.'"[13]

The Force commander's guess, as it happens, was not far off the mark.

19

"Picked men of first-class physique"

At 5:30 p.m. on August 5, 1943, the former luxury passenger liner *Queen Mary*, holder of the Blue Riband for crossing the Atlantic, slipped its moorings on the Clyde estuary in Scotland and set sail for Halifax, Nova Scotia. On board were a "Colonel and Mrs. Warden" and a "Lieutenant M. Warden," cover names for the British prime minister Winston Churchill, his wife Clementine and daughter Mary. Also traveling were the British Chiefs of Staff, their senior planners and two intrepid war heroes that Churchill thought Roosevelt would like to meet: Wing Commander Guy Gibson, who was awarded the Victoria Cross[*] for leading 617 Squadron's famous Dambusters raid on the Ruhr's Möhne and Eder and Sorpe Dams on May 16; and Brigadier Orde Wingate, a "born military genius with a mystical fire about him, according to Mountbatten, who had gained a reputation for taking the fight to the enemy with his daring [operations] behind the lines" in Ethiopia and Burma. All were part

---

[*] Gibson had also won a Distinguished Service Order and Bar, and a Distinguished Flying Cross and Bar. This collection of gallantry medals was unique.

of a 250-strong British party heading to the latest inter-Allied conference, code-named Quadrant, at Quebec City in Canada.[1]

Highest on the conference's agenda was the planning for the twice-postponed cross-Channel invasion of France, now known as Operation Overlord. For months, the Allied staff of COSSAC (the office led by the British lieutenant general Freddie Morgan, chief of staff to the Supreme Allied Commander) had been working on all aspects of the scheme to land troops on the Normandy beaches, a location first favored by Mountbatten. But this voyage was the first time Churchill would be briefed in detail on the "whole coherent plan," particularly its innovative use of two artificial harbors — an idea originally mooted by the prime minister a year earlier — to land troops, vehicles and supplies once the initial beachheads had been secured. At one point two COSSAC staff officers used the large bath in Churchill's bathroom to illustrate the effect that blockships would have on the sea, one flapping his hand in the water at one end "to simulate a choppy sea," while the other "stretched a lilo across the middle to show it broke up the waves." And all the while Churchill, "a stocky figure in a dressing-gown of many colors, sitting on a stool and surrounded by…'Top Brass,'" looked on.[2]

Churchill was delighted with the Overlord briefing, declaring the whole project "majestic." Yet he was worried about the maintenance of air superiority over the beachheads and thought a floating airfield might be the answer. Among the various options discussed during the voyage was one that had been developed by Geoffrey Pyke, the originator of Project Plough, who was still on Mountbatten's staff. Pyke's new idea — code-named Habakkuk — was, in Churchill's words, "to form a structure of ice, large enough to serve as a runway for aircraft." It would be "of ship-like construction, displacing a million tons, self-propelled at low speed, with its own anti-aircraft facilities, with workshops and repair facilities," and with a refrigeration plant to prevent the ice from melting. That aim would be aided by adding wood pulp to ordinary sea ice to produce a material known as Pykrete, after its inventor, that was both extremely tough and an effective insulator.[3] As Pyke was not part of Britain's Quadrant delegation, the pitch to Churchill and the other chiefs of staff was done by Mountbatten. Sir Alan Brooke, for one, was unimpressed. "To Hell with Habakkuk!" he declared. "We are about to have the most difficult time with our American friends and shall not have time for your ice-carriers."[4]

Looking to move on from Combined Operations, which he thought he had taken as far as he could, Mountbatten was angling for the command of a big ship. But not before he had tied up any loose ends, and one of them was Project Plough. So on August 8, three days into the voyage, he gave his fellow chiefs of staff a memorandum on the future use of "Plough Force." The unit—made up of "picked men of first-class physique," all trained parachutists, skiers and experts in winter warfare—was "being used in a commando role" for the US Army to gain battle experience. But it could easily be reassembled "for its proper role" with snow vehicles "before the winter."

His suggestion, therefore, was to use the Force to initiate a series of raids in Norway that would tie down German troops and even cause them to be reinforced. Such a "strategic role would," declared Mountbatten, "be a useful complement to OVERLORD." There were two options: insert the Force by land (Russia), sea or air for a specific operation and later withdraw it; or let it hide in a hollowed-out glacier from which it would "emerge periodically and attack selected objectives." Combined Operations would prepare the necessary plans in conjunction with the Force's staff. Before that could happen, he needed the British Chiefs of Staff to approve his proposal so that it could be submitted to the Combined Chiefs of Staff during Quadrant. If they were in agreement—and he had already received the thumbs-up from Britain's influential Joint Planning Staff (JPS)—then the Force would be sent to Norway in the winter of 1943/44.[5]

By the time the chiefs of staff met to consider Mountbatten's proposal on August 13, the *Queen Mary* had docked in Halifax and the whole Quadrant delegation had moved on by train to the Citadel in Quebec, where the conference would officially open on the 19th. Churchill, meanwhile, had left on a two-day trip to President Roosevelt's country estate at Hyde Park, New York, where the two leaders agreed, among other things, to share their respective work on the atom bomb but to concentrate the research and manufacture in the United States (the so-called "Tube Alloy" memorandum).[6]

Without Churchill's backing, Mountbatten was always going to struggle to win support among his fellow chiefs of staff for his Norway scheme. Hoping to head off opposition from the RAF, he told them the Force would probably be "landed by sea and make its entry through Russia." Thereafter it would be supplied by air, and the whole value of the plan "lay in its relation to 'OVERLORD' since it might contain and divert German forces." The chiefs were unconvinced. Even the maintenance of the Force by air, said Portal, might prove a "heavy commitment" that the RAF was unable to meet without sacrificing other, more important targets. Moreover, since there was a general shortage of troops trained in snow and mountain warfare, the Force might be better employed in the Apennines or Alps. It was therefore agreed at the meeting on August 13 that the Joint Planning Staff would be asked to put forward proposals for the use of the Force in Italy that could then be discussed at the Quadrant conference.[7]

This priority given to the Italian campaign was influenced by recent developments: the success of the Allied invasion of Sicily (it was finally captured on August 17); and the arrest on July 25 of Italian dictator Benito Mussolini on the orders of King Victor Emmanuel III. Then, a couple of days after the BCOS meeting, Mussolini's replacement, Marshal Pietro Badoglio, put out secret peace feelers to the Allies. Churchill was now convinced that an immediate invasion of Italy would knock the Axis power out of the war and secure airfields for the strategic bombing of occupied Europe. "Should Naples be captured in the near future," he wrote in Quebec on August 17, "we shall have a first-rate port in Italy, and other harbours, like Brindisi and Taranto, will fall into our possession thereafter. If by November our front can be established as far north as the Leghorn-Ancona line, the landing-craft in the Mediterranean will have played their part."[8]

On August 18, having received a generally pessimistic report from the JPS on the possible use of the Force in the mountains of Italy, the British Chiefs of Staff gave their American counterparts two options: deploy the Force in Norway, "as originally planned," where, if the maintenance commitment was "not too great," it might be used for a specific operation "in conjunction perhaps with Operation OVERLORD"; or send it to Italy, where it could be used "in the Apennines, or better still in the Alps if we get as far north," or even in collaboration with Yugoslav partisans "in the mountains of the Dalmatian Coast." Their recommendation was to send full details of the Force and its capabilities to both General Eisenhower (the Supreme Allied Commander in the Mediterranean) and General Morgan (in charge of planning for Overlord), who could then state their preferences to the Combined Chiefs by October 1.[9]

It was this memorandum that had caused the US Joint Chiefs to order Frederick to return the Force to San Francisco "without delay." The following day, August 19, at the conference's first plenary session with Roosevelt and Churchill, the Joint Chiefs agreed with their British counterparts that Eisenhower and Morgan should be asked if the Force "could be usefully employed in their theaters." When the telegrams went out on August 24, the two generals were also asked what extra provisions of air transport or ancillary units might be needed, while Eisenhower was told to consult the commander in chief, Middle East, General "Jumbo" Maitland Wilson, on the possible use of the Force on the Dalmatian coast. The unit, the generals were told, comprised three combat regiments of 417 men each. It had had "extended mountain, winter and commando type training, and limited amphibious and parachute training." It was "well qualified for guerilla activities in rugged snow terrains" and had trained with "tracked amphibious vehicles," 600 of which would be available by December 1. Its morale was of the highest order.[10]

With the Force now definitely earmarked for the European Theater of Operations, the man who had played a key part in its creation could bow out gracefully. But Lord Louis Mountbatten was not going back to sea. Instead, Churchill had asked him to consider taking up the new post of Supreme Allied Commander in South-East Asia. "I feel," Mountbatten said after the meeting, "as though I have been pole-axed."

It was an extraordinary opportunity for such a young officer, and he was never going to turn it down. Once Roosevelt and the US Joint Chiefs had given their assent, the appointment was announced on August 24. "Mountbatten has unique qualifications," Churchill cabled the Dominion premiers, "in that he is intimately acquainted with all three branches of the Services, and also with amphibious operations." He had enjoyed, in addition, a year and a half on the Chiefs of Staff Committee, and thus knew "the whole of our war story from the center." Lastly, he was "a fine organizer, and a man of great energy and daring."[11]

Mountbatten's close-to-last act as chief of Combined Operations was to take advantage of a lull in proceedings during the first plenary session at the Quebec City conference to give an unscheduled demonstration of Pyke's special ice mixture, Pykrete. A large dumbwaiter was brought into the room bearing two three-foot-high blocks of ice. Mountbatten then asked the strongest man present to attack each block with an ax. The burly General "Hap" Arnold, commanding the USAAF, was given the job. Taking off his coat and rolling up his sleeves, he took a two-handed swing at the block of ordinary ice and split it in two. Smilingly confident he would do the same to the Pykrete, Arnold took a second swing and yelped in pain as the ax bounced off the tough surface. Both elbows had been "badly jarred."

Then, in a ludicrously irresponsible act of bravado, Mountbatten drew a revolver from his pocket and shot at the ordinary ice, which shattered. "He then fired at the Pykrete," recorded Churchill, "which was so strong that the bullet ricocheted, narrowly missing Portal."

Already alarmed by the sound of the blows and the scream of pain from General Arnold, the gaggle of staff officers waiting outside were horrified by the gunfire. "My God!" shouted one. "They've now started shooting!"[12]

But despite Mountbatten's spirited and dangerous advocacy of Habakkuk, the Americans were unconvinced—not least because technical problems made the introduction of these iceberg/aircraft carriers unlikely before 1945. By then there would be more than enough conventional carriers, as well as long-range fighters and bases in the Azores. Even Churchill lost faith when he discovered that the cost would be six times the original estimate of £1 million.[13]

20

"We had a swell 3 decker cake"

Before leaving Amchitka, Colonel Williamson complained "so loud and long that his [2nd] regiment had been left out" of the Kiska operation that Frederick promised him "the first crack in the next engagement." Thanks to the Quadrant deliberations, it was bound to be in Europe—exactly where had yet to be decided.[1]

Returning to Adak on the *John B. Floyd*, the 2nd Regiment continued its voyage to San Francisco in the much faster USS *Heywood*. It was, noted 1-2 Company's diary, "a 7-day pleasure cruise" compared to their journey out. When not on guard duty, the men spent their time eating and sleeping. Reaching San Francisco on September 1, there was no opportunity for the "coming home" party that Ed Thomas and the others had planned. Instead the men were immediately loaded on a river ferry and taken up the Sacramento to the large US Army staging area at Camp Stoneman. There, as thanks for the $5,418.80 that the Forcemen had donated on hearing of the sinking of the light cruiser USS *Helena* in the Pacific in early July, they found waiting for them a number of cases of Johnnie Walker Black Label whisky that had been sent by the Helena authorities. Ed

Thomas drank his share and, next morning, gorged on the "feast" of a breakfast provided. It was a "big mistake after the night before," and he became "very sick." He was not the only one.[2]

At Stoneman, Frederick gave half his men—chiefly those from the West Coast—ten days' leave with orders to report back to their old stamping ground, Fort Ethan Allen in Vermont. The rest would get their leave when they reached Burlington.[3] Though the Force had failed to see any action on Kiska, Frederick was delighted with the largely calm and professional way it had carried out its tasks, as were his superiors. "They performed all missions according to plan," wrote Major General Corlett in a letter of commendation on August 24:

> And even though no actual enemy was encountered, their missions were difficult and dangerous. They landed in rubber boats at unknown beaches during hours of darkness against what was presumed to be a hostile shore. They moved across difficult terrain and positions where cleverly concealed explosive traps had been left by the enemy. They reached their objectives on schedule exactly according to plan.

Because of the need to move quickly, the Forcemen had not carried packs that provided "the ordinary comforts of soldiers in the field." They, as a consequence, were "exposed to extreme discomfort for long periods of time." For all these reasons, Corlett wanted to commend all the officers and men of the Force "for their fine spirit and unselfishness," and particularly their commander, Colonel Frederick, who had shown "splendid leadership and devotion to duty." The Force, Corlett was convinced, would be of "great value in almost any difficult battle situation."[4]

Among the 1-2 Company men who were given immediate leave from Camp Stoneman were West Coasters like Ray Holbrook, Howard Van Ausdale, Clarence DeCamp, Harry Deyette and Don Fisher from

Marysville, Washington. Deyette's leave was not a moment too soon: His wife, Ida, had recently given birth to their first child, Henrietta, and he could not wait to hold her in his arms. During a blissful week at home, he had a photo taken of the three of them—Ida smiling and holding the baby, Harry looking pensive—to remind him of what he was fighting for.[5]

Holbrook went home to Spokane but spent just 24 hours with his family before leaving for Helena to see his on-off girlfriend Dorothy. "I'm not sorry that I gave myself only one day at home," Holbrook wrote to his sister Gladys on September 16, "because I had such a swell time in Helena. Dorothy really showed me a good time. I guess I darn near danced both our feet off." Holbrook's only regret, he told his sister, was that he would have liked to have a couple more days in Helena with Dorothy who, despite his obvious devotion, was "still in love with the Sgt. in Africa." The train journey from Helena to Vermont—via Chicago and Montreal—was, he added, "awfully rugged," with Holbrook forced to "ride in a day coach all the way."[6]

Two other company men who went straight to Helena, riding part of the way with the 2nd Regiment men bound for Vermont, were Joe Glass and Lorin Waling. Aware they were about to be sent overseas, Joe was desperate to spend as much time as he could with his heavily pregnant wife, Dot. Lorin, no doubt influenced by Joe's happiness, had decided to propose to Steffie. She was in her bedroom when Lorin arrived unannounced at her house. Spotting him from the upstairs window, she opened it and shouted, "Waling, is that you?"

He nodded. "I wasn't going overseas without having you as my wife."[7]

They were married two days later in Steffie's local Roman Catholic church in East Helena after Lorin, to please his bride-to-be, had agreed to bring up any children they had in her faith. This time Joe stood up for Lorin who, because they were in Canada, had none of his family present. They heard the news by telegram, with more details sent later in a letter. "I hope," Waling began, "you are as happy to have Steffie in the family as I am to have her for a wife." He added:

> When we found we were able to be married in a church I sure was happy. The priest said to Steffie that seeing I was from the Special Service Force he would make it special and he sure did. The church was all decorated and was sure full of people. I never realized we had so many friends... We had a lot of cars in the parade and it went around town a couple of times, then to "Frank's," our brother's place, where we had a grand party. Chicken, ham and, oh, everything, plus a party in the bar where we drank all we had, which wasn't much due to the ration...
>
> We had a swell 3 decker cake with a soldier and bride top piece. Talk of gifts, we were piled with them that night and Steff says she is still getting them. It was sure swell Mom and we sure are happy. Our only and deep regret was that you couldn't be there and we couldn't even get to see you.[8]

Among their wedding gifts was the loan of a '41 Studebaker sedan and a full tank of fuel. They used it to drive to a one-room cabin in the mountains for their brief honeymoon, which they shared with their best friends Joe and Dot. For privacy, they hung a blanket between the beds. "My parents were in one bed," said Waling's son Dave, "and Joe and Dorothy in the other. So they all spent my parents' honeymoon together. You have to be very close to do that."[9]

Lorin ended his letter from Fort Ethan Allen by admitting he was doing "KP (kitchen police) or flunky for being three days late in getting back but I don't mind at all as I don't go out anymore except to a show in the post theater and have a beer or two at the PX."[10] Waling and Glass were among hundreds of Forcemen who overstayed their furlough. Another was Geoffrey Hart, a 22-year-old acting sergeant in Gordon's 2nd Platoon, who returned two days late from visiting his family in their modest homestead in the Peace Country of rural

British Columbia. With his father struggling to make ends meet during the depression, Hart, the eldest of four children, had left school at 14 to work as a farm laborer and a tractor driver. The army must have seemed an attractive option, and after enlisting in late 1941, he completed basic training and an engine artificers' course before volunteering for the Force. A confident young man with hazel eyes and thick brown hair, Hart was an ideal recruit: physically strong, used to an outdoor life and experienced with engines. Furlough was always going to be a problem because of the huge distance he had to cover, and this may have been taken into account when Hart kept his stripes and was only docked two days' wages as a punishment for going AWOL.[11]

Others were not so lucky. Knowing it would take so long to reach Winnipeg that he would only have a matter of hours with his family before he had to leave, Joe Dauphinais ignored the deadline and stayed an extra few days. On returning to Vermont, he and two other late men from his section — Howard Van Ausdale and Tom Fenton — were told to report to the battalion commander, Tom MacWilliam, newly promoted to lieutenant-colonel.* Just keep your mouths shut and take the punishment, they were told by their section commander. But when it was Dauphinais's turn to hear how disappointed MacWilliam was with his behavior, he listened for a time and then exploded: "When we were in Helena, they twice threatened to kick me out! So go ahead and kick me out! I don't give a shit what you do!"

Convinced the angry young Canadian was about to punch MacWilliam, the escort grabbed his arms. They need not have worried: he had said his piece and was beginning to regret it. MacWilliam had been sitting when Dauphinais started to speak. Now he stood up, his face "as white as a sheet," and told Dauphinais exactly what he

---

* On September 16, senior Force officers received the following promotions: regimental commanders to colonel; battalion commanders to lieutenant colonel; and battalion second-in-commands, or XOs, to major.

thought of him. But no, he continued, he wasn't going to throw him out. Instead he was busting him back to private with no possible promotion for six months. Moreover, when the time came, he would be given "hazardous duty." Dauphinais was unconcerned. To a member of the Force, dangerous duty came with the territory.[12]

It was around this time that Ed Thomas, now a major, engineered a move to MacWilliam's battalion. He had become increasingly frustrated working for Lieutenant Colonel Robert S. Moore, who commanded the 2/2nd Battalion, and had a much better relationship with MacWilliam. So when he heard that MacWilliam's XO was leaving the Force because of "foot problems," Thomas asked if he could replace him. MacWilliam agreed, as did Adams and Frederick, and Thomas became the XO of the 1/2nd Battalion.[13]

Frederick, meanwhile, was enjoying a couple of days with his wife, Ruth, and two young daughters in their rented home in Washington, DC. To do her bit, Ruth had become an air warden—one of six million Americans who, by early 1943, had volunteered for public protection roles. When the sirens wailed, her job was to strap on her white warden's helmet, grab a flashlight and patrol the neighborhood to make sure the blackout was being enforced. If she found anyone stranded on the street, she led them into her basement, which— stocked with water, cots and bandages—was serving as the local air-raid shelter. Before returning to Fort Ethan Allen in early October, Frederick urged his wife to get a large dog to protect her on her night patrols. She eventually bought a Doberman pinscher called Donner who, thanks to its general unruliness, would be rechristened Donner the Terrible.[14]

Frederick was back in Vermont when he received word, on October 7, that the Force would soon leave for North Africa, where it would come under the orders of General Eisenhower's Allied Force Headquarters in Algiers.[15] That of course meant, though it had not yet been confirmed, that its probable combat role was on mainland Italy, where two Allied armies—Sir Bernard "Monty" Montgomery's British

Eighth and Mark W. Clark's US Fifth—had made successful landings at, respectively, Taranto on September 3 and Salerno on September 9. The day before the Salerno landings, the Italians had surrendered to the Allies, prompting German forces to occupy Rome, and Marshal Badoglio and the Italian royal family to flee to Brindisi, where they set up an anti-fascist Italian government.[16]

21

"This excellent and specially trained force"

The decision to send the Force to the Mediterranean had happened almost by default. The Combined Chiefs of Staff's cable of August 24, asking if the Force "might usefully be deployed in their theaters," had been sent to both Generals Eisenhower and Morgan. But only Eisenhower provided a timely response (on September 8). Having spoken to Lieutenant Colonel Sandy Wedderburn, who had flown in to Algiers a few days earlier, Eisenhower believed the Force would "prove invaluable for reconnaissance and raiding during [the] methodical advance up [the] leg of Italy which German build up will probably force upon us."

His initial plan was to use the Force's regiments as "strong reconnaissance units, for flank protection in the Apennines and for raids behind enemy lines." Looking ahead, the Force could be of "greatest assistance" in the "French Alps next spring when mounting our diversion to OVERLORD." Fortunately, said Eisenhower, none of these missions would require additional transport aircraft or auxiliary units. He had been asked to consult with General Wilson on whether the Force would be better employed in Italy than on the Dalmatian coast of Yugoslavia—and he was doing that. In the meantime, he hoped that preliminary arrangements could be made for the Force to reach the Mediterranean by mid-November.[1]

Wilson's response to Eisenhower's query, sent a couple of days later, was that the Force "would be ideal both for independent guerilla and sabotage activity in Balkans and for support of resistance groups." Its use, moreover, would pay "high dividends in containing enemy forces and interrupting communications and industry" for a "relatively small outlay." He therefore wanted the Force to be assigned to his headquarters for use in Yugoslavia.[2]

On September 11, at a meeting in the White House, General Marshall spoke to Winston Churchill about the Force. The British prime minister had stayed on in North America after the Quadrant conference to receive an honorary degree from Harvard University and also, as he put it, to "be in close contact with our American friends at this critical moment in Italian affairs."[3] Well aware of Churchill's "particular interest" in the Force, Marshall explained that there had been a request for the Force to be "made available for employment in the Southeast Asia Command." This bid had undoubtedly been made by Mountbatten, the new supreme commander of that theater.* But it was never likely to succeed because the climate and terrain did not suit the Force's training. In any case, said the US chief of staff, Eisenhower had suggested the use of the Force "in the Apennines."

Churchill seemed to approve but added that the Force "might be usefully employed in the Balkans to help out the patriot forces." Yes, said Marshall, but he preferred the Italian option because the Force "was trained in snow conditions." Though it had seen no combat in Kiska, the landing there had been "a very good battle exercise and excellent training." The Force was now back in the United States, and

---

*   In late September 1943, Sandy Wedderburn wrote to Frederick from London that Mountbatten "hopes to have you with him for use in Burma after your campaign in Italy or the Balkans is completed" (Frederick Papers, Box 8).

an early move to the Mediterranean would, in Marshall's opinion, "raise its morale even higher still."

Churchill agreed, adding: "What I certainly wouldn't like to see is this excellent and specially trained force used in the steaming jungle."[4]

There was little chance of that. On September 13, by which time he had received Wilson's cable, Eisenhower informed Marshall that there were two possible uses for the Force in the Mediterranean— either in Italy or the Balkans—and that the "choice between them would depend upon future developments." The most likely scenario, however, was that it would first be needed in Italy, and that it needed to be sent to the Mediterranean without delay.[5]

Marshall and the US Joint Chiefs endorsed this recommendation, as did the British Chiefs of Staff on September 16, though they had not yet heard back from General Morgan at COSSAC.[6] That same day, Morgan informed the Combined Chiefs that the Force would not be needed for Operation Overlord. It "could well be used" in a possible expedition to Norway—Operation Jupiter—but as that would not happen before the summer of 1944 at the earliest, and there was a greater need for it in the Mediterranean, he was happy for it to go there.[7] With this last obstacle overcome, the Combined Chiefs cabled Eisenhower on September 17 that the Force would be "assigned to your Command without delay."[8]

On October 13, six days before the Forcemen were due to leave Fort Ethan Allen for Camp Patrick Henry, near the Hampton Roads Port of Embarkation in Virginia, Lorin Waling wrote to his mother and siblings in Alberta:

> *Boy are we having a stay here. We have been on the alert for the past three weeks, stuff all loaded ready to move, and still we are here. We don't know where we are going but each of us has an idea, but no idea when. Last night we went on a 35 mile march*

and boy it was a tough one. The last four and a half miles we walked in 55 minutes. If you don't think that is fast after walking 30 miles just ask some soldier and see.

Turning to more personal matters, Waling complained that he still had not heard from his father and wanted "to know the reason." He was particularly aggrieved that his father had not written to Steffie to "let her know how he felt about having her for a daughter, that's what makes me so mad." His wife, on the other hand, was an excellent correspondent and had written him a letter a day since their first meeting, even when he was at "ski camp in Helena." He added: "I only wish she could make a visit and meet you folks. You will all like her, I know. I can say I have one of the best little wives in the world, [and] my only regret is that I can't be with her." He then gave an update on the Glass pregnancy. "Joe and Dorothy," he wrote, "will be father and mother this month. The doc said it would be about the 20th and a girl, but Joe and I are hoping against that. He and I put our arms around each other and cried together after the wedding. That's just how happy we were."[9]

Among the officers' wives who traveled to Vermont to spend a last few days with their husbands in the Burlington Hotel were Evelyn Becket and Bobby MacWilliam. On October 18, the day before the Force set off for Virginia, Bobby had a farewell dinner with her husband, Tom, and his new XO, Ed Thomas, in a restaurant in the town of Underhill, where she was due to catch the train to Montreal, en route to her parents' home in Moncton, New Brunswick. After dinner, she and Tom said a tearful goodbye at the station.[10]

A few days later, Tom wrote to Bobby's father:

We had a wonderful time at our last camp but it was all too short and I can't tell you how sorry I was to leave. I did hope that we would have a little more time before we set out on our next "jaunt" but the "powers that be" thought otherwise and, after all,

*the sooner we get at this job and get it done, the sooner we will all
be home again and able to settle down to a decent life again.*

*I hope someday you will know what a wonderful help Bobby
has been to me. It gets harder and harder to say farewell but she
is such a Darling—never once has she sent me off without a smile
and I know how much it takes to do it. Knowing that she is in such
good hands helps a lot too and I'm afraid I shall never be able to
express how very very grateful I am to you both for all you have
done for me.*[11]

Another Forcemen making an emotional farewell on October 18
was Dick Daigle, the former US Airborne soldier from Massachusetts.
As an Easterner, he had taken his leave after returning to Vermont in
early September, and spent the last afternoon of this precious time at
home, talking in "low, serious tones" with his father in the backyard.
Next morning he returned to Burlington, where he contacted student
nurse Rae Bourgeois, who was surprised and delighted to hear he was
back so soon—and in one piece. They spent as much free time as they
could together before a last dinner in Burlington on Sunday, October
17, and parted at the entrance to Rae's nursing dorm in Winooski Park
on the edge of town. Dick promised to look after himself and to write
regularly.[12]

By the time the first of six trains pulled out of the siding at Fort
Ethan Allen in the morning of the 19th, carrying the Force HQ
and part of the Service Battalion, Colonel Frederick was already in
North Africa, having flown to Algiers to discuss the Force's next assignment with General Eisenhower. Rothlin's 1-2 Company traveled
in the third train, with Tom MacWilliam acting as transportation officer. One soldier wrote of the journey: "In familiar intimacy, men
are sitting and lounging about in all forms of dress or undress. Some
are kidding, the old horseplay, one is chewing an apple and viewing
the scenery. Most are engrossed in current nickel and dime
literature...Who would ever dream that this coach full of calm, quiet

men was hurtling towards a point of embarkation and a blazing theatre of war?"[13]

After two uncomfortable nights on board, the men were detrained
and marched the short distance to Camp Patrick Henry, 12 miles
north of Hampton Roads. The next few days were taken up with
clothing parades, packing baggage, medical inspections and final inoculations.[14] But the contrast between the Forcemen's new camp and
the "paradise" they had just left was stark. "The food here," wrote
Lorin Waling to his mother and siblings (now in Edmonton), "is as
bad as the camp and we have to stand in line nearly all of our meal
hour. I hope to God we don't stay here long."

Here, explained Waling, was "somewhere on the East Coast." He
could not be more specific. Instead he waxed lyrical about Steffie, his
"darling wife," who still wrote to him daily. Marrying her was the best
thing he had done. In fact, he admitted, the longer they spent apart,
the deeper his love for her grew. "I go to bed and pray every night that
I may soon be home with her and we can plan and build our future.
This war can't be over too soon for me and I will sure do my part to
end it."

About to leave for war, Waling had a couple of things he needed to
get off his chest. He knew that he and his father were the two "black
sheep" of the family. Yet he wanted his mother to know that he had
changed since meeting Steffie, and no longer lived a "fast life." His
father, on the other hand, was still as self-centered as ever. "Boy," he
wrote, "I have stood about all I can of that fellow. He hasn't written to
Steffie or I since we got married…I hate to write and tell him what
a hell of a poor man he turned out to be. He seemed happy enough
when I told him I was going to marry Steffie when he was in Helena
but now I'm not so sure."[15]

22

The *Empress of Scotland*

Lieutenant-Colonel Bill Becket rose early on October 28 and made a quick tour of the woods where his men had bivouacked. As he did so, he saw two WACs—members of the Women's Army Corps—crawl out of a couple of Forcemen's sleeping bags and race off into the woods. He thought about disciplining the soldiers involved, but decided to be lenient. The day before, while setting up camp on the edge of Hampton Roads, the Forcemen had been delighted to learn that two companies of WACs—some 360 women—would be traveling on the same ship as them. According to Jack Callowhill, a WAC officer had asked "if a bunch of our guys could do guard duty to keep the blacks away from their girls." There was, of course, no shortage of volunteers—and some had clearly taken their protective duties a little too seriously.[1]

Once up and breakfasted, the whole Force—recently brought up to its establishment strength of 164 officers, 7 warrant officers (senior NCOs) and 2,286 enlisted men[2]—was paraded in companies for the march to the docks. Officers and men were dressed in woolen olive-drab shirts and baggy mountain pants with large cargo pockets, the pants tucked into parachute boots. Over their shirts they wore the new thigh-length M-1943 field jacket made from light olive-drab cotton and with a detachable hood, drawstring waist and large pockets on each breast and skirt. The jacket had a separate liner in faux fur for extra warmth in winter. Each Forceman was also wearing the standard infantry helmet known as the M1, a one-size-fits-all steel construction with chin strap and a hard inner plastic liner with an adjustable sweatband and cotton webbing for comfort. He also had his personal weapons (including knife, pistol and rifle or carbine), a gas mask, water bottle and first-aid kit. On his back he carried a heavy rucksack with sleeping bag, shelter half, tent pole, mess gear, raincoat and toilet articles, and a barrack bag with, among other things, a change of clothes, a woolen cap, a mosquito net and an overcoat. His remaining kit—extra clothes, flashlight and electrical equipment—was transported separately.[3]

At the docks the heavily loaded Forcemen were confronted with, as one passenger put it, "the largest, tallest, fanciest ship I had ever seen in my life." She was the *Empress of Scotland*, "one of those luxury liners known as 'millionaire troop carriers,' converted to carry soldiers overseas."[4] Built in Scotland in 1929 for the transpacific service between North America and Asia, and originally named the *Empress of Japan*, the 25,000-ton ship was designed to carry just under 1,200 passengers in four classes of varying comfort. Her celebrity passengers had included baseball star Babe Ruth, who traveled to Japan from Vancouver in 1934. Requisitioned as a troopship at the outbreak of war, she was renamed after the attack on Pearl Harbor and, by late 1943, was "considered a lucky ship, evacuating women and children through bombing raids and surviving U-boat attacks." She still had her original British captain, J. W. Thomas, and merchant crew, but her company paint scheme of white and gold had long since been changed to battleship gray, and antiaircraft guns were placed at the bow and stern.[5]

For this voyage she would carry just over 4,900 passengers: Forcemen, WACs and GI reinforcements. They boarded at the base of the ship and worked their way up the interior stairways to their assigned decks. Only officers and WACs had access to the top—or sun—deck, much to the annoyance of the enlisted men who were kept well away. "The boys look up at them on the next deck just like a bunch of wolves," a 3rd Regiment sergeant noted in his diary, "and I think the gals look a bit the same way."[6] The WACs could be "seen not visited," recalled Percy Crichlow, and this prompted many comments in his section about the "selfishness of the officers." Certainly some of the officers took advantage of their privileged position to socialize with the WACs. Ed Thomas, for example, had a number of conversations with a WAC called Jane Ebey, a "friend" he knew from Helena. Bill Becket got to know a "very attractive" enlisted female who, it turned out, was the daughter of the governor of New York. They would go for regular walks on deck together until Becket was warned by his regimental commander, "Cookie" Marshall, that their fraternization had not gone unnoticed. Aware that the gossip might hinder the girl's military career, Becket told her gently that their walks would have to end.[7]

Though "heavily guarded from any roaming Romeos," the WACs still provided some entertainment for the enlisted men below. "We went up to the front of the ship," recalled Jack Callowhill, "and got a kick out of looking up and seeing the WACs coming out on the deck above. The first thing they had to do was lift up their skirt. The MPs were making sure they had pants on or they couldn't get out."[8] Another Forcemen witnessed a similar scene when, to get some air, he climbed up to the starboard boat deck—the port being out of bounds—and saw Forcemen and GIs, gathered in groups of 20 to 30 people, "their eyes straining up to the sun deck" where groups of WACs in their green coveralls were carrying on loud conversations.

"Edith," said one, "wait till the water gets rough—you'll be sick."

"No, I won't. Wait and see."[9]

Belowdecks, the enlisted men were crammed into a space that might have been "generous for some six hundred or so civilian passengers" but not to accommodate more than 4,000 servicemen. The floor-to-ceiling height of just seven feet had been filled with rows of three-tier canvas bunks. The aisle between the rows was just 20 inches wide. "Into this crowded space," noted a Forcemen in his diary, "each soldier has brought his rucksack, his barracks bag, rifle, steel helmet and all his personal equipment. With him on his person he has at all times his life preserver and rifle belt containing water bottle."

Just moving down these narrow corridors in a Mae West life preserver, while soldiers were trying to get dressed and find things in their packs, was a "feat in itself." Far worse, however, were meal times when the men, carrying their mess gear, formed long lines of sweating humanity as they waited to be "carried by the crowd behind into the mess hall." Eventually they entered a large, well-ventilated room, still sporting its "peace-time murals and ceiling decorations," and sat at narrow tables where food containers for each platoon were placed. Often as not, the greedy "chow-hounds" closest to the containers left the others hungry. Having queued again to wash their mess gear, the men fought their way out of the mess hall and, if it was breakfast or lunch, took the opportunity to get some fresh air on deck. "But after dinner," wrote the diarist, "no such luck. Troops are not allowed on the deck during blackout."

A typical sight below deck was of Forcemen lying in their narrow bunks, "clad only in underwear, despite standing orders to sleep fully clothed. Some sit on the top tier, their feet dangling down into the faces of those beneath them." Apart from "the wreckage strewn in the aisles"—sleeping bags, rucksacks, respirators and discarded candy-bar wrappers—the men showed great "variety and ingenuity" in the way they hung up all types of equipment.[10] With so many people packed into a small space, and no air circulating, an "aromatic fog" soon became a "serious stench." To escape it, some Forcemen tried to sleep in the corridors and stairways. But as the crew needed them clear in case of an emergency, MPs were given the unwelcome task of moving the sleeping soldiers. "It was," wrote one MP, "a bit like facing a biting boar, or a sow with piglets." Every night he had to "gut it out" with a new bunch who did not go easily. He kept thinking: Why not save your aggression for the Krauts?[11]

The diary for 1-2 Company noted that the weather during the voyage was "very hot and the quarters stifling." Even so, it was a vast improvement on the earlier trip to the Aleutians, with calmer seas and even some entertainment. On November 1, for example, the Red Cross put on three showings of Ian Hay's *All at Sea*, a play about a lovestruck young man who pretends to be a famous writer to impress a girl during an ocean cruise. The lead roles were played by soldiers and WACs.[12]

If the Forcemen had a concern, it was the lack of a naval escort. Bill Becket, for example, had already crossed the Atlantic twice during the war—to and from the United Kingdom—and been up to the Aleutians and back. All four voyages had been accompanied by warships. Yet on this journey the *Empress of Scotland* traveled alone because, with twin screws and a top speed of 21 knots, she was considered relatively safe from U-boat attack as long as she moved in a zigzag rather than a straight line. But this lack of an escort "bothered" Becket,[13] as did the air-raid scare and "call to quarters" on November 3 as the ship approached the West African coast and became a target for long-range Axis bombers. Fortunately it was a false alarm and the "all clear" was sounded: the "hostile" plane was a USAAF Liberator bomber on anti-submarine duty.[14]

Next day, having passed the Portuguese island of Madeira, the Force officers were told by Colonel Adams that they were heading for Casablanca, French Morocco, and would disembark on the 5th. This was no great surprise: the inoculations, mosquito nets and issue, on the third day at sea, of a little booklet called *A Language Guide to North Africa* had largely given the game away. "We knew we were going somewhere warmer," recalled Jack Callowhill, "because we got into hotter and hotter weather." The real question was: Where would they fight? The battle for North Africa had ended the previous May with the Allied capture of Tunis. Sicily had fallen in August and, since then, Eisenhower's troops had invaded southern Italy and were making slow progress up the peninsula. Would they join that campaign? Or were the commanders planning a behind-the-lines mission more suited to their winter training, in Italy or somewhere else in the Mediterranean? Only time would tell.

November 5 was a "grand morning": bright, warm and calm. An hour after passing a small convoy of ships—including a small aircraft carrier—the *Empress of Scotland* came in sight of the "gleaming" city of Casablanca, its buildings a mixture of white and brown stucco. As they approached the harbor, Forcemen and GIs were hanging over the rails, hoping to see the superstructure of the French battleship *Jean Bart*, which had been partially sunk by US dive bombers during the Torch landings in November 1942. But before it came into view, the "call to quarters" was sounded and the men headed below deck for disembarkation.[15]

At 11:00 a.m., an hour after tying up at the Gare Maritime, the heavily laden Forcemen were the first to leave the ship. One of them was missing: a member of the Service Battalion had disappeared that morning while on gun watch, leaving only his Mae West and webbing to be found by the relief. He was thought to have committed suicide, having tried once before, and was reported "missing at sea." Onshore, where they were welcomed by Colonel Frederick, the Forcemen were shocked by the obvious signs of poverty: dock workers wearing nothing but palliasses—cotton mattress covers—with holes cut for the head and arms; ragged and filthy children "hollering for bonbons"; and raw sewage in the streets. "They shoveled it into 'honey wagons,'" recalled Jack Callowhill, "and used it for fertilizer. That's why there was so much sickness." It was, complained Larry Piette, "a dirty place."[16]

The plan was for the Force to travel by rail from Casablanca to the port of Oran in northwest Algeria and on from there by ship to Naples in Italy, where it was scheduled to arrive on November 15. It would be "ready for operations," noted Eisenhower's assistant chief of staff, around ten days later.[17] The Force was heading for Naples—the chief supply port for Lieutenant General Mark Clark's US Fifth Army— for two main reasons: Eisenhower's staff had concluded, after much consultation, that Italy offered the best opportunities for utilizing the Force's winter training; and Clark himself had asked for the Force to be "sent to Italy to work in the difficult mountain terrain."[18]

With freight trains in short supply, the Force was moved to Oran over three days. While they waited their turn, the 2nd Regiment men were bivouacked in a transit camp on the edge of Casablanca, little more than a collection of tents surrounded by concertina wire to keep out thieves. "We hadn't been there more than five minutes," remembered Jack Callowhill, "when girls appeared on the other side of the wire, trying to get in. They were prostitutes. A lot of guys wanted to be with them, and it was stupid, because there was so much VD."[19]

The following day, the 2nd Regiment was taken to the station and put on a train for Oran. It was a rickety old model with a wood-fired engine, a couple of "old and shabby" day coaches for the officers, and 40 or so small freight cars known as "8 chevaux ou 40 hommes" (8 horses or 40 men) for the men. "We slept on the floor," recalled Jack Callowhill. "We didn't have blankets or anything. We just put our heads on the pack. Every so often you'd get a double toot on the train and it would slow down and we had to get off to go to the washroom. You would very seldom hit the ground before some of the natives were there already begging. The Americans would throw empty ration cans out, and they would grab them and see if there was anything to eat."[20]

Some of the Forcemen sold their sleeping bag liners to the locals for as much as 500 francs each (the equivalent of US$10), a profit of at least 700 percent. They used the money to buy alcohol, though it was not always needed. When the 2nd Regiment's train stopped next to a flatcar loaded with barrels of wine, the Forcemen jumped down and used knives and bayonets to get at the booze, filling water bottles and even helmets. As ever, Larry Piette's rowdy 3rd Platoon was in the thick of the mischief. Piette was furious: he had "very high standards of morals that he held himself, and his men, to." Placing the chief culprits on a charge, he bawled out the rest. But it would have little effect on their behavior.[21]

The two-and-a-half-day journey across North Africa—the train traveled at around 11 mph—was, for most of the Forcemen, a torturous experience. One exception was Classics teacher Percy Crichlow, who found the trip "vastly interesting," particularly its glimpses of Arab life, the Atlas Mountains and fortress towns such as Taza in northern Morocco and Sidi Bel Abbès in northern Algeria (the training base for the Foreign Legion). When the 1st Regiment stopped at Sidi Bel Abbès, Bill Becket and the supply officer, Orval Baldwin, went to have a look at a "native village which lay a short way down the tracks," its "narrow unpaved streets lined with adobe huts." Becket recalled:

> Here we are, fully armed in battle rig, with revolvers in full view in our holsters, walking into this seemingly peaceful but somewhat troubling village. Veiled women advancing towards us stepped off the so-called sidewalk—men lying hunched down, smoking hashish in water-pipes in front of their huts. We very soon began to sense that we were not exactly welcome so we turned about and walked sharply back.

It was only when they returned to the station platform that an excited group of French officers pointed to a sign that said, "in bold letters," the village was strictly out of bounds to all military personnel, particularly Allied troops. "You don't know how lucky you are," said one officer. "A few of our soldiers went into that village and have not been seen since."[22]

At Oran the Forcemen set up their tents in a "beautiful olive grove" on the edge of the port—Staging Area No. 1—while the officers were quartered in nearby Nissen huts. That first night, Bill Becket returned from checking the men to find the last berth was by the open back door. He sat on a "miserable looking straw mattress" to take off his parachute boots and felt movement under him. "I shifted my weight slightly," he recalled, "looked down, and to my horror saw the head of a snake emerging out of the edge of the mattress an inch or so from my right leg." It was huge, with a head larger than an egg and at least four feet long. Rigid with fear, Becket stared in horror as the snake slithered past the top of his boot and onto the floor. Only when it was through the open door did Becket jump up, draw his pistol and run after it. The noise of the gunshot woke the hut, causing one or two officers to leap out of bed. "I was *not* popular, nor, even when some of them saw the snake lying there, was I considered a hero."[23]

Once again the Forcemen were confined to camp for security reasons. But many "sneaked out" anyway, including Percy Crichlow and some other 6th Section men. They ended up in "a crowded, smoky little room where a dark-haired, olive-skinned girl served wine to us and French soldiers in old C-ration tins." The following night, remembered Crichlow, "those who tried to go out were caught and put in a stockade and charges laid against them."[24]

23

"There was utter destruction"

On November 13, with all the regiments reunited, the Forcemen were trucked to Oran's harbor and loaded onto three naval transports (including one, the USS *Thomas Jefferson*, they knew from their Chesapeake training). But engine trouble postponed their departure, and it was not until November 16 that they set a course for Naples. The 2nd Regiment traveled with Force HQ on the USS *Barnett*, a "swell ship" that had shot down three Japanese planes and one German and had a "torpedo patch" on its port side. There was a minor scare when a hostile plane was spotted, but it soon cleared off when the antiaircraft guns opened up.[1] The threat, however, was real: just over a week later, the British troopship HMT *Rohna* was bombed and sunk by German planes after leaving Oran. Of the 1,100 lives lost, more than a 1,000 were US servicemen (the worst loss of American troops at sea during World War Two).[2]

The transports reached the Bay of Naples on November 19 and nudged slowly into a harbor that had been badly damaged by German demolition teams and, later, air raids. Describing the port on the day of its capture by his US Fifth Army, Mark Clark wrote: "There was utter destruction of ships, docks, and warehouses, such as not even ancient Pompeii, through which we had passed earlier in the day, had ever seen." Clark had feared the harbor would not be usable for weeks. But thanks to the tireless efforts of US engineers and laborers—who removed tons of rubble and converted sunken ships "to foundations for emergency piers"—the first supplies were landed within 72 hours, and soon the port "was handling over 20,000 tons daily."[3]

When the Force transports arrived, they tied up against one of the sunken ships and wooden catwalks were used to get to the shore. Though the worst of the debris had been removed, the scars of war were still obvious. "The Germans had destroyed everything," noted a wide-eyed Jack Callowhill. "The electricity, the water, the staircases, the buildings." Shouldering their heavy packs, the Forcemen set off for their temporary bivouac to the west of the city. At one point, passing through a tunnel that the locals had been using as an air-raid shelter, they had to hold their noses as the pavement and gutters were still strewn with human feces. Everywhere they encountered desperate Italians begging for food or trying to sell them nuts and oranges. The children would cry, "Caramelli? Joe, Joe, caramelli?" Or even—in an attempt to sell sex with their mothers and sisters—"Joe, Joe, signorina? Fiki Fiki?"[4] As they set off in trucks for the last leg of the journey, Jack Callowhill could see a woman sitting on the ground with a baby. She seemed to be dressed in black. It was only when they passed the woman that they realized she was naked from the waist up and covered in flies. "She didn't even have the strength," noted Callowhill, "to swat them away. There was nothing we could do. We just kept on going."[5]

After two days in Naples, the Forcemen were trucked 25 miles to their new base in a former Italian Artillery School barracks in the medieval town of Santa Maria Capua Vetere, built on the site of ancient Capua (a city that, in Roman times, was second only in size and influence to the capital itself). As the trucks moved north and closer to the front, through roads crowded with peasants, many pushing "all their worldly goods on a bicycle or two wheeled cart," the skies cleared and the sun shone on the rock-strewn Italian countryside. Taking advantage of the good visibility, two German fighters strafed the column as it neared its destination, wounding two Force drivers who became the first casualties of the campaign. "We had only been there a short time," recalled Sam Boroditsky of the 1st Regiment's HQ Detachment (which had preceded the combat echelon), "when there was a series of explosions and the sounds of airplanes buzzing and firing. Lieutenant Eiwen came in to where we were all laying out belongings with an order. 'This is the real thing—steel helmets to be worn at all times!'"[6]

The previous occupants of the barracks were soldiers from a German panzer division. Before they withdrew, their engineers demolished all the staircases, washrooms and kitchens and partially blew up most of the buildings. But as these shattered structures still provided some shelter from the winter rain and sleet, they were assigned to each Force regiment, while "one of the few nearly whole buildings in the compound" was reserved for Force HQ. The men slept in sleeping bags on the hard marble floor. "It was better," said Jack Callowhill, "than being outside."[7]

Lieutenant General Mark Clark's command post was located five miles from Santa Maria in the grounds of Caserta Palace, the former residence of the Bourbon kings of Naples. Built in the 18th century to rival Versailles, it was a huge Baroque confection with five floors, 1,200 rooms and four interior courtyards. The southern face alone was 134 feet high, 830 feet long and boasted almost 250 windows. The place was so cavernous that one staff officer complained it was the only place he had had a hat blown off indoors; another likened it to Alcatraz "without the bay."[8]

Clark had moved his Fifth Army HQ from Naples to Caserta on October 24. But he decided not to move into the "magnificent

A married schoolteacher and reserve officer from the maritime province of New Brunswick, Lieutenant-Colonel Thomas C. MacWilliam, OC 1st Battalion, 2nd Regiment (1/2nd), was a talented athlete with born leadership qualities. *Courtesy of Tom MacWilliam Jr.*

A likeable fellow with an easy grin, Private Jack Callowhill, 19, from Hamilton, southern Ontario, joined the Force to "get out from under" his family and look "for a bit of adventure." *Courtesy of Jack Callowhill*

Sergeant Geoffrey Hart (far right) and Private Joe Dauphinais (far left) with two other unidentified members of 1-2 Company, outside their tent at Fort Harrison, Montana, in the summer of 1942. Both 22 years old and from the prairies of Canada, they had qualified as mechanics before volunteering for the Force. *Courtesy of John Hart*

Major Ed Thomas, 23, from Spartanburg, South Carolina, attended Georgia Tech before he was called to active duty in 1941. Having volunteered for airborne training, he was a company commander in the 505th Parachute Infantry Regiment when he received orders to report to the Force, "a strange unit" he had never heard of. *Courtesy of Ann Thomas*

Private Richard "Dick" E. Daigle (right) of Lynn, Massachusetts, and a friend pose in their uniforms of the 506th Parachute Infantry Regiment, the unit that would be featured in the book and miniseries *Band of Brothers.* Shortly after this photo was taken, Daigle was unexpectedly posted to the First Special Service Force, a move he had neither asked for nor wanted. *Courtesy of Ken Beaton*

A Forceman practices the rock-climbing techniques that would make the assault up the north face of Monte la Difensa possible. *US National Archives*

A Forceman trains on skis at Blossburg, Montana, in the winter of 1942–43. The novice skiers, typically Americans from the South, described the ordeal as "the battle of the slabs." *Library and Archives of Canada*

Sergeant Harry N. Deyette, his wife, Ida, and their two-month-old daughter, Henrietta, share a few rare hours together in September 1943 during Harry's last home leave before the Force shipped out to Europe. *Courtesy of Ken Beaton*

Steffie and Lorin Waling on their wedding day, East Helena, October 1943. "I wasn't going overseas," he told her, "without having you as my wife." They honeymooned in a one-room cabin in the mountains with their best friends Dot and Joe Glass, with only a blanket hung between the beds for privacy. *Courtesy of the Waling family*

Captain Lawrence J. Piette, the son of a millwright from Appleton, Wisconsin, was a private in the Corps of Engineers when the army identified his potential and sent him to the Officer Candidate School at Fort Belvoir, Virginia. He volunteered for the Force because "it sounded good" and "we were going to be a select group," but he was not eager to leave behind his sweetheart (soon to be his fiancée), Marin deGravelles. In this 1946 photo, Lawrence, readjusting to civilian life, and Marin enjoy their honeymoon in the Roosevelt Hotel, New Orleans. *Courtesy of Dan Piette*

A Forceman hauls a load of water and rations up a mountain in southern Italy. So rugged and steep were the slopes of Monte la Difensa that mules were useless for resupply, and manpower was the only option. *Courtesy of Nathan Gordon*

Lieutenant Joe Kostelec (left) and a fellow officer outside the Force Clearing Station in Italy. Kostelec would be KIA at Anzio in March 1944. *Library and Archives of Canada*

The path from the village of Mignano to Monte la Difensa runs up Ridge 368 to the point at which the northern cliffs were scaled by the men of 1/2nd Battalion, marked by the dot. *Courtesy of John Hart*

The final section of Monte la Difensa's rock face, scaled by the Forcemen on December 3, 1943, was especially treacherous. *Courtesy of the author*

Major Ed Thomas and the 1/2nd command group surge into Rome—the first Axis capital to fall to Allied troops—on June 4, 1944. *Courtesy of Ann Thomas*

palace" because he knew it was earmarked for his boss, British general Sir Harold Alexander, who commanded the Fifteenth Army Group (composed of Clark's US Fifth Army and the British Eighth Army under General Sir Bernard Montgomery). Clark was also mindful of his staff living in relative luxury while the frontline troops suffered in the mud and rain of an Italian winter, and he wanted to be in a position "to move forward at a moment's notice." So he had the tents and trailers of his command post placed in a large forest behind the palace and used an adjacent road as a landing strip for his Piper Cub plane.[9]

A tall, loose-limbed man with a long beaky nose, thick lower lip and prominent Adam's apple, Clark was a military brat who had entered West Point in 1913 as the youngest in his class. Dark in complexion—a legacy of his maternal ancestors, who were Romanian Jews—he was nicknamed Contraband by his fellow cadets because of his ability to smuggle candy into the barracks. With his studies interrupted by illness, Clark graduated 110th out of a class of 139 in 1917 and hardly seemed destined for senior rank. Yet he had befriended an older cadet, Dwight D. Eisenhower, who would prove to be a most valuable ally and mentor.

Unlike Eisenhower, Clark saw frontline service toward the end of the First World War as a junior officer with the 11th Infantry Regiment in the Vosges Mountains, and was quickly promoted to captain and acting battalion commander. But his war ended when shrapnel from a German shell tore through his shoulder and upper back, knocking him unconscious. He saw out the war as a supply officer and spent much of the interwar period in staff and training roles. But promotion was slow: he did not become a major until 1933 and had to wait another seven years to reach the rank of lieutenant colonel. By then he had passed through both the Command and General Staff School at Fort Leavenworth and the Army War College in Carlisle, Pennsylvania. In the summer of 1941, skipping the rank of colonel, he was promoted brigadier general and made Marshall's assistant chief of staff (G3) with the task of training the rapidly expanding US Army. Clark's meteoric rise continued in early 1942, soon after Pearl Harbor, when he was appointed deputy chief of staff and, soon after, chief of staff to Army Ground Forces, a job perfectly suited to his talent for organization. By now he was, at 46, the youngest major general in the US Army.

His friendship with Eisenhower bore fruit in the summer of 1942 when he became the latter's deputy, first in the UK and then in the Mediterranean Theater of Operations where Clark did much of the detailed planning for the Torch landings in North Africa. He was rewarded with promotion to lieutenant general and, in January 1943, command of the newly formed US Fifth Army, though it was not used in either North Africa or Sicily. This caused much jealousy among older officers with more operational experience, such as George S. Patton, then commanding the I Armored Corps, who later wrote of Clark: "If you treat a skunk nicely, he will not piss on you—as often."[10] But Eisenhower had no doubt the promotion was deserved. "The best organizer, planner and trainer of troops that I have met," he wrote to Marshall. "In preparing the minute details, he has no equal in our Army."[11]

Clark's first test as a field commander was at Salerno in southern Italy, where his Anglo-American troops—drawn from the British X Corps and the US VI Corps—made a successful amphibious landing on September 9, 1943. But rapid counterattacks by German panzers almost split his army in two, and on September 13, when the fighting was at its fiercest, he asked his staff to draw up two contingency plans for evacuation, each involving the withdrawal of one corps before it was relanded to reinforce the other. He also wired Eisenhower that he was thinking of moving his headquarters from the beachhead to a ship offshore, from where he could better direct the battle. This latter signal caused panic at the Allied Forces HQ in Algiers, with Eisenhower insisting that Clark should stand and fight and, if necessary, go down with his command like a naval captain. Had it been a mistake, he wondered, to put his old friend in charge?[12]

In a desperate attempt to stop the German panzers reaching the sea, US artillery fired over open sights, and noncombat soldiers—drivers, cooks and clerks from Army HQ—were given rifles and told to fight. The line held, just, and by September 15 the crisis was over. The following day, Clark's troops linked up with advance elements of Montgomery's Eighth Army, which was advancing up from the toe of Italy. Clark would later deny that he had ever seriously considered evacuation. "The only way they're going to get us off this beach," he vowed, "is to push us, step by step, into the water."[13] That was written later. At the time, Clark had panicked, and only the stoicism of his subordinates had prevented a disastrous retreat. But someone had to carry the can, and that man was Major General Ernest J. Dawley, commanding the US VI Corps. On Clark's recommendation, Dawley was sacked and replaced with Major General John P. Lucas (who would also prove unequal to the task). For Clark, Eisenhower had only praise. "You and your people have done a magnificent job," wrote the supreme commander on the 14th. "We are all proud of you."[14] Despite the doubts that Eisenhower had voiced on the 13th, he never seriously considered sacking Clark, either then or later when his friend "continued to disappoint." Why? Because, wrote Eisenhower's biographer, "he liked and respected Clark" and blamed the Combined Chiefs for not providing heavy bombers to disrupt the German counterattacks.[15]

On September 21, with the beachhead secure, General Alexander visited Clark's command post at Salerno to outline the Fifteenth Army Group's future plan of operations. Tracing his finger along a map of Italy, Alexander indicated the boundary between Clark's Fifth Army and Montgomery's Eighth Army. "The Fifth Army was to seize Naples," recalled Clark, "without pause cross the Volturno River and work up the western side of the mountainous peninsula while Montgomery advanced along the eastern side." The

Allied strength would be about 14 divisions, a slight numerical advantage over the number of German divisions in opposition.[16] As
Italy would soon become a secondary front to the main Allied effort
in Normandy, the overall strategy was to fight, noted Eisenhower,
"with economy and caution so as to avoid unnecessary diversion of
units and supplies that could be used in Overlord." The plan was
to "avoid reverses, costly attacks, and great expenditure of supplies,"
yet still keep the enemy "uneasy" and unwilling to move troops
from Italy "to reinforce his position in northwest Europe." This was
easier said than done.[17]

In Clark's opinion, the German commander Generalfeldmarschall
Albert Kesselring was a "master of delaying tactics" whose use of
artillery was "highly effective in the mountainous region through
which we had to pass." Small detachments of German motorized infantry would site machine guns on hillsides, while riflemen on higher
ground forced the Allied troops "to make wide time-consuming envel-
opments almost every mile of the way." Meanwhile, enemy artillery
targeted Allied columns. "Often," noted Clark, "one 88-mm. gun,
properly placed, could deliver fire along an entire valley-floor and
might not be knocked out for many hours." Mud and rain were a
constant problem, and "with trucks bogged down soldiers and pack
mules had to move supplies over rugged hills." Wrecked bridges and
minefields were "constant problems." Each hillside was a conundrum
that could only be solved "by careful preparation" and the inevitable
"spilling of blood." Progress, as a result, was painfully slow. It took
Clark's 100,000 combat troops more than three weeks to capture
Naples, just 30 miles north of Salerno, and a further two weeks to
cross the Volturno River. Then the weather got even worse. From
mid-October, wrote Clark, the "rain came down in torrents, vehicles
were bogged above the axles, the lowlands became seas of mud," and
his army's progress was slowed by the carefully sited German rear-
guard.[18]

Perhaps the best description of the challenges facing the Allied soldiers was provided by 43-year-old Ernie Pyle from Indiana, the famous American war correspondent whose column about life at the front for ordinary GIs—or "dogfaces" as he affectionately called them—was syndicated to more than 300 newspapers. The war in Italy was "tough," wrote Pyle, because "the land and the weather are both against us." Incessant rain turned roads into quagmires and washed out temporary bridges. The country was "shockingly beautiful" but just as "shockingly hard to capture." Hills rose "to high ridges of almost solid rock." You could not go around them "through the flat peaceful valleys," because the Germans "look down upon you and would let you have it." The only option was "to go up and over." Yet a "mere platoon of Germans, well dug in on a high rock-spined hill, can hold out for a long time against tremendous onslaughts."

Meanwhile, the GIs were suffering unimaginable discomforts. Thousands occupied the "fertile black valleys," knee deep in mud, and had "not been dry for weeks." Thousands more suffered in the high mountains "with the temperature below freezing and the thin snow sifting over them." Sleeping in "little chasms and behind rocks in half caves," they lived "like men of prehistoric times, and a club would become them more than a machine gun." The Allies had some consolations, including air superiority. "All day long," reported Pyle, "Spitfires patrol above our fighting troops like a half-dozen policemen running up and down the street watching for bandits." It helped too that the "fiendish rain of explosives" fired by US artillery pieces was lowering German morale. "They've always been impressed by, and afraid of, our artillery and we have concentrations of it here that are demoralizing." Lastly, however cold the mountains, wet the snow or sticky the mud, the GI's knew it was "just as miserable" for the Germans.[19]

But the Germans enjoyed the biggest advantage of all: fighting in a rugged environment more suited to defense than attack. This was why they were hurriedly constructing a double-layered defensive system to guard the approach to Rome. The main position, known as the Gustav Line, rested on the Garigliano, Gari and Rapido Rivers, and was protected in its center by the rocky hill of Monte Cassino. But just as important was the "strong outpost" to the Gustav, known to the Germans as the Bernhardt Line or *Winterstellung* (Winter Line).

24

The Winter Line

The seeds of the German decision to fight south of Rome were planted on July 26, 1943, when a twin-engine Junkers Ju-88 bomber landed at the military airfield at Rastenburg, East Prussia. It was carrying Generalfeldmarschall Erwin Rommel, the legendary "Desert Fox" whose German-Italian Panzer Army had for much of the war in North Africa run rings around its British and Commonwealth opponents. Rommel had been inspecting Axis defenses in Greece when he received an urgent telephone call from the *Oberkommando der Wehrmacht* (OKW, the High Command of the German Armed Forces) on July 25. The Italian dictator Benito Mussolini had been arrested, he was told, and he was to return at once to Hitler's *Wolfsschanze* ("Wolf's Lair") field HQ near Rastenburg to discuss the crisis with the Führer.[1]

Met at Rastenburg airfield by a staff car, Rommel was driven five miles to the Wolf's Lair in the gloomy Masurian woods. Built in 1941 as Hitler's temporary field headquarters for the invasion of Russia, the complex consisted of three concentric security zones: a heavily fortified outer area (Zone Three), protected by a minefield and the soldiers of the elite *Führerbegleitbrigade* who were manning guard houses, watchtowers and vehicle checkpoints; a middle area (Zone Two) that housed a military barracks and the quarters of several Reich ministers, including Albert Speer and Joachim von Ribbentrop; and the inner sanctum, known as "Security Zone One," consisting of the Führer Bunker and ten other camouflaged bunkers built from two-meter-thick steel-reinforced concrete to house Hitler and his inner circle, including Generalfeldmarschall Wilhelm Keitel, chief of the OKW, Hermann Göring, head of the Luftwaffe and deputy Führer, and Martin Bormann, Hitler's personal secretary. The Führer Bunker, the largest, was at the northeastern end of the complex to protect it from the glare of the sun.[2]

Having passed through the inner security checkpoint, manned by black-uniformed soldiers of the SS *Reichssicherheitsdienst* (RSD), Hitler's personal bodyguard, Rommel was dropped outside the long, narrow conference room,[*] close to the guest bunker in the west half of the compound. Inside, the noon situation briefing was already in progress, attended by Hitler and all the "leading men of the Services, State and Party," including Grossadmiral Karl Dönitz, foreign minister Joachim von Ribbentrop, Reichsführer-SS Heinrich Himmler, Reichsminister Joseph Goebbels, Göring, Bormann and Generalfeldmarschall Günther von Kluge, commanding Army Group Center in Russia, who was there to report on the situation on the Eastern Front where, earlier that month, a major German offensive—Operation Citadel—had failed to pinch out the Red Army's salient at Kursk. Hitler was poring over maps on a long oak table when Rommel entered the room.

"Ah, Rommel," said Hitler. "We must talk about the situation in Italy. It is still obscure. Nothing is yet known of the circumstances of

---

[*]   The same conference room in which, just under a year later, Oberst Claus von Stauffenberg would attempt to assassinate Hitler by detonating a briefcase bomb in the so-called July Bomb Plot. Hitler was wounded but survived.

Mussolini's downfall. Marshal Badoglio, who has taken office on the command of the king, has assured me that the change of government is an internal matter, and that Italy is loyal to the Axis cause and will fight on. I don't believe him. What do you think?"

"I don't believe him either, *mein* Führer."[3]

"In that case," said Hitler, "we need to move reliable troops to Italy as quickly as possible to disarm the Italian Army, which is bound to betray Germany sooner or later. That means taking Waffen-SS Divisions from Manstein's army group in southern Russia." Addressing von Kluge, he added: "I'm sorry, Herr Feldmarschall, but you will have to give up some of your divisions to reinforce Manstein's weakened front."

"But *mein* Führer," protested von Kluge, "if I do that, how can I stop the Soviet offensive at Orel?"

"Do your best. We are not master here of our own decisions. As for Italy, I want the city [Rome] occupied and the king, Badoglio and members of the new government arrested and flown to Germany. While you're at it, you can also remove those swine in the Vatican. They were part of the plot against Mussolini, I'm sure of it."

"*Mein* Führer," interjected Rommel, "I would urge caution. The situation is complex and calls for a carefully prepared response. This might take at least eight days. It is important not to drive the Italians into the arms of the Allies but instead be ready to act if they try to make peace."[4]

The meeting ended with Hitler undecided. But by the following day, he had come around to Rommel's point of view. He told the Feldmarschall that while it was obvious the Italians were about "to turn traitor," it was not yet possible to march troops into Italy "for political reasons." Rommel's task, therefore, was to prepare for such an eventuality by massing troops on the frontier.[5]

Ordered to set up his HQ in Munich, Rommel received official confirmation from OKW on August 1 that he would command all German troops in Italy if Operation Axis—the disarmament of the

Italian Army—was ordered. To prepare for that, German troops were moved surreptitiously into Italy. But for the time being, Rommel was ordered by Hitler to remain on German territory.[6] "The Führer," noted Rommel on August 9, "is still unwilling to allow me into Italy, as he imagines this would be tantamount to a declaration of war."[7] This had changed by August 15 when Rommel was ordered to fly to Bologna and set up Army Group B's HQ on Lake Garda. When news of the Italian surrender reached him there on September 9, Rommel authorized Operation Axis, and within ten days his men had disarmed and interned 82 Italian generals, 13,000 officers and 402,600 soldiers, of whom 183,300 were transported to Germany.[8]

But the real crisis was in the bottom half of Italy, where the German Army Group South was commanded by Generalfeld-marschall Albert Kesselring, a jovial 57-year-old Bavarian known by his soldiers as "Smiling Albert." Kesselring had commanded air fleets in Poland, France, the Battle of Britain and Russia, and been shot down no fewer than five times. In late 1942, he was sent to Italy to command all German armed forces in the Mediterranean—bar Rommel's German-Italian Panzer Army in North Africa—and had been there ever since. Unlike Rommel, who only had to concentrate on the disarmament of Italian troops north of the Alba-Ancona line, Kesselring had the additional responsibility of repelling the Allied landings in the south and a possible coup de main against Rome itself. The difficulty of his position on September 9 was summed up by his chief of staff, General der Kavallerie Siegfried Westphal, who knew that the two German divisions near Rome "could not conceivably neutralize the five Italian divisions there" and fight off an expected landing by Allied troops both on the coast and from the air.

To lose control of the road and rail network that passed through Rome would, Westphal knew, condemn the forces farther south— chiefly von Vietinghoff's Tenth Army—to almost certain destruction, because it would be impossible to resupply them with fuel, food and ammunition. Everything depended on the behavior of the Italians

and, unable to coerce them by force, Westphal came up with the idea
of inviting them to surrender. Incredibly, they accepted this offer and,
having handed over their arms, they were allowed to return to their
homes. Kesselring was later criticized for not incarcerating the disarmed soldiers, as Rommel had done. But Westphal knew this would
have provoked bloodshed. "What other inducement to capitulation,"
he asked, "could have been offered to the Italian troops in Rome who
were largely superior in numbers and arms?"[9]

Released from anxiety over Rome, Kesselring could concentrate
on defending southern Italy. As early as September 10, he drew on
the map a series of defensive lines in the event of a withdrawal
that were, as it happened, "more or less kept to." He felt that they
must be prepared for "a considerable sacrifice of ground, but that
it might still be possible to go over to the defensive south of Rome,
perhaps on a line running through...Mignano [the Winter Line]
or on the Garigliano-Cassino Line [the Gustav Line]." It was up
to Generaloberst Heinrich von Vietinghoff's Tenth Army to buy
Kesselring the time needed to prepare these defenses. "Vietinghoff,"
recalled Kesselring, "and his brilliant operations chief, Wentzell,
carried out the retirement in exemplary fashion and fought a delaying action on the Volturno till 16 October." By November 1, the
Generalfeldmarschall had authorized the withdrawal of all troops to
the Winter Line and had "full confidence" in holding this "naturally very strong position" for some length of time, "perhaps till the
New Year, to be able to make the rear Gustav Line so strong that the
British and Americans would break their teeth on it."[10]

Encouraged by Rommel, Hitler's original intention had been to
defend only northern Italy from a line across the Apennine
Mountains. He had promised to make Rommel the supreme commander and transfer Kesselring to another theater. But when the
expected disaster in southern Italy failed to come about, he "began
to favor the idea of not relinquishing Rome voluntarily but holding
out as long as possible to the south of the city." As Kesselring's stock

rose with Hitler, Rommel's fell. Asked for his opinion, Rommel said that the "amphibious capabilities" of the enemy were so pronounced that to hold a line too far south would leave a whole army group in danger of being cut off by a landing farther up the peninsula. Hitler vacillated for some time and eventually decided to back Rommel. He ordered OKW to prepare a document to that effect. Before signing it, however, Hitler allowed Kesselring to put his case at Rastenburg on October 21. Kesselring must have been persuasive, because a few days later, Hitler told OKW to draw up a new document giving him the supreme command in Italy. Henceforth, Kesselring was known as Commander in Chief, South-West (or Army Group C). Rommel, meanwhile, was ordered to France to inspect the Channel defenses. He did not return. "The duality that had long bedeviled the German leadership in Italy," wrote Westphal, Kesselring's chief of staff, "was now over." Had there been a single commander at the time of the Salerno landings, noted Westphal, the outcome might have been very different.[11]

So the decision was made to hold the Winter Line, which ran from the Gulf of Gaeta, just north of the Garigliano River, to the "great blocks of Monte Camino and Monte Sammucro, that stand like watch-towers commanding the approaches to Cassino," and on through yet more mountainous terrain toward the Sangro River. The obvious route of attack for the Allies was along Highway 6 and through the Mignano Gap, a hill pass that runs between the 3,160-foot-high Monte Camino massif on one side and the even taller Monte Sammucro, at 3,953 feet (1,205 meters), on the other. The pass is further subdivided by two smaller features, Monte Lungo and Monte Rotondo, at 1,151 and 1,171 feet (351 and 357 meters) respectively, while yet another impressive peak, the 3,870-foot-high Monte Cesima, dominates the pass from the east.[12]

The siting of defensive positions on the Winter Line was the responsibility of a special engineer HQ under General Hans Bessell. Its sappers sowed more than 75,000 antipersonnel and anti-tank mines, almost half of them on the immediate approaches. On the line itself, the intention was to create "a system of mutually supporting positions organized in depth to permit penetrations to be sealed off quickly." Supplies and materials were carried up the peaks by mules and Italian civilians, "who were paid good wages plus a bonus of tobacco and food." On the ridgeline they began constructing a chain of strongpoints, manned by machine gunners, riflemen and artillery spotters. As the hard ground was unsuitable for trenches, they constructed sangars with stones and used explosives to blast weapon pits and bunkers from solid rock. The latter were roofed with timber.[13]

The man tasked with defending the Winter Line was General der Panzertruppe Fridolin von Senger und Etterlin, a cultured 52-year-old former Rhodes scholar at Oxford University who spoke fluent English and French. Von Senger had fought in the Battle of France and on the Eastern Front, and for a time commanded German troops in Sicily and later in Sardinia and Corsica. In the latter role he used SS troops to attack and disarm four recalcitrant Italian divisions. But when Hitler ordered him to shoot all the mutinous Italian officers, he refused and was later reprimanded. But by then he had overseen the successful evacuation of the 10,000-strong German garrison on Corsica to Italy, and his disobedience was forgotten. In early October 1943 he was appointed commander of the XIV Panzer Korps—part of von Vietinghoff's Tenth Army—with its headquarters in the medieval hill town of Roccasecca at the head of the Comino valley. He admired von Vietinghoff, "an old Prussian infantryman of the Guards," who he felt was "competent, sure of himself and adaptable," and "an excellent intermediary between the fighting troops and the High Command."[14]

When von Senger took over the XIV Panzer Korps, it consisted of just four and a half divisions: the 3rd and 15th Panzergrenadier Divisions, the 94th and 305th Infantry Divisions, and a battle group of parachutists (part of the 1st Parachute-Panzer Division "Hermann Göring"). By early November, the four complete divisions were all holding sectors of the Winter Line. On the extreme right, guarding the Garigliano River from the sea to near the Camino massif, was the 94th Infantry, an understrength division, barely 13,500 men strong, that was composed chiefly of elderly reservists who were "neither experienced nor well trained."[15]

Next, defending the crucial right shoulder of the Mignano Gap, was the 15th Panzergrenadier Division, which had been formed in Sicily in June 1943 from the remnants of the old 15th Panzer Division, a unit that had served Rommel so well in the desert. It had only narrowly avoided encirclement by the US 1st Infantry Division in a six-day battle near the town of Troina, Sicily, in early August 1943 and, having escaped across the Strait of Messina, fought at Salerno in early September before withdrawing to the Winter Line. The panzergrenadier division—introduced in 1942 as an upgrade to standard or motorized infantry—was a formidable all-arms formation with two regiments of truck-mounted infantry, a battalion of tanks, and the usual complement of artillery, pioneer and reconnaissance units, numbering 14,700 men in all. But few German divisions were at full strength at this stage of the war, and the 15th was no different. It had been formed without a reconnaissance battalion, and by the time it reached the Winter Line, its two panzergrenadier regiments (PGRs)—the 104th and 129th—had been reduced by battle casualties to around 50 percent.

But the 15th still contained many veterans from the fighting in North Africa and was commanded by the hugely experienced 47-year-old Generalleutnant Eberhard Rodt, an officer von Senger knew well from their time in the same cavalry regiment. At Stalingrad, Rodt had commanded the 22nd Panzer Division, a formation that was all but destroyed by the huge Soviet counteroffensive (Operation Uranus) that encircled the German Sixth Army. Rodt and a few survivors were lucky to escape. Von Senger appreciated Rodt's "quiet and confident if somewhat dispassionate manner" and felt he could rely on his division. The impression was reinforced on October 29 when von Senger and army commander von Vietinghoff inspected part of the

Mignano Gap defenses and found Rodt's regimental commanders—particularly Oberst Karl Ens of the 104th PGR, which was holding part of the Camino massif—competent and dependable. He admired the way the two battalions on the massif had dynamited bunkers "shaped like swallow nests" out of the solid rock, before covering them with railroad ties. They had a much wider field of fire than the bunkers made by Bessell's engineers and were mutually supporting.[16]

Less satisfactory, however, were the defenses held by the neighboring division, the 3rd Panzergrenadier Division, in the center and on the left shoulder of the Mignano Gap. One of its two regiments, the 8th, was defending Monte Cesima and the town of Mignano, sited in the gap itself, close to Highway 6; while the other, the 29th, was dug in on Monte Sammucro. In most places, von Senger discovered defenses that were unfinished and inadequate. They were, he wrote, chiefly "single strongpoints, all weak and uncoordinated." His experience in Russia had taught him that such positions are all too often "traps rather than useful defensive works," and he was determined not to "worry very much about the loss of this or that 'position.'" Far more worrying for him was the issue of shelter in such a "rugged mountain district." If the troops did not have any, "then their capacity for resistance would soon diminish." They would "feel that conditions were much better behind the lines, and that would be disastrous."

Von Senger was also concerned by the quality of the 3rd Panzergrenadier Division. Many of its men were *Volksdeutsche*—ethnic Germans from Poland—who were serving in the Wehrmacht on probation. Though eligible for gallantry awards, they could not be promoted until their period of probation was over, and their morale had been further dented by complaints from relatives in Poland that they were being mistreated by local Nazi Party officials. Moreover the division as a whole had been "exposed to the severest trials," and von Senger was convinced that "even the German elements among the troops had been shaken by the many reverses and uninterrupted withdrawals." So poor was discipline during the withdrawal from the Volturno that an officer and two soldiers from the 29th Panzergrenadier Regiment had no compunction murdering nine children and six women in a farmhouse near the village of Caiazzo, during the retreat on October 13, because they suspected the occupants of trying to help approaching US troops.[17] (In 1993, almost 40 years after the murders, two of the three former soldiers—Leutnant Wolfgang Lehnigk-Emden and Kurt Schuster—were charged with murder by German prosecutors but were acquitted on a technicality.)[18]

Von Senger had fewer qualms about the division holding the left of his front, the 305th Infantry. It was made up of "effective fighting men" from Württemberg-Baden who would "show their mettle in the critical battles that lay ahead." It helped that their commander, General Haug, was a "very conscientious and zealous officer, who took any reverses most seriously to heart."[19] Yet the key sector, in von Senger's view, was the Mignano Gap. "We assumed," he wrote, "that the enemy would attempt to capture the pass, send his tanks over it and overrun the broad valley of the Liri at Cassino and southwards, thus preparing the way for a bold operation to capture Rome."[20]

25

"Met at every turn by rifle and machine-gun fire"

For a time in late October 1943, fully aware of the potential cost of a frontal assault on the Winter Line, Mark Clark considered an amphibious landing farther north. His favored target was the beach west of the coastal city of Gaeta. But it and other options were dropped because, as Clark put it, "the beaches were unsuitable and small and usually dominated by defended mountains."[1]

So Clark turned his attention back to the Winter Line. His first plan, proposed at a conference at his Caserta command post on October 26, was to ignore the predictable route of attack—along Highway 6 and through the Mignano Gap—and instead send tanks from the US 1st Armored Division down a secondary road that led from the town of Venafro to the village of San Pietro Infine at the base of Monte Sammucro, just a short distance from Highway 6. By taking this oblique angle of advance, Clark hoped to outflank the German defenses at the Cesima, Rotondo and Lungo mountains. When it was pointed out to Clark that the zigzag route was commanded by peaks on either side, particularly the imposing Monte Sammucro, and that to send tanks down the road without first taking the heights would invite disaster, he agreed to drop the matter. Major General Lucian Truscott, commanding the US 3rd Infantry Division (and Clark's eventual successor as Fifth Army chief), felt that Clark lacked that instinctive "feel" for battle that all successful field generals seem to possess. Truscott was right. Clark had commanded neither a division nor a corps in combat, and the fact that he even considered sending tanks down a road overlooked by high ground shows how little he knew about the effective use of armor.[2]

Brought to his senses, Clark agreed to take the more conventional approach of capturing, one after another, the mountains dominating the Mignano Gap. Twelve miles behind the gap lies the entrance to the Liri valley, the gateway to Rome. But to reach it, noted the US Army's official history, Clark "had first to clear the shoulders of the Mignano gap, then take Cassino, and finally cross the Garigliano and Rapido Rivers." If his men could "crack the defenses at Mignano, they might be able to rush across the intervening ground to the Liri valley."[3]

The plan worked out by General John P. Lucas's US VI Corps was for a three-division attack: Truscott's US 3rd Division would attack the gap itself while, farther north, the US 34th and 45th Infantry Divisions crossed another bend in the Volturno and assaulted the XIV Panzer Korps's left flank. Truscott's men began their advance on October 31, and by nightfall of the following day, fighting patrols from the 15th Infantry had entered the Mignano Gap, causing the German defenders at the base of Monte Cesima to withdraw to new positions on Monte Lungo. A furious Kesselring signaled von Vietinghoff that he was failing to carry out his orders "with the energy and farsightedness required of the situation." The army commander responded with a long letter rejecting Kesselring's criticisms and stating his intention, as of November 4, to take six weeks' sick leave in Germany. He was replaced first by Kesselring himself and then, two days later, by Generalleutnant Joachim Lemelsen.[4]

More setbacks followed for the Germans. An attempt on November

4 to reinforce the lone company of panzergrenadiers on the summit of Monte Cesima was broken up by artillery fire, and soon after, the company withdrew, allowing Truscott's troops to occupy this vital feature. "A local failure of the Panzer Grenadiers," noted a disappointed Kesselring, "suddenly gave the enemy possession of the massif."[5] Farther north, men from the US 45th Division crossed the Volturno and took, in turn, the towns of Venafro and Pozzilli, while the US 34th Division managed to turn the flank of the German 305th Division. Von Senger, who was visiting the Pozzilli sector when the attack took place, was impressed by the performance of the US troops. "I noticed," he wrote, "that the enemy was swift in attack and did not shun close-in fighting. Evidently the Americans were no longer affected by the novelty of battle."

The overall effect of these American attacks was serious: the Winter Line had been pierced north of the Mignano Gap, and there were no other troops between Pozzilli and Cassino. To seal the breach, Kesselring rushed over the "famous and above average" 26th Panzer Division from the Adriatic sector, and von Senger placed it between the "somewhat shaken infantry" of the 3rd Panzergrenadier Division and the 305th farther to the north. This did the trick and the crisis, in this sector at least, was over.[6]

The focus shifted back to the Mignano Gap. Climbing Monte Cesima with Truscott on November 5, Clark could see the whole German defensive system laid out before him, notably the nearby peaks of Sammucro, Rotondo, Lungo and the triangular-shaped Camino massif on the left shoulder of the gap. Eight miles long and four miles wide, the massif's series of peaks included, from left to right, Monte Camino (3,160 feet or 963 meters), Monte la Difensa (3,150 feet or 960 meters), Monte la Remetanea (2,975 feet or 907 meters) and Monte Maggiore (2,030 feet or 619 meters).[7] The two highest peaks—Camino and la Difensa—posed separate problems. Camino has two fairly easy ascents: one up a mule track on its southeastern face, the other up a long exposed path from the south. An attack up either would put troops on a plateau 1,000 feet below the summit. But the plateau is overlooked by a series of small peaks and ridges, as well as by the main peak, putting attackers at the mercy of the defenders above them. Only carefully coordinated attacks by a sizable force could hope to take the main position.

Monte la Difensa—a name denoting a strong defensive position that had its origins in Roman times—was an even tougher nut to crack. The obvious approach route was via a gulley that ran up its eastern face. But the open terrain would expose an attacker to direct fire from the summit above, and to enfilade fire from machine-gun nests that had been cleverly sited on a spur that ran down the mountain. The alternative was to scale the near-vertical 200-foot cliffs that topped part of the eastern and northern faces, but that was only an option for trained mountaineers with ropes. If an attacker did get to the top, however, the mountain was his—unlike Camino, Difensa has no false summit—and he would be well placed to advance west along a spur and capture the lower Monte la Remetanea. Once Remetanea had fallen, any defense of Monte Maggiore, the massif's remaining peak, would be untenable.[8]

Clark planned a series of new attacks to capture both shoulders of the Mignano Gap, using the US VI and British X Corps. Truscott had wanted to use his 15th Infantry to take both Rotondo and Lungo on November 6, with the 30th Infantry waiting in reserve to exploit any breakthrough. But the initial plan was scuppered by the corps commander, General Lucas, who persuaded Clark to move the 30th Infantry farther north to support simultaneous attacks on other peaks. When Truscott complained, Lucas authorized him to use a battalion of the 30th to attack Rotondo. Unfortunately there was no time for proper reconnaissance, and both attacks failed. Even worse, that night a strong German patrol descended from Monte Rotondo and shot up men from the 30th asleep in their bivouacs.

Also on November 6, two battalions of the British 201st Guards Brigade—part of Major-General Gerald Templer's 56th Infantry

Division—attacked Monte Camino. Told the mule track up Camino was unfeasible, the British commander had identified two alternatives: a jagged ridge that led to the base of the mountain's peak, dubbed "the Razorback," and an easier but longer and very exposed approach from the south up a spine dubbed the "Bare Arse." He chose the latter. It was, noted one guardsman, "steep solid rock leading God knows where." To prepare the ground, Scots Guardsmen captured the village of Calabritto, on the flank of the Bare Arse, and then Grenadier Guardsmen made some progress up the ridge. Everywhere they encountered "strong enemy defenses," wrote an admiring Mark Clark, "mines, and booby-trapped approaches to strongpoints." Somehow the advance continued and, by the night of November 8/9, the Grenadiers had taken Hill 727,[*] the first of the two peaks that led to Camino's summit. But after three days of combat, the guardsmen were showing signs of exhaustion and the weather had turned cold and wet. On November 10, a battalion from a sister brigade—the 168th—passed through the Grenadiers and, despite its leading companies suffering 60 percent casualties, fought its way to the top of Hill 819, the last obstacle below the peak. However, it was driven off by a fierce German counterattack.[9]

On November 12, Clark visited the HQ of the British X Corps and was told by its commander, Lieutenant General Sir Richard McCreery, that the crippled 56th Division was no longer strong enough to take Monte Camino. Its men had fought for four days and five nights with "only a 24-hour haversack ration, an emergency ration, and one water bottle per man." Having lost most of their officers, the survivors had been "forced to leave their wounded lying on the ground without blankets, despite the freezing temperature." The division as a whole had been in action since Salerno and badly needed a rest.

---

[*] US military practice is to name high ground after its height in meters, hence "Hill 727."

This was not what Clark wanted to hear. He had hoped the British capture of Camino would set off a chain reaction across the massif, enabling the Fifth Army to seize the high ground on both sides of the Mignano Gap and open up the route to the Liri valley. It was not to be and, acknowledging that the 56th Division was tired and needed to be reorganized, and that the problem of resupplying the troops on the mountain had become acute, he authorized a withdrawal. "This was," noted Clark, "almost as hazardous as the ascent, but, with remarkable skill, the British veterans pulled out at night so quietly that the Germans continued for forty-eight hours to shell positions they had left."[10]

The British failure to capture Monte Camino was not helped by events farther along the massif, where two battalions of Colonel Harry Sherman's US 7th Infantry Regiment—part of Truscott's 3rd Division—had assaulted the equally formidable Monte la Difensa. Having cleared German outposts from the foot of the mountain on the 4th, Sherman's men spent the next 24 hours scouting a route to the summit. The colonel eventually decided on a two-pronged attack, with one battalion climbing up the easier eastern face, the other attempting to scale a gully up the cliffs on the northern face. Neither worked. The easier route was too exposed, and the GIs were cut down long before they neared the ridge; the tougher route proved impossible to find at night and, once they were spotted by German lookouts at the foot of the cliffs, the men were machine-gunned and mortared at will. "They met at every turn," wrote the Fifth Army's official historian, "rifle and machine-gun fire from holes blasted in the rocky slopes and accurate mortar and artillery fire directed from commanding heights." Resupply was also a major problem in a landscape "cut by deep gorges and precipitous ridges." Everything had to be carried up, and a man could manage "only a small amount when he needed both hands for climbing." Attempts were made to drop supplies from planes, but unsuccessfully. It took six hours to bring down the wounded. Meanwhile the men on the mountain "suffered from exposure to rain and cold and from a lack of proper food and clothing."[11] The two battalions of the 7th Infantry were eventually withdrawn on November 10, having lost 91 killed, 538 wounded and an unrecorded number of men hospitalized with trench foot and exposure. But as many of the dead were in exposed locations, halfway up the mountain, they could not be recovered for burial and lay where they had fallen.[12]

Truscott's division had better luck when two battalions of the 30th Infantry captured Monte Rotondo on November 8. But a simultaneous attack by the 15th Infantry on Monte Lungo, guarding the center of the gap, could only secure a toehold on the lower slopes.[13] Aware of the importance of Monte Rotondo, the Germans counterattacked fiercely but were beaten off by, among others, Maurice "Footsie" Britt, a 24-year-old platoon leader and former football star from Carlisle, Arkansas. During the fight, Lieutenant Britt's "canteen and field glasses were shattered; a bullet pierced his side; his chest, face, and hands were covered with grenade wounds…for which he refused to accept medical attention until ordered to do so by his battalion commander following the battle." He had personally accounted for five dead Germans and wounded many more, and but for his "bold, aggressive actions, utterly disregarding superior enemy numbers," the German counterattack would have succeeded. For the example he set that day, Britt was awarded the Medal of Honor, the US military's highest award for distinguished acts of valor.[14]

In just over ten days of fighting, the 15th Panzergrenadier Division had lost 334 killed, 547 wounded, 194 missing and 501 sick. Its losses in officers, in particular, had been heavy. On November 14, Kesselring and Lemelsen attended a conference at von Senger's HQ in Roccasecca to discuss future strategy. Only a few days earlier, von Senger had complained to Kesselring that he did not have enough men to man the Winter Line, and that the 3rd Panzergrenadier Division, in particular, needed to be replaced. Kesselring had agreed to release reinforcements to von Senger's reserve, but not to relieve the 3rd—at least not yet. His emphasis then had been on the need for rapid counterattacks to recover lost ground. At the conference on the 14th, however, Kesselring accepted that the Winter Line could not be held indefinitely, and that it was better to concentrate their efforts on strengthening the coastal defenses and the Gustav Line proper. But a firmer line was taken by Hitler, who ordered, later that day, that while it was no longer necessary to regain the Winter Line's "main line of resistance"—notably the peaks of Cimino and Rotondo—von Senger had to maintain his "current position," and that to do so he needed to prepare the "necessary reserves."[15]

In truth, von Senger's men had fought well in difficult circumstances, particularly the 15th Panzergrenadier Division, which had won an impressive defensive victory on the Camino massif. It was this setback, as much as anything, that forced Clark to suspend offensive operations against the Winter Line while his battered divisions licked their wounds. "I directed," he wrote, "that the Fifth Army should pause for reorganization and regrouping until around the end of November, taking strong precautions against counterattacks."

The news did not go down well with General Alexander, who grumbled, on a visit to Clark's HQ a few days later, that it would now "be harder than ever to get Mount Camino and Mount Maggiore." Clark could not disagree but added that "three times X Corps had attempted to take Mount Camino and ... there had been three failures." Once his army had regrouped, Clark promised, it would take the "hill masses." Alexander was not quite so optimistic. It would be, he said, a "hard fight for them and it might be wise to wait awhile."[16]

26

A "Herculean" Task

On November 22, the day after arriving at Santa Maria, Colonel Frederick was driven five miles by jeep to Clark's command post in the woods at Caserta. The pair had first met in the War Department in late 1941 when Clark was assistant chief of staff, G3 (Operations and Training), and Frederick was in the War Plans Division. A few months later, as chief of staff of Army Ground Forces HQ, Clark had recommended that Colonel "Skeets" Johnson be given command of the Force. That appointment had not worked out. But all that mattered to Clark now, as he pondered the challenges ahead, was that Frederick and his versatile Force had reached Italy and were available to spearhead the latest attempt to break through the Mignano Gap.

Clark wrote later that he was "especially pleased" at the arrival of the Force, a unit "trained to do anything from making a ski assault to dropping by parachute on the enemy's rear." On learning from Eisenhower of the Force's availability, he had requested that it be attached to his army "to work in the difficult mountain terrain." Now that it had arrived, he had the ideal job for it: to help the Fifth Army "drive the Germans off the Camino hill mass," puncture the Winter Line and open up the road to Rome.

Welcoming Frederick into his command trailer, Clark gave a quick résumé of the recent fighting before turning to the layout of the front and the Force's specific role in the planned offensive. "I now have three corps in the front line," he said, pointing to a map. "On the left is McCreery's British X Corps, which extends from the sea to Mount Camino. In the center is the newly formed US II Corps, under [Major General Geoffrey T.] Keyes, covering the smallest sector, just five miles, from Camino to Mount Rotondo. On the right is Lucas's US VI Corps, with responsibility for 15 miles of mountainous terrain from Rotondo to a point near Castel San Vicenzo, its junction with Monty's Eighth Army. Keyes has one division forward, General Walker's 36th Texans,* and you will come under Walker's command for the battle ahead."[1]

The forthcoming operation to pierce the Winter Line, explained Clark, had been code-named Raincoat, an ironic reference to the heavy rainfall that typically fell in the mountainous terrain during December. It would be launched in three phases: the first would consist of a joint attack by X and II Corps on the "Mount Camino–Mount Maggiore hill mass," the southern shoulder of the Mignano Gap; once that was secure, II Corps would switch its attention to Monte Sammucro, the northern shoulder; with both shoulders in Allied hands, all three corps would take part in a joint attack into the Liri valley to create an opportunity for an armored breakthrough. "Because of their expertise," explained Clark, "your boys will play a critical role in all three phases."[2]

---

* During the night of November 16/17, Major General Fred Walker's 36th (Texas) Division had relieved Truscott's 3rd Division in the front line. After 59 days of near constant combat, the 3rd had suffered 3,265 battle casualties, with a further 12,959 men hospitalized for a variety of ailments. Such a high sick rate was partly down to the fact that Truscott's men had landed at Salerno without their bedrolls, groundsheets, greatcoats or shelter halves, and had to make do with a single blanket (Bowlby, p. 85 and note).

The first phase would begin on November 29. The date had been selected, said Clark, because his meteorological section had predicted it would be preceded by two consecutive days of clear and sunny weather, thus giving Allied air support a brief window of opportunity to bomb the German defenses and disrupt their supply routes before the attack began. The plan was for a preliminary assault by the British 56th Division to recapture the two peaks below Monte Camino— Hills 727 and 819—during the night of November 28/29. If successful, they would move on to the main peak itself. "Your task, Frederick," said Clark, "is to capture the neighboring peaks of Difensa and Remetanea. It won't be easy. A whole regiment of infantry—two and a half thousand men strong—tried to take Difensa earlier this month and failed. The final climb is up near-vertical cliffs, but your men have trained for that, haven't they?"

"Yes, sir."

"Good. Your men will have to go up Difensa at night and begin their assault at first light on November 29. Once Difensa is in your hands, you're to move on at once and capture Remetanea. Speed is of the essence, because this second attack will coincide with another by the 142nd Infantry on Mount Maggiore. As Remetanea looks directly down on Maggiore, it won't end well for the 142nd if your second attack fails or is delayed. Do you understand?"

"I do, sir. Don't worry. We won't let you down."

"I'm sure you won't. Just remember: we can't advance into the Liri valley until those peaks have been taken. I hear your men performed well on Kiska without seeing action. Well now's their chance to prove themselves against a real opponent."

"I appreciate you giving us the opportunity, sir."

"Fine. Well, I'll leave you to refine your plan of attack with General Walker. Good luck."

"Thank you, sir."[3]

What Clark did not mention—because he was not aware of it himself—was the lack of faith that the Anglophobic Walker had in the

British general who would command the attack on Monte Camino, Major General Gerald Templer of 56th Division. After their first conference, Walker noted that Templer was "not enthusiastic about doing anything on his part, but quite enthusiastic about following up any successes I could attain." Walker would "cooperate with him in every way possible" but did not think he was "going to do anything except talk." He was no more optimistic after visiting Templer on the 22nd. The British general "promises great things," he noted in his diary, but "will do little to help us." Walker would, as a result, "go on the assumption that I shall receive no help from him."[4]

That evening, in the battered building that housed his HQ, Frederick briefed his three regimental commanders—"Cookie" Marshall, Don Williamson and Edwin Walker—on the Force's first mission in Italy: the capture of Monte la Difensa and Monte la Remetanea. Turning to Williamson, he said: "Don, I promised you the first crack at the next opponent, and I'm keeping my word. Second Regiment will lead the assault on Difensa. I want you to reconnoiter the different approaches to the summit and decide on the direction of attack. Third Regiment will be Force Reserve, with one battalion designated as litter bearers and supply carriers. At General Walker's request, I've agreed to put First Regiment into divisional reserve in case the 142nd Regiment needs help on Maggiore. You'll all move your men into concealed positions on the mountainside after dark on November 27, D-Day minus two. Second Regiment will begin its final ascent on the night of November 28/29, ready to attack at first light. All clear?"[5]

"Yes, sir," said the three colonels in unison.

Delighted that his regiment would spearhead the attack, Williamson wasted no time briefing his battalion commanders, Tom MacWilliam and Bob Moore, and their XOs, Ed Thomas and Sulo Ojala, a 33-year-old son of Finnish immigrants from South Range, Michigan. "We have been given the job," he told them, "of leading the Force in its first combat mission in Italy. Our first objective is

Mount la Difensa. From there we'll continue on to take the peak behind Difensa, Mount la Remetanea. Then, we'll have the privilege of watching the greatest show on earth as Fifth Army's tanks roll through the gap below us and on towards Rome. Our attack will be preceded by the greatest artillery barrage yet fired by the guns of Fifth Army. While we strike one end of the Camino massif, the British 56th Division will attack the other and seize Mount Camino. Tom," said the regimental commander, addressing MacWilliam, "your battalion will lead, with Bob's in support. D-Day is November 29, and we need to be in our concealed bivouac area on the mountain by first light the day before, so time is short. Send out patrols tomorrow and decide on the best route up the mountain. Get to it."

MacWilliam, in turn, gathered his company commanders and explained their mission. He designated Rothlin's 1st Company to lead the assault, with "2nd and 3rd Companies following in that order." Ed Thomas was told to scout Difensa and select the route to the top. To assist him, Rothlin had assigned his best scout, Howard Van Ausdale. Despite his age—he was, at 38, even older than the Force commander—Van Ausdale had never complained during the tough training regime. "He was always in terrific shape," recalled Joe Dauphinais, "because he had tramped around mountains all his life." The younger Forcemen would sometimes poke fun at him. "You old bugger," said one, "you're old enough to be my father!" But Van just laughed and said, "Somebody has to take care of you young kids!" His chief talent, however—and one that made him ideal for the job at hand—was that he was a "king among scouts" and "could read terrain like a book."[6]

It was cold and wet as Thomas and Van Ausdale set out by jeep the following afternoon, November 23. After making a brief courtesy call at General Keyes's HQ, where they were "buzzed by a pair of enemy aircraft," they continued on in near darkness to the command post of the 142nd Infantry, situated behind a cemetery close to Pescia Creek, about a mile from Highway 6. The 142nd, noted Thomas, was the "unit that held as much of Mt. Difensa as was under our control" and "through which we would make our attack." Arriving in the late afternoon, Thomas reported to the regimental commander, Colonel George Lynch, and was told a guide would take him to the 142nd's forward positions in the morning. Meanwhile, he and Van Ausdale could sleep in the "regimental guesthouse, an old barn with a straw-covered floor." They did so, and were eaten alive by lice.

The 24th "dawned bright and clear" and, led by their guide, Thomas and Van Ausdale worked their way through an olive grove and a dry riverbed before reaching Difensa's lower slope. From there they got their "first good view of the mountain and the first concept of what was to come." The height of the peak, and the "grim rocky wall" that loomed above them, "was breathtaking." A little to their right, a ridgeline ran from the valley floor to the first false crest of the mountain, about 1,000 feet from the actual peak. For two-thirds of its length, the ridge formed the 142nd Infantry's front line, so that the GIs' outposts looked "down on the valley at the enemy some distance away." A closer threat was from German troops on top of Difensa, "off to their left flank and somewhat to their rear." That flank, in any event, was unprotected as far as the British positions on the Camino end of the massif.

It was now, as he surveyed the steep rocky ground in front of him, that Thomas appreciated for the first time the enormity of his battalion's task: "to climb behind and beyond the 142nd at night, make the scramble up the rocks and cliffs, and secure Difensa and then Remetanea as the preparation for the Fifth Army's attack along the main highway." Such a climb would, he thought, be difficult enough in daylight and unopposed; at night, with an enemy waiting on top, it would be nothing less than "Herculean."

Scampering across an open slope, they had just reached the entrance to the tree-covered trail that ascended the back of the ridge—the main supply route for the GIs in this sector—when the guide heard the whine of an artillery salvo and shouted, "Get down!" All three of them went to ground, trying to burrow a little deeper in the damp earth as explosions shook the ground and "whistling shrapnel" struck nearby trees. This baptism of fire was, for Thomas, a "mind-searing experience, never to be forgotten." He had been told by veterans that the artillery shell you need to fear is the one you did not hear. But that dictum "did not relieve the apprehension when rounds were exploding nearby."

Back on their feet, they had begun moving up the trail when they were met by the incongruous sight of several US Navy sailors, in their distinctive bell-bottoms, coming the other way. They were, discovered Thomas, from a ship in Naples and had come to the front "to collect any souvenirs they could find or buy from the men on the line." He soon had other concerns, as several times during their slow progress up a trail that rose in switchbacks through rock and scrub brush, more shells exploded nearby, forcing them to hit the dirt again. But nothing was as sobering as meeting a party of GIs descending with pack mules. "On each mule," noted Thomas, "was lashed a human-sized form in a mattress cover. We did not have to ask questions as to the contents."

After a "rocky, rough and long climb," they finally reached the battalion Command Post (CP) "located in a hole hollowed out of the back side of the ridge." Hearing about their mission, the lieutenant colonel gave what advice he could, though his "knowledge of the terrain beyond his left flank was scant." So they set out to reconnoiter the ground on which the Force would fight its first battle as best they could. Thomas considered the combat conditions on the mountain even worse than he had imagined. The men on the ridge were "dirty and exhausted." Even the simplest task became "one of some magnitude because of the terrain." All rations were the US Army's "Type C," three individually boxed meals for breakfast, dinner (lunch) and supper that included simple menus of biscuits, crackers, a tin of meat, a fruit bar, powdered coffee, chewing gum, cigarettes and toilet tissue. They all had to be packed up the trail in wooden boxes, each containing three meals for eight men, as did all the water supplies.

Thomas asked the troops on the ridge the best way up the mountain, but he got little assistance. The forward artillery observer was "gaunt, dirty, bearded" and had the "first case of combat shakes" that Thomas had encountered. That evening he and Van Ausdale went out with a patrol "seeking a route to the top" but "found no easy way." The ground had already been fought over "quite bitterly, with battlefield debris testifying to the several Allied attacks that had failed to take the peak." Thomas was moving across one "small rock-strewn flat" between two of the 142nd's units, when mortar rounds forced him to take cover behind a boulder. There he found a dead German "sitting against a rock with a rifle across his knees." He moved on as soon as he could.

That night, they bivouacked in sleeping bags on a patch of ground suggested by their guide, and continued their reconnaissance at first light. It was now that Van Ausdale's "inborn sense of terrain, probably due to his Indian blood," came into its own. "He and I," wrote Thomas, "ventured into no-man's land as far as we felt wise and he selected a final assault route in which I concurred, a route from a direction that should surprise the enemy."

The route crossed not just the first ridgeline but also the one after that, so that the final approach to the summit was directly up the 200-foot cliffs on the north face, an approach that the German defenders had discounted as too difficult and one that would be, Van Ausdale and Thomas surmised, largely unprotected. Van Ausdale even pinpointed a cleft, or chimney, up the center of the cliffs that would be possible to climb once ropes had been fixed. All that remained was the selection of the assembly area or jumping-off point. This was needed because the Forcemen would be unable to accomplish the march to the base of the mountain and the climb to the top in a single night. It was eventually identified by Thomas and Tom MacWilliam, commanding the assault battalion, who came on one of the "three or four other trips to the target area" that his XO made in the next few days. Together they spotted a grove of scrub pine above and behind the ridgeline held by the 142nd Infantry, about a third of the way up the northeast face of Difensa. It was just about big enough to conceal the two battalions of Williamson's 2nd Regiment—the 1st, which would make the assault, and the 2nd, which would take over the defense of Difensa when the 1st moved on to capture Remetanea—but both would need to be under the tree canopy by dawn on D-1 or the game would be up.[7]

27

"Difensa or Bust"

Colonel Frederick approved Van Ausdale's route of assault after making a personal reconnaissance over the target area in a Piper Cub light plane. "To attain surprise," he told the Fifth Army planners, "we'll use the back door of Difensa at night."[1]

He then instructed his staff to work out the finer details, including the passwords for each day of the mission, the supplies that needed to be stockpiled at the assembly area, the amount of equipment each Forceman would carry up the mountain, and the latest intelligence on the number and identity of the German soldiers holding the two peaks. He also got them to build a clay model of Monte la Difensa and its approaches so that key personnel could be briefed on the plan. Meanwhile, the Forcemen caught up on their conditioning and training, with Rothlin's 1-2 Company and the rest of MacWilliam's 1st Battalion sent on regular "field exercises and marches through the Italian hills to regain some of the edge lost on the trip from Ethan Allen to Santa Maria." They also practiced rock climbing and tested their weapons in live-firing exercises on a wooded plateau about a mile east of their base at Santa Maria.[2]

Despite Allied air supremacy, the Forcemen were still vulnerable to occasional German air raids. One took place after dark on November 26, prompting a storm of antiaircraft fire that was, noted a private in 2-2 Company, "just like the Fourth of July with the tracers and ack-ack guns bursting above the clouds." Marker flares were dropped that "lit up the whole camp." But no bombs followed, causing the private to conclude that the German planes must have been lost. One came below the clouds and was shot down—"how could they miss?"—while the others eventually dispersed. "It was sure pretty," he wrote in his diary. "This fire, it must have lasted almost an hour and we seen all of it."

Next morning, persistent rain—and the forecast of more to come—caused Clark to postpone Operation Raincoat for two days. "Somebody," wrote a Forceman, "has forty-eight hours more to live."[3] Bill Becket took advantage of the respite to give his men "a last crack at weapons training with live ammo" on the plateau above the valley. Mortars were fired in one area, bazookas in another, and "in a third location the men were attempting to approach a dummy enemy machine-gun position on their bellies under covering fire."[4] About an hour into the exercise, one of the bazookas misfired, and the man in charge—Sergeant George Wright of 1-1 Company—ordered the gun team to lay down the weapon and walk away. This prompted the company commander to intervene. "What is the matter with that bazooka, sergeant?" he asked.

"It misfired, sir," replied Wright. "I will carry it onto the range and blow it up, as there is something wrong with either the gun or the rocket, and I understand they should not be played with if they do misfire."

The officer was having none of this. "Take your crew back out there and fire it," he insisted.

"Sir, I'm not in the habit of disobeying orders," said Wright. "But I have to this time, as I'm not going to put my life or my gun crew's life in danger for the sake of a bazooka."

"I shall deal with you later, sergeant," said the officer, before ordering two men from another group—Sergeant John Gibbon from Nova Scotia and North Carolinian Malcolm McFee—to refire the bazooka after he had checked it over. Acting as gunner, Gibbon put the bazooka on his shoulder and aimed, while McFee replugged two wires into the battery and signaled it was ready to fire. Gibbon pulled the trigger and, as the sergeant in charge had feared, there was a huge explosion as the rocket—capable of penetrating two inches of steel plate—"blew up in the tube."[5]

Hearing the noise, Becket ran over, shouting "Medic! Medic!"

It was far too late to help Gibbon, who had had his head "blown off." So Becket concentrated on the youngster McFee who, despite severe wounds to his neck and chest, was "still conscious" and looking at his battalion commander with "no fear in his eyes at all." As the medic dressed McFee's neck wounds, Becket held the young private in his arms and tried to reassure him. "You are going to be all right, soldier—and you *will* be invalided home. Think of that."

McFee smiled. "I'll see my mother, sir?"

"You will see your mother, son, and I'll be writing to her soon too."

McFee grinned a second time…closed his eyes and died.

As Becket stood up, tears streaming down his face, he noticed blood "all over the left arm" of his leather flying jacket; it was a reminder of a "fine young soldier" that he would never wash away. The tragic accident had affected Becket "deeply," and he was grateful for the kind words spoken to him that evening by Colonel Frederick. "I think that I know how you feel, Bill," said the Force commander, "but you can't take the blame—it was a faulty weapon."[6]

Frederick was right, but the deaths could have been avoided if the company commander had not arrogantly ignored his sergeant's advice to destroy the bazooka. He paid the price, as he was also wounded by the explosion, and Wright "never saw him again after they loaded him in the ambulance."[7]

In a letter written that day to his mother and siblings, Lorin Waling

made no mention of either the tragedy or the upcoming mission. Instead he tried to reassure them that all was well. "We are," he wrote,
"getting along fine and hope to keep on that way. As yet we can't say
or even give a hint where we are so don't ask. When I can let you
know I will tell you." He added the news this his wife, Steffie, had
recently moved to Spokane, Washington, to take up a job as a schoolteacher, and that he had recently received four letters from her, the
first in more than three weeks. He ended the letter by bemoaning
the fact that he was not with Steffie in Spokane. "It seems strange to
have been married two and a half months and be so far separated. Of
course that is war and all we can do is hope it is over soon and we are
together again."[8]

The following morning, just hours before Waling and the other assault troops were due to leave for the front, the "long-awaited" mission
orders—in the form of Field Order No. 14—were issued to all senior
officers involved in the first phase of Operation Raincoat. The key
sentence stated: "The First Special Service Force will capture Mt. LA
DIFENSA (HILL 960) and Mt. LA REMETANEA (HILL 907) and
will hold the heights until relieved." The attack would be carried out
by the 2nd Regiment, which "will move from current bivouac" to a
"concealed bivouac" on the slope of Difensa after dark that evening,
D-2. It would remain there "until dark on the night of D-1/D-Day at
which time it will advance up Ridge 368 and seize HILL 960 by day-
break on D-Day." Once in possession of Difensa, the 2nd Regiment
"will immediately advance to capture HILL 907." It would, moreover, "assist by fire the attack of the 142nd Infantry on Mt. Maggiore
(HILLS 510, 639 and 619)."[9]

As the commander of the assault battalion, MacWilliam then
briefed his company and platoon officers, and they, in turn, spoke to
the men. "We, the Second Regiment, has two hills to attack," wrote a
2-2 Company private in his diary. "I hope we do it." If successful, they
would have a "ringside seat" to watch "the 5th Army push up through
the valley."[10]

The plan was for Rothlin's 1-2 Company to lead the assault on Difensa, supported by 2-2 Company. Then, once Difensa was secure, 2-2 would spearhead the capture of Remetanea, with 3-2 Company in reserve. Rothlin's men were under no illusions as to the difficulty of the task they had been set. "Attempts to take the mountain had been made previously," noted 1-2 Company's diary, "and by experienced troops, but without success. Now the Force was to do the job, and no turning back…[1-2 Company] was to be the first in the Force to see action and proud the men were of that fact."[11]

Tradition dictated that the company's senior platoon, the 1st, should be given the honor of leading the assault on Difensa. But Bill Rothlin selected Piette's 3rd Platoon instead. Why? Joe Dauphinais felt it was Rothlin's way of punishing the platoon for all the disciplinary trouble it had given him during the previous 16 months. "All of us bloody buggers had been pretty hard on him in the past," recalled Dauphinais. "We were always in trouble, so maybe this was his payback."[12]

Maybe. But was the company commander really capable of such petty-minded spite? It does not seem to fit his character and this, after all, was war and not a game. Two much more likely explanations for Rothlin's decision were provided by young Don MacKinnon of 5th Section. "Did he feel," wrote MacKinnon, "we were the toughest and most likely to succeed? Or, perhaps it was because the two scouts assigned to get us as close as possible to the Germans without detection were 3rd Platoon members, [Tommy] Fenton and [Howard] Van Ausdale. Both were prospectors before the war, effective in working their way across rough terrain. Van Ausdale was part Indian from the state of Arizona. He had prospected throughout the northwest and, like most Indians, he moved carefully and quietly. Tommy Fenton was also a good tracker with prospecting experience in mining country."[13]

It is possible, of course, that Dauphinais was partly right: Rothlin *did* choose 3rd Platoon to lead the assault because it was full of cussed characters. But not out of spite; rather because he knew instinctively that, when the chips were down, he could rely on them and they would shirk no challenge. Such men would be needed on Difensa.

The identity of the platoon officers might also have been a factor. Shortly before leaving the United States for North Africa, the 1st Platoon leader had been replaced by a young Second Lieutenant, Karl D. Kaasch from Scottsbluff, Nebraska, who had joined the company as an extra officer in January 1943. Kaasch's lack of familiarity with the men of his platoon was not ideal for an assault. Larry Piette, on the other hand, was known and respected by his men and highly regarded by Rothlin, who considered him to be an excellent officer, tough and dependable. Now he would get his chance to prove himself in battle. When Piette heard his men were going up the hill first—using the "insurmountable" back side, the steep side, the cliff side—he told them: "This is what you've trained for. Use your training."[14]

More bad weather—"dull and wet"—and a delay borrowing artillery for the attack from the Eighth Army prompted another two-day postponement. December 1, however, dawned "bright and cool" and the word went round that the assault troops would depart as planned at 3:30 p.m.[15] Rothlin and his men spent the remaining hours cleaning and checking their weapons and equipment and preparing mentally for the ordeal ahead. "This was," wrote Don MacKinnon, "the critical test for the FSSF as a unit, and for each of us as an individual, facing a formidable challenge which had defeated earlier attacks by units already blooded in battle."[16] Ordered to leave all personal letters, diaries and other written documents in the barracks at Santa Maria—in case they were captured and gave vital intelligence to the enemy—many penned a final message to families and sweethearts. Fearing he might be killed, Larry Piette wrote "what he thought might be his last letter to the young beauty in Louisiana," Marin deGravelles, proposing marriage.[17]

Shortly before 1:30 p.m., the Force officers gathered in a courtyard to hear a final pep talk by the corps commander, Major General

Geoffrey T. Keyes. As the minutes ticked past the appointed time, the officers "stood around, talked quietly, said little, waited impatiently." There was, noted Lieutenant Colonel Burhans, the Force intelligence chief, "a certain gathering tenseness" among the group. To relieve it, one junior Canadian officer asked Williamson the relative order of Canadian and US decorations for bravery. "To hell with that," interjected Tom MacWilliam. "Give me the long service medal any day."[18]

At 2:15 p.m. there was still no sign of Keyes, so Frederick ordered all 2nd Regiment officers to go for an early meal. They missed the talk that the corps commander gave when he finally arrived at 2:30 p.m. To the remaining Force officers, the 55-year-old Keyes cut a surprisingly unmartial figure: tall and thickset, graying at the temples, and with a genial grin that made him seem more bank clerk than warrior. But looks could be deceptive. Born in Fort Bayard, New Mexico, the son of an army officer, Keyes had joined the US Cavalry after graduating from West Point—where he had excelled as a football player— in 1913. Three years later he took part in the Pancho Villa Expedition in Mexico, and since then had served as a staff officer, an instructor at West Point and the Cavalry School at Fort Riley, Kansas, and as chief of supply in the War Department. But it was his stint in 1940 as chief of staff at the 2nd Armored Division, commanded by another cavalryman, George S. Patton, that put him on the road to high rank.

Patton considered Keyes to have "the best tactical mind of any officer I know." When Patton took command of I Armored Corps in North Africa in 1942, he asked for and got Keyes as his deputy. That arrangement continued in Patton's next command, the US Seventh Army, for the invasion of Sicily. During that campaign, Keyes was put in charge of the Provisional Corps, which advanced 125 miles in five days through challenging mountainous terrain and eventually captured the Sicilian capital of Palermo. Keyes was rewarded with the Distinguished Service Medal and mentioned favorably in Eisenhower's reports to Marshall.[19]

The "impetuous, vitriolic, histrionic Patton," wrote one officer, "is considerably leavened by the calm, deliberate, circumspect Keyes."[20] The latter, moreover, was known for his tact and compassion and for his strong adherence to the Roman Catholic faith. But as he stood before the Force officers at Santa Maria, he misjudged both the tone and content of his speech. He began by welcoming the Force to II Corps and adding a few pointless platitudes like: "You will all have new experiences to look forward to." This caused more than a few officers to shift their stance uneasily, and none to smile. But it was the general's next ill-chosen comment that was to lead to lasting bitterness. "You have," said Keyes, "been preceded by a great reputation, but you haven't been blooded yet. War isn't Hollywood glamor stuff and men do not die dramatically."

Some lieutenants frowned; others whispered uncomplimentary remarks from the corners of their mouths. Who the hell did this bumptious oaf think he was talking to? They knew perfectly well that they had not been tested in battle. They also knew that their training was second to none and that, when the time came, they would live up to the hype—or die in the attempt. As Burhans put it: "There was enough humility among them to obviate the necessity of debunking a reputation that none had thought much about. They would long resent the 'Hollywood' reminder."

Thankfully, Keyes kept his talk short and ended it by wishing the Force luck in the battle ahead.

Meanwhile, the men were writing letters, talking, joking and playing crap games in their barracks. There was "no bragging and few hazarded any guesses" as to what might happen on the mountain. Some "just sat holding rifles and Tommy guns, not speaking." In one 3rd Regiment hallway, a soldier who was a talented artist "was busy with charcoal converting a wall to the mural of a man in baggy pants, pockets bulging with ammunition, grenades, rations." On the figure's back the artist had drawn "a packboard that towered high above him and bulked far behind him—a load that dwarfed a man and which contained boxes of rations, ammunition, sleeping bag, rifle, machine gun, mortar and battle miscellany." It was a depiction of the job given to one of the 3rd Regiment's battalions to act as litter bearers and supply carriers. When the call came for chow—the final meal before the operation—the artist wrote above the burdened figure: "Freddy's Freighters—Difensa or Bust."[21]

28

The Defenders

Thirty miles to the north of Santa Maria, the German troops defending the Camino massif were cold, wet and hungry. Robert Burhans, the Force intelligence chief, would later claim that the 2nd Regiment knew what it was up against on the "Difensa-Remetanea eminences" because "II Corps had sized up the enemy with fair accuracy."[1] In fact, Burhans's prebattle knowledge of German strength—and, more important, the siting of their machine-gun nests—was sketchy at best.

As the Force was not yet in the front line, most of its information was gleaned from intelligence reports and debriefs compiled by higher headquarters. On November 18, for example, seven Germans surrendered to General Walker's 36th Division. Wearing summer uniforms, they were cold and wet and lacked motivation. "They said they were sick and tired of the war," noted Walker in his diary, "had had nothing to eat for two days and were through with it."[2]

On the 23rd, after the debrief of these and other prisoners, a Fifth Army intelligence summary noted the presence of companies of the 104th and 129th Panzergrenadier Regiments on the Camino massif, and that they were "part of a group of 300 recently discharged from hospital."[3] A day later, Clark's intelligence staff reported that two Italian civilians, "considered reliable and competent," had given vital information about the enemy's defenses in the Winter Line. They had been part of a group of 300 to 400 Italians who had been "impressed to do manual labor for the Germans and working with German soldiers on defense installations from 4 October to 2 November." In that time they had helped to construct numerous "small forts" or pillboxes "made of lumber and covered with concrete, size 2 meters by 1 meter" and all armed with at least one machine gun.[4]

The only extra information that Clark's intelligence people were able to provide about the 104th's 3rd Battalion, believed to be holding Difensa, was that its 9th Company was 50 to 60 men strong and armed with ten MG 42 light machine guns (first introduced in 1942 as an upgrade to the MG 34 and capable of firing 1,200 rounds a minute from belt or drum).[5]

Piecing this information together, Burhans thought the Camino massif was being defended by two Panzergrenadier battalions with another in reserve. In fact there were now three German battalions on the massif and another nearby. Three of the four were from Oberst Ens's 104th Panzergrenadier Regiment: the 1st Battalion (I/104th) was holding Monte Camino and its subsidiary peaks, Hills 819 and 727; the 3rd Battalion (III/104th) was dug in on Monte la Difensa and Monte Maggiore; while the 2nd Battalion (II/104th) was stationed a short way behind the massif, in case it was needed for a counterattack.[6]

The other battalion, the 115th Armored Reconnaissance (*Panzer-Aufklärungs-Abteilung 115*), was bolstering the positions on Difensa and the saddle that led to Monte Camino. It was not mentioned in any of the various Allied intelligence reports, because it had only recently been deployed on the massif. Raised just two months earlier in Germany and Italy from a core of veterans who had served in North Africa with the 33rd Armored Reconnaissance, the new battalion consisted of five companies of infantry mounted in armored cars and trucks. The main cadre had begun its training in early October at a camp near Paderborn, northern Germany, with most of the vehicles arriving on the 22nd. Just over a week later, as pressure began to build in the Mignano Gap, Generalleutnant Rodt requested that the 115th, three companies of which were already in the Italian theater, be assigned to his division. This was granted, though it would take time for the rest of the battalion to complete its training and travel down from Germany.[7]

The first senior officer to arrive from Paderborn was Rittmeister Walter Freiherr von Gienanth, the descendant of a humble man from Eisenberg in the Palatinate who was ennobled after making a fortune in iron foundries. Von Gienanth's father, Curt, a senior officer in the Wehrmacht, had commanded German forces in the General Government in Poland until he was relieved of his post in 1942 for protesting about the economic absurdity of removing Jews from the arms industry. The son, meanwhile, was distinguishing himself in North Africa, where he was awarded the German Cross in Gold—a gallantry award that could only be won by men who already held the Iron Cross First Class—for outstanding leadership while serving with the 33rd Armored Reconnaissance.[8]

Von Gienanth left for Italy on November 10, to get a "feel for the area of operations from Oberleutnant Gerlach von Gaudecker, who was already there."[9] Five days later, Rittmeister Alhard Freiherr von der Borch arrived at Paderborn to take command of the 115th. Just 27 years old, von der Borch had been brought up in his mother's family home of Schloss Sophienreuth, near Schönwald in eastern Bavaria, after her father, Graf von Arnim-Boitzenburg, was killed by revolutionaries in 1918. It was a pampered if emotionally deprived childhood in which young Alhard spoke only French for the first five years of his life, spent most of his time with his nanny (and later tutor) and saw his parents for just 15 minutes each day. At 14 he was sent to a private school in Bayreuth where he later passed the *Abitur*, the German qualification needed for entrance to further education.

Instead of going to university, however, von der Borch joined the interwar German Army, the *Reichswehr*, as a junior cavalry officer in the elite 17th Horse Regiment. Though the regiment was partially motorized in 1939, he and some of his colleagues served in the Polish campaign as horsed reconnaissance troops.

Such a socially exclusive cavalry regiment was dominated by officers from Bavarian noble families: they included Oberst Claus Schenk Graf von Stauffenberg and four others who would later be executed for their part in the bomb plot to kill Hitler in July 1944. Might von der Borch have been an anti-Nazi too? There is no evidence for this. He was not implicated in the bomb plot and, like many professional soldiers, was a proud patriot who was probably happy to turn a blind eye to the worst excesses of Hitler's regime while Germany's armed forces were carrying all before them. That was no longer the case in late 1943, still less in 1944, and it is likely that von der Borch and his officers fought on because, as von Gaudecker put it, they were "doing their soldierly duty."[10]

Earlier that year von der Borch—an extremely handsome, intelligent and cultured man with a deep love of classical music and the poems of Goethe, Eichendorff and Hölderlin—had married Ruthmaria von Radowitz, who was pregnant with their first child by the time her husband joined the 115th.[11] Yet whatever concerns he may have felt about the future course of the war and the likelihood of seeing his future child grow to adulthood, he kept them to himself. To his subordinates, he was the ideal commander who "often succeeded in preventing the battalion from being needlessly 'run into the ground,'" and whose "careful execution of the highest orders saved the health and lives of many." As a result, "an esprit de corps arose in the battalion," noted von Gaudecker, "for which we were often envied by other units" and "many, who had been soldiers since the beginning of the war and longer, only began to understand fully what is meant by the term 'military home' once they had joined the battalion."[12]

On November 16, the day after taking command at Paderborn,

von der Borch supervised the loading of the 115th's new cadre on trains for Italy, arriving at Rome's eastern train station six days later. From there von der Borch and his men drove south to Rodt's HQ, where he was informed that his battalion, "which still had not completed its activation process, would also be committed immediately." The fact that his men would serve not in the role for which they had been trained—as a fast-moving and hard-hitting armored reconnaissance battalion, the "eyes" of a division—but rather as infantry in a "high mountain terrain" was a surprise for von der Borch. "It was," he noted, "rocky and filled with cliffs, and the only way to provide logistical support—in a very laborious manner, to boot—was by means of mules and backpack." Yet he and his men knew they could not simply stand around with their hands in their pockets while "the grenadier regiments of the division were involved in extremely heavy fighting."

Leaving the armored cars of the HQ (Reconnaissance) Company as a mobile reserve at San Giovanni Incarico, west of Cassino, von der Borch led his other four companies, the men still dressed in their tropical summer uniforms, up a narrow winding mule track— the main route of resupply—to the top of the Camino massif. Two companies were deployed in support of the troops already on Monte la Difensa, the other two at Monte Camino and on the saddle that connected it to Difensa. Von der Borch, meanwhile, set up his command post at an altitude of 2,600 feet "in a cold and wet cave" at the rear of the saddle. He and his staff dubbed it, with wry humor, the "Camino Bar." For the first few days the positions occupied by his men were approached only by Allied patrols: "Americans to the left and Tommies to the right." The Allied artillery and fighter-bombers were also "very active," but they did not have "much of an effect initially." All the while, von der Borch's combat engineer platoon was trying to improve the various defensive positions, though the work "moved forward slowly due to the meager means and forces available." It did not help, noted Oberleutnant von Gaudecker, commanding 4th Company, that the rocky limestone terrain was "completely free of vegetation" and all the machine-gun posts had to be built "from stones."[13]

This was particularly the case on Difensa, where the reconnaissance battalion's 110-strong 2nd Company, under Leutnant Wolff, had joined a weak company of the III/104th to provide a total garrison of around 175 men. Some were manning machine-gun posts on the rocky ridgeline that covered the eastern approaches to the mountain, or sheltering in bunkers and caves in the shallow depression, barely 40 yards across, that lay just below the summit. The largest cave—with room for up to eight people and accessed by a narrow gap between two slabs of rock—was located on the southern side of the depression and served as a platoon headquarters. The balance of the garrison had taken cover in a broad ravine that led, via the saddle, to Remetanea, protected from artillery fire but ready to reinforce the soldiers on the peak in the event of an attack. Not that the garrisons were inactive. "Reconnaissance and combat patrols were carried out on foot," recalled von Gaudecker, "and [Leutnants] Mann, Kessler, Bensel and Wolff became specialists in this kind of work."[14]

In most German accounts of the battle there is little mention of the weather. Clad in summer uniforms, however, von der Borch's men would have been particularly susceptible to the freezing rain and plummeting temperatures. For those in the front line, it was almost impossible to keep warm and dry, and the intermittent supply of rations did not help. And all the while, their positions were subjected to regular artillery bombardments and air attacks that took their toll on the men's nerves and lives. The defenders knew, moreover, that sooner or later the Allies would launch another major attack to drive them from the heights. The only question was: When?

It was a question also being asked by Hitler and his senior generals at the Wolf's Lair in East Prussia. On November 27, Generalfeldmarschall Wilhelm Keitel, chief of the OKW, had sent a message "on behalf of the Führer" to Kesselring in Italy. He, in turn, forwarded it to Generalleutnant Joachim Lemelsen. It began: "In the very near future, severe enemy attacks on the 10th Army are to be expected. These must end in bloody failure." Reinforcements were being sent, and Kesselring was to ensure that combat strengths were maintained "at the required level even in the case of heavy losses." He could do this by keeping steady the ratio between fighting troops and supply troops in each division. If it fell to the detriment of the combat troops, "the rear services and combat trains must be reduced and thinned out accordingly." Henceforth, only the "physically unfit," "specialists in staff units, or in rear or supply services" and those who "cannot be spared from the home front" would avoid frontline duty. "These measures," insisted Keitel, "are to be prepared with ruthless consistency and to be implemented if the need arises."[15]

Three days later, von Senger ordered all battalion commanders "to save ammunition, in order to have reserves ready in case of large-scale enemy attack."[16]

29

"A wet and forbidding mountain"

Just after 3:30 p.m. on Wednesday, December 1, the first of a convoy of 27 US Army trucks pulled out of the gateway of the artillery barracks at Santa Maria Capua Vetere and headed northwest in bright sunshine toward Highway 6. In the lead vehicle, denoted by a white flag, was Colonel Don Williamson, commanding 2nd Regiment, and his staff. Next came Lieutenant-Colonel Tom MacWilliam, his XO Major Ed Thomas and the rest of the 1/2nd Battalion's command group. Then came the battalion's three companies—1-2, 2-2 and 3-2—each occupying four trucks, a section and a half per truck. The pattern was repeated for Lieutenant Colonel Bob Moore's 2/2nd Battalion, its last vehicle marked by a green flag. "It was," remembered Ed Thomas, "a most uncomfortable ride and seemed to last forever. We were too crowded to sit."[1]

This was because each officer and enlisted man was wearing a camouflaged steel helmet and an extra-warm combat uniform of woolen gloves, socks, drawers, baggy mountain pants, vest, shirt and high-necked sweater, topped off by the thigh-length M-1943 cotton field jacket with hood and faux-fur lining and a red-and-white FSSF spearhead on each shoulder. On their belts were slung pistols, fighting knives and canteens, while a first-aid kit, grenades and magazines for their personal weapons were stuffed into the various pockets. Each man carried, in addition, a blanket roll over his shoulder with a mountain sleeping bag and a shelter half and poles, plus a field bag containing emergency rations, toilet articles, extra socks and a poncho. As well as their specialist weapons—rifle, Tommy gun, machine gun or mortar—the enlisted men also carried extra ammunition or five-gallon cans of water, a total load of up to 100 pounds. They had left their metal-framed rucksacks, filled with a change of underwear and socks, mess gear and remaining toilet articles, back at Santa Maria.

The 89 officers and men of Rothlin's 1-2 Company were riding in four trucks near the front of the column: Lorin Waling was in the first with the bulk of Kaasch's 1st Platoon (all of the 1st Section and half of the 2nd); Jack Callowhill rode in the second with half the 2nd Section and all of the 3rd; in the next truck was the 4th Section and half of Hugh McGinty's 5th, including Geoffrey Hart, Ray Kushi, Jimmy Flack and Syd Gath; the rest of the 5th Section and all of Percy Crichlow's 6th—among them Herby Forester, Joe Glass, Clarence DeCamp, Johnny Walter, Ray Holbrook, Harry Deyette, Dick Daigle, Joe Dauphinais and the company scouts Howard Van Ausdale and Tommy Fenton—were in the fourth truck.

For young Canadian Don MacKinnon, riding with Hugh McGinty in the third truck, it was a long, rough and, at times, hair-raising journey, "sometimes at breakneck speed, the driver nervous and anxious to drop us off and get the hell out of there and back to safety." As the light began to fade, the sky "lit up sporadically with great flashes of light" as the Allied artillery bombarded the German positions. "The noise was deafening," recalled MacKinnon, "and as the sky was illuminated we could see the surrounding mountains and lower clouds. There was a menacing feeling about it." They had started off in unseasonably fine weather, but as darkness fell, so did the rain, causing the truck to skid "dangerously on the slick and muddy road as it kept up with the vehicle ahead," the way lit only by narrow blackout head-lamps. Only luck prevented MacKinnon's truck from "being pitched into a ditch."[2]

The plan was to reach the detrucking point—about 30 miles from Santa Maria—at 7:00 p.m. and the covered bivouac on Difensa's slopes four hours after that.[3] But they were already two hours late when the first trucks disgorged their loads behind a hill just off High-way 6. "The usual confusion surrounded the detrucking with grunts, groans and curses, and the clank of weapons," noted Ed Thomas, "as bodies stiff from the long, cold ride, and burdened with heavy loads, hit the ground." It was chilly and wet, and the men could hear the "constant bark" of artillery fire from a battery in the next field. For many, it was the first time they had heard guns firing in anger. "Finally," wrote Thomas, "the sections, platoons and companies got organized in the dark. Then, led by a guide from the 142nd, we moved off single-file across the road and into a streambed, angling to-ward the base of the mountain."

Wading through "ankle-deep water" and across broken terrain in the dark, 2nd Regiment's progress was painfully slow. It seemed to take an age even to reach "the vicinity of the 142nd CP" where Ed Thomas's guide duties began. "My great problem," he recalled, "was to guide the regiment along paths with which I was not too familiar even in daylight, and reach the assembly area before light, else we would be on the exposed slope under observation. This would surely lead to destructive shellfire, and by now there was no safety margin left in the timing." His difficulties were exacerbated by a problem he had not anticipated—the mental state of the regimental comman-der, Don Williamson, who, with his command group, was marching just behind Thomas at the head of the column. Williamson "cursed, complained and criticized" Thomas for the delay in reaching the "rel-atively safe haven of the assembly area located in a small woods."[4]

Tempers were fraying throughout the column. Rothlin's 1-2

Company—marching in ponchos in order of platoons—was getting more strung out as it negotiated fields, rocky creek beds and muddy trails. Piette's 3rd Platoon would arrive just as a five-minute break was finishing, forcing it to go without rest. The platoon leader was "furious," and Sergeant Herby Forester threatened to "tear off his stripes" if matters did not improve. "We were afraid," recalled MacKinnon, "that we would be too exhausted to be much use in battle. The sky continued to flash and roar with artillery fire and it continued to rain off and on as we scrambled, slid and clawed our way, passing by artillery emplacements firing at targets near and far."[5]

When the head of the column stopped, Thomas would range ahead to make certain he was moving in the right direction. With the rest over and the regiment on the move, he spent as much time trying to calm Williamson as he did searching for the right trail. "I do not know," he wrote later, "if anyone else in the column knew the critical nature of the timing. I certainly did not confide this to Williamson because his state of mind was already impossible. As daylight grew near my tension built and I strained trying to see trees in the dark that would not appear."[6]

It was a hellish march that tested the Forcemen, weighed down by full combat loads, to their limit. As they began moving up Difensa's lower slopes, they passed through the 142nd Regiment's outer pickets. "They had never heard of the FSSF," remembered MacKinnon, "and skeptical remarks were heard about our prospects of taking the mountain."[7] That was one way of putting it. The warning made to Jack Callowhill, in a thick Texan drawl, was typically blunt: "You're going to get your ass shot off."[8] Ignoring the comments, the Forcemen just kept marching and, finally, the head of the column reached the grove of scrub pine, having covered a distance of more than ten miles.

Thomas waited at the entry point to watch the companies coil their way in. All except 6-2 Company. His temper flaring anew, Williamson ordered his intelligence sergeant, Canadian Bill Story, to hurry it along. But when Story located the company a short way down the track, he was astonished to find its commander, a lieutenant from Hackensack, New Jersey, asleep under his shelter half. The lieutenant's feet had been "killing him," Story was told, and he refused to go a step farther. Story was warning 6-2's first sergeant of the consequences of staying where they were when the lieutenant overheard the conversation and got up. Furious at Story's apparent insubordination, he threatened him with a court-martial. But Story stood his ground and eventually the lieutenant gave the order to move. Dawn was breaking as the last of his men reached the tree line. It was a "hairbreadth" escape and Thomas's relief was "immense."[9]

Ordered to get some sleep, the men of 1-2 Company found it impossible to dig into the rocky ground. So they strung up their shelter halves as best they could, took off their boots and sodden socks and lay down in their sleeping bags. Preoccupied with thoughts of what lay ahead, many enjoyed only a fitful rest. "Each of us," remembered Don MacKinnon, "dealt with the knowledge that we were about to face the real thing and we tried to subdue the fear we felt with an ache in the pits of our stomach." He, like others, thought of family back home—of his mother and father in Saint-Lambert, Quebec— and how they were blissfully unaware that he was "on a wet and forbidding mountain in Italy," about to go into action and "maybe never to return." It was a long way, he mused, "from the safety of home, family and friends." He was just 18.[10]

Men looked at pictures of wives and girlfriends, uncertain if they would meet again. A few, like Harry Deyettte, thought of their children. Having left before the birth of his infant son Charles ("Chuck"), Joe Glass prayed that he would live long enough to see him in the flesh. Tom MacWilliam might have done the same, but the letter from his wife, Bobby, informing him that she was pregnant arrived at Santa Maria after his departure.[11] Some had keepsakes that reminded them of loved ones. Dick Daigle, for example, was carrying the Buck folding knife inscribed with the name of his sweetheart, Rae Bourgeois. In the lining of his helmet was the photo his sister had sent him of his young nephew Ken.[12]

After a couple of hours of fitful sleep, the Forcemen woke to bright sunshine. They breakfasted on C rations—eaten straight from the can—and spent much of the day in the woods recovering their strength, drying their clothes and cleaning their weapons. Yet always, remembered Ed Thomas, "the shadow of what was to come" was in "our minds—some of us would only see one more dawn."[13] Sporadic Allied shelling and bombing of the heights could be heard all day. But the main air effort was directed against the distant Cassino and Acquafondata sectors, where 700 sorties dropped more than 500 tons of ordnance in an effort to disrupt resupply and divert the Germans' attention from the Mignano Gap.[14]

Colonel Frederick, who had set up his command post in a ravine a short way down the valley the night before, spent part of the morning of December 2 sending radio messages and visiting the 1st and 3rd Regiments in their separate bivouac areas.* "Make sure you keep your feet dry," he told one group of soldiers. "Change your socks at regular intervals."[15] At 10:00 a.m. he met Clark, Brigadier General Wilbur (assistant commander of the US 36th Division) and Colonel Lynch in the 142nd Infantry's CP to go over last-minute details and to hear the welcome news that, the previous night, the British 46th Division had captured its preliminary objective of Hill 360 on the approach to Monte Camino. The British 56th Division, added Clark, was ready to attack that night alongside the Force. Having shaken hands with Clark, Frederick returned to the Force CP.[16]

---

* They had had almost as bad a time as the 2nd Regiment. "Got off," wrote one 3rd Regiment sergeant, "and carried 70 lb packs through mud and slime for 8 miles, one of the toughest grinds in my life...We climbed up steep banks and slid down others, and just made our bivouac area before daylight, a march of twelve hours altogether" ("Diary of Sergeant A. W. Ovenden").

Meanwhile, Joe Dauphinais was "basking in the sun" when he was told to report to Piette. "What have I done this time?" he asked himself. The answer was nothing. He had, however, been selected with his former adversary and now buddy, Johnny Walter, to help the scouts Van Ausdale and Tom Fenton fix ropes "on the trail just ahead of our assembly area to make it easier to ascend a small vertical cliff." Was Dauphinais's long record of misdemeanors and insubordination finally catching up with him? It may have been. After all, MacWilliam had warned him after one outburst at Fort Ethan Allen that he would be first in line for "hazardous duty." This was certainly that.

Accompanying the four men carrying the rope were three officers: Rothlin, MacWilliam and Thomas. The latter pair went along because, according to Thomas, the job would have a "critical impact…on our movement that night." As it was still daylight, the decision had been made to put rope on only the first cliff. But it was still tough carrying the long pieces of heavy rope up the steep, slippery terrain. Dauphinais consoled himself with the knowledge that he was doing an important job and that it would give the battalion "something to work with." Fortunately for him, the hardest and most dangerous part—climbing and roping the actual cliff—was done by the scouts Van Ausdale and Fenton.

They went right to the top with their ropes, recalled Dauphinais, "and we tied ours to the end of theirs." Dauphinais and Walter narrowly avoided injury when a German shell exploded nearby and a piece of shrapnel passed between them. "Gee," said Dauphinais, with feigned insouciance, "they're getting careless with that scrap iron and we haven't even got near them yet." It was a relief to return to the cover of the trees at around 3:00 p.m.[17]

Watching them walk in was Private Bob Davis of 2nd Platoon. "I still don't know how they did it—how they went up and came down, then went up again. It was an ordeal doing it just once."[18] Ed Thomas spent the next hour talking quietly with Tom MacWilliam, who was suffering from a cold; earlier, during the climb, the battalion commander had complained about chest pain. They talked, remembered Thomas, about "home and family, and some of the things we would rather be doing, but not too much about what was ahead." Yet it still overhung both their thoughts.[19]

Shortly before 4:30 p.m., a runner arrived in the bivouac with a final message for Williamson from Frederick. It gave the latest British positions and reminded 2nd Regiment of the artillery fire plan and the ban on the use of firearms until 6:00 a.m. on the 3rd, when the 142nd Infantry would begin its attack on neighboring Maggiore. Before that time, fighting knives and bayonets would have to suffice unless the troops were "definitely pinned by the enemy." The message was passed on by Williamson to the battalion commanders, and from them to their officers and men.[20] MacWilliam also ordered his men to eat a last C ration meal, stack their blanket rolls—to make the climb a little easier—and get ready to leave. Ed Thomas remembered "an air of tense anticipation as packs were slung, weapons checked for the last time, and the men scrambled into position to start the long climb upward." Each man would take with him one lightweight K ration—three boxed meals of candy, hard biscuits and canned processed meat, totaling 2,830 calories—to be consumed the following day, and a D ration (made up of three high-energy bars) for emergencies.

30

The Climb

As dusk fell, the 281 men of 1/2nd Battalion moved off in single file with scouts Van Ausdale and Fenton in the lead, followed by Rothlin, Piette and the rest of 3rd Platoon. Next came MacWilliam and his forward command group, 1-2 Company's remaining platoons, then 2-2 Company, Thomas and the rest of the battalion staff, and finally 3-2 Company. Moore's 2/2nd Battalion, weighed down with even heavier loads, would follow at a more leisurely pace. Even without their blanket rolls, MacWilliam's men were groaning under the weight of their packs, weapons and extra loads. Jack Callowhill, for example, had his rifle, pistol, knife, four grenades, a belt of .30-caliber ammunition (for the Browning machine gun) and a five-gallon water container strapped to his back. It was the water that just about killed him. "The slope was about 60 percent," he recalled. "Luckily we were in shape."[1]

For 16 months these teak-tough young men had been put through a military training regime as punishing as any in the world. They had been taught a multitude of skills—rock climbing, survival in a winter climate, marksmanship with a bewildering variety of weapons—

that would now be put to the test. Each platoon was bristling with firepower. The 27 men of Piette's 3rd—who would spearhead the assault—had one M1 carbine (platoon leader), two Tommy guns (section leaders), 18 M1 Garand rifles, four M7 rifle grenade launchers (which could be attached to the Garand and fired with blanks), two Johnson light machine guns, two Browning .30 medium machine guns, two bazookas, one M2 60mm mortar, 27 V-42 fighting knives and 27 semiautomatic pistols.

Following the route agreed with Thomas, Van Ausdale led the men obliquely upward over Ridge 368 and away from the east side of the mountain "to the north-facing cliffs, the approach that the Germans would not anticipate." En route they passed the bloated bodies of 7th infantrymen who had been killed in the previous attempt to dislodge the Germans. It was a sobering moment. "Who's next?" wondered Don MacKinnon.

At 8:00 p.m., as they climbed, 925 Allied artillery pieces of all calibers opened up on the "Camino-Difensa-Lungo island," the heaviest concentration of the campaign, "perhaps the heaviest in the war." The attack on Difensa alone was supported by more than 340 guns, including the tank destroyers of the US 1st Armored Division and two battalions of the new eight-inch howitzers whose huge shells were supposed to be capable of penetrating even the best-protected enemy bunkers. The Germans responded by plastering the known supply trails with medium and heavy artillery and mortars. The combined noise was ear-splitting. "Shells roared overhead in both directions," recalled MacKinnon, "like fast freight trains, one after another."

While Allied shells were "crashing into the enemy positions on the top of Difensa," the Germans were using howitzers and mortars to hit "positions down the mountain behind and below us." The mortars were being directed by German machine guns shooting tracer bullets at "twice the number of rounds per minute" that the Forcemen's Johnny guns were capable of. "So much," noted MacKinnon, "for the morale-building speeches we had received on the superiority of our weapons."[2]

Watching from the Force CP below, Lieutenant Colonel Burhans was awestruck by the effect of the bombardment. "A murderous seething and crackling thundered along the Camino-Difensa ridge," he recalled. "The batteries along the road behind the command post were firing four and six guns at a time."[3] It seemed to Private Bob Davis of 2nd Platoon as if the mountain "was on fire." The shells were "bursting on that slope all over the place, and continued to do so over and over again." He noted: "You wouldn't think an ant could crawl out of it alive." To Corporal Joe Glass, climbing near the head of the column, the barrage—the heaviest of his time in the service—was a "beautiful sight" that would, with luck, knock out most of the German resistance before they even arrived. It was the sheer number of shells fired on Difensa that caused Glass and others to dub it the "Million-Dollar Mountain."[4]

The opposite emotion was felt by General von Senger, the German corps commander, who happened to be visiting positions on nearby Sammucro that evening. He was "astonished and dismayed" by the sight and sound of shells exploding on the Camino massif, and had not witnessed a bombardment of such intensity "since the big battles of the First World War."[5] It was far worse, of course, for the panzer-grenadiers and armored reconnaissance troops on the massif. "We and our poor companies," wrote Rittmeister von der Borch, "experienced massive barrage fire." Luckily they were well protected in their rock bunkers and caves from all but direct hits and suffered remarkably few casualties.[6]

Meanwhile, the Forcemen continued their climb with full combat loads, its difficulty "compounded by the dark night and the wet, treacherous terrain." Ed Thomas recalled: "Scrambling in the dark up the rocky trail with every foot and handhold doubtful, demanded superhuman effort by men loaded with weapons, ammunition, radios and litters. To our ears, every rock displaced clattered downhill with sound magnified a thousand times and raised the question in our minds, 'Did the enemy hear this?'" It was "a not very comforting thought."

Thomas was worried that the strung-out nature of the approach would not allow the Forcemen—when they eventually did make contact with the enemy—"to employ the battle technique we'd been so intensely trained in—setting up a base of fire with a maneuver element charging in." He also worried that the huge physical and mental strain of climbing the mountain, on top of the Herculean effort the night before, would eventually take its toll and, "after a break, a dozing and exhausted man might not move off with the column, and the battalion would be split in the night on the face of the mountain."[7] With similar concerns, Tom MacWilliam spent the whole time "moving up and down the column," even when others were resting, to ensure there were no stragglers. "He went round encouraging the fellows," recalled a private in 2-2 Company, "who were pretty near fagged out."[8]

As the head of the column neared the base of the final 200-foot stretch of cliffs, Van Ausdale spotted a German sentry above him. He was manning a stone bunker at the tip of a spine of rocks that jutted down from the summit, and in daylight would have easily seen the Forcemen. But it was dark and, having halted the column, Van Ausdale used all his tracker's stealth to stalk, climb behind and silently kill the sentry with his knife. Resuming his position as lead scout, Van Ausdale led the column round to the base of the cliffs and told Rothlin and the others to wait there while he and Fenton went to find and rope the best route up the rock face. It was the latest in a series of halts that had caused the men farther down the trail much uneasiness. "But," noted Ed Thomas, "we had to have faith in the column leaders."

He was right to do so. Van Ausdale's skill in reading the terrain had "deeply impressed" Thomas during their early scouting missions, and his guiding of the route they had visualized "beyond the terminus of our reconnaissance" was, in the XO's opinion, "what got us to the top that night." The company diary agreed: "But for the excellent scouting of Sgt. Van Ausdale, it is doubtful whether the [company] would have been able to get in so close to Jerry's main position. Van knew his stuff and did an admirable job in leading [us] around the enemy outposts."[9] When Van Ausdale and Fenton returned from roping the final stretch, they had good news. They had found a way up the rock face that was sheltered from view and easily climbable without ropes. Van later admitted that, while roping this last section, he "could hear a German giving orders or directions above him." Fortunately the German did not look over the precipice. If he had, the mission would have ended in disaster.[10]

It was well past midnight, and the main bombardment of Difensa had moved on to other targets, when Van Ausdale and Fenton led Rothlin, Piette, MacWilliam and the assault troops up the final rope climb. "Knuckles, shins and knees took a terrific beating," remembered Don MacKinnon, "but fear and urgency gave us the adrenaline and strength necessary to keep moving up."[11] Staff Sergeant Percy Crichlow, who was climbing just behind Piette, soon began to struggle with his heavy load and would never have made it "without the help of the ropes" and the assistance of Sergeant "Pop" Lewis. Even Lewis, a tough former miner, found climbing the ropes an ordeal with the extra burden of rifle grenades. "I kept spinning," he recalled, "and swinging around and around because of the weight I was carrying. It was a rough climb for me." It did not help that it was raining and pitch black. "The conditions were just terrible," noted Lieutenant Piette, "and we continued climbing—one foot after another."[12] Van Ausdale was the first man to slither silently over the lip, followed by Fenton. They knew from their study of the clay model that they were facing south and that the peak lay some 200 yards to the left—or east—along a gently rising scree slope. The plan was to concentrate the whole company before they advanced on the German positions, so they took up post behind the nearest rocks, weapons at the ready, while they waited for the others to appear.

It took more than an hour to get all Rothlin's men up the ropes. During that time at least two men from 2nd Platoon lost their helmets, including Jack Callowhill, who like many others had failed to do up his chinstrap because it made it harder to breathe. He held his breath as the helmet clattered down the slope, fearful it might alert the enemy. Fortunately, the noise had been partially masked by the continued artillery bombardment of Remetanea, and there was no response from above. Callowhill spent the remainder of the battle wearing just a little woolly hat and his helmet liner, neither of which were capable of stopping a bullet. As one by one the men climbed over the lip, they were told by their section leaders to drop their loads, check their weapons and deploy for battle. Lieutenant Piette then instructed 3rd Platoon: "Fix bayonets, fellas."[13]

31

"All hell broke loose"

With Van Ausdale and Fenton leading, Rothlin's company—in order of platoons 3rd, 1st and 2nd—began edging silently "along a narrow, rock-strewn path toward the German positions, which were located in a saucer-like area near Difensa's summit, a short distance from the top." Still unsure exactly where the German machine guns were, the scouts moved at a snail's pace, stopping frequently to listen for movement up ahead. "The whole company had reached the top without detection," wrote Don MacKinnon. "We had got further than any earlier assaults and had achieved the element of surprise."[1]

They were nearing the saucer when Staff Sergeant Crichlow, leading the rest of 6th Section just behind the scouts, heard a German voice shout a challenge. Either the scouts had been spotted or, as Don MacKinnon believed, someone had dislodged a rock with his foot and the sound had been detected. The two scouts "hit the dirt" and one of them—probably Van Ausdale—loosed off a shot with his Garand that dropped the sentry, who then rolled down the slope and came to a halt beside Lorin Waling of 1st Platoon. "He was gasping for air," recalled Waling. "That was my first initiation in combat... But there was nobody that had bad feelings about the killing; it was just the way it was."[2]

That single gunshot alerted the rest of Wolff's defenders who, realizing the enemy were almost on top of them, displayed extraordinary professionalism by firing flares and swiveling their MG-42 machine guns to face this unexpected threat from the rear. Others leapt from their bivouacs and opened up with Schmeisser machine pistols. The stillness of the night was shattered by the roar of German machine-gun fire, fired mostly blind but no less deadly for that as it pinged off rocks and sent lethal fragments in all directions. "All hell broke loose," remembered Crichlow. He dived for cover behind the nearest rock, while his men started to crawl into position on his left. "Crich," shouted Lieutenant Piette from just behind him. "Get your men to lay down a base of fire. I'll tell McGinty's section to work their way in from the right."

This was the classic "fire and movement" battle drill that the men had been taught earlier that year and that Ed Thomas had feared could not be used. "My section started to return the Jerry's fire," wrote Crichlow. "In the dark it seemed that there was a kind of fort ahead of me from which came the flashes of German machine guns and submachine guns. There was a quick intake of breath nearby and I knew somebody was hit. I kept firing my Tommy gun at the gun-flashes ahead of me and then the firing spread to my right. Apparently McGinty's section was getting into action."[3]

The man hit was "Pop" Lewis. He had just told Piette he was about to use one of the rifle grenades he was carrying, when he saw a figure rise up in front of him, barely ten yards away. Even in the half-light, he could see from the figure's square helmet that he was a "Kraut." Lewis tried to raise his rifle but was beaten to the draw by the German's machine pistol. Three 9mm bullets ripped through the right side of his back as he instinctively turned his body, severing the lumbar muscle, opening up a nine-inch gash and exposing the fatty tissue around his kidney. One slug missed his backbone by a quarter of an inch. "I went down," recalled Lewis, "like an ox that had been hit on the head with an axe. It was just the force of the hits...If I hadn't had those rifle grenades on me, I would have got him."[4]

Meanwhile Rothlin, having lost contact with both scouts, ordered Joe Dauphinais and Johnny Walter to find them. The pair crawled forward, keeping as low as possible and taking advantage of the fact that the Germans were concentrating their fire on the muzzle flashes of their colleagues. They soon found the scouts, sheltering from a hail of fire behind rocks. "What in the hell have you been doing, Van?" asked Dauphinais.

"I've been pinned down," replied Van Ausdale.

Dauphinais took stock. The German fire was still "pretty heavy," but he was convinced they did not know what they were shooting at. "Maybe," he said, "they couldn't believe we were that audacious. How could anybody come in your back door?"[5]

German defensive tactics relied on their quick-firing Spandau machine guns and mortars putting down a curtain of fire that was hard for attackers to penetrate. But at Difensa they had three disadvantages: the attackers were coming from a direction they had not anticipated, so they wasted time turning their weapons; the fight was at such close quarters they could not, at least at first, use mortars for fear of hitting their own men; and the opposition was not willing simply to take cover and return fire. "The key," said Jack Callowhill, "was our aggression. When they opened up, we didn't just go to ground. That's what surprised them."[6]

Back down the trail, Major Ed Thomas was climbing just behind 2-2 Company when a burst of German machine-gun fire "broke the silence" at around 5:00 a.m. "Tracers speared the darkness overhead," he recalled, "and echoes rolled down the mountainside. Then our rifle and machine-gun fire joined in, telling us that the lead company had made enemy contact and the firefight had begun." It was this "sound of enemy fire" in his general direction that brought home to Thomas, for the first time, the reality of war. Knowing that "every stride upward would bring us closer to the point of contact," his mouth filled with a "coppery taste." He recalled: "Then a problem arose of a kind that I never expected to have to handle. The battalion supply officer, a lieutenant with me in the rear section of the command group, suddenly went hysterical. With great difficulty I got him quieted but it was a cowardly display, particularly for an officer, and a poor example for other ranks witnessing this performance."[7]

The supply lieutenant, however, was not the only officer who lost his nerve as he approached the summit. Even farther down the trail, Colonel Don Williamson was climbing with his regimental command group at the tail of Bob Moore's 2/2nd Battalion. "As we went higher," recalled Sergeant Bill Story, "Williamson got more edgy. The Germans were sighting in their guns, using both Schmeisser and MG-42s to sight down the trails that the previous attacks had come up. So as soon as this firing started up, Williamson got very upset."[8] When the top of the final cliff came in sight, the colonel became particularly agitated. "He was extremely afraid of being fired on from the cliffs," noted his intelligence officer, Captain Eino Olson. As one German machine pistol began to fire tracers down the mountain, Williamson drew his pistol and fired back. Soon after this incident, Williamson received two messages from a platoon leader in 5-2 Company. The first was the welcome news that MacWilliam's men had captured Difensa. Though incorrect—the battle was still raging above—it was immediately relayed by radio to Frederick's advanced CP lower down the mountain. "First obj (960) taken," read the message. "Proceeding according to plan—little resistance." Frederick passed the premature news, in turn, to Brigadier General Wilbur, the assistant commander of 36th Division.[9]

But it was the second piece of news—that Moore's battalion had lost contact with MacWilliam's—that seemed to unhinge Williamson. Convinced that the plan was unraveling, and that the earlier message about the capture of Difensa was incorrect, he decided he needed to make his way down to Frederick's CP in person to correct the error. His main concern, he claimed later, was that the 142nd Infantry would launch their attack on Maggiore while Difensa was still held by the Germans. Yet it was his decision to take the message in person that most horrified his command staff, particularly his XO, Major Walter Gray. "You can't go back, sir," Gray pleaded. "Your place is up here."

Gray even offered to go forward to find out what was happening. But Williamson was determined to head down the hill, and his staff were powerless to stop him. So Gray ordered Bill Story to go with him and make sure he got there safely. "Okay," said Story, grudgingly, "I'll go down." Before departing, Williamson spotted men on the cliff above and again opened fire. According to another sergeant on his staff, the men Williamson was shooting at were Forcemen from 1/2nd Battalion. So rapid was Williamson's descent that he fell at least twice, and on the second occasion lost his pistol because he had failed to do up his holster flap. Farther on, he became convinced that there was a German sniper hiding behind a rock and would not proceed until Story had checked. When they finally appeared at Frederick's CP, sited just behind Major George Evashwick's forward casualty station, the Force commander was aghast. "Colonel Williamson," said Frederick, "*what* are you doing here?"

As Williamson tried to explain, Frederick pulled him away so they could talk in private. He eventually left Williamson to "recuperate" while he "went up to the head of the column to see what was going on."[10]

Back near the summit, aware that most of Piette's men were pinned down by machine-gun fire, Lieutenant-Colonel Tom MacWilliam sent Kaasch's 1st Platoon to outflank the German positions on the left, while Gordon's 2nd Platoon did the same on the right. "Keep your heads down," Staff Sergeant Art Schumm told his 2nd Platoon men as he directed them forward. "There are snipers up ahead."[11]

With 1st and 2nd Platoons moving quickly into action, the fire the

Forcemen were able to bring to bear on the German positions was increasing all the time. Private Ken Betts used his Browning machine gun to shoot "anything that remotely resembled a Kraut." Once he was through his "few belts of ammo," he "grabbed a rifle from one of the guys who was lying there dead" and moved forward. "I think," he remembered, "it was because I was scared and very, very busy that I don't really remember too much of what happened that first few minutes."[12]

Meanwhile, with firefights now on both flanks, Joe Dauphinais had continued his crawl toward the main German position, assuming Walter and the others were following in his wake. The ground he was passing over was rocky and uneven, with the odd sprig of undergrowth. Reaching one low bush growing between two rocks, Dauphinais crawled over it and was at once targeted by three German machine guns. He could see from the muzzle flashes that the machine guns—probably MG-42s—were on higher ground. His only hope was to keep his head down and pray. But pinned down in the open, he knew "it was only a matter time" before they got him.

He was right. The next burst of machine-gun bullets hit the flesh of his upper left arm and slammed into his rifle stock. The pain was so intense he almost passed out. Once over the shock, he had enough sense to play dead. "I didn't move a muscle," he recalled, "and when they raised their fire to take on the guys behind me, I made my move and got the hell out of there." Dauphinais had imagined the whole skirmish line had moved forward with him. It had not and, for a short time, he had been out on his own. It was only later that he noticed the stock and breech of his Garand had been shattered by bullets and the weapon was unusable.[13]

One of the "guys" behind Dauphinais was Percy Crichlow, who could see the muzzle flashes from "a strongpoint ahead of me and to the right and another to the left just below the very crest between boulders." He and his remaining eight men—including Sergeants Don Fisher and Harry Deyette, Corporal Ray Holbrook and Privates

Dick Daigle and Clarence DeCamp—had been firing everything they had at the German positions for more than an hour. Deyette and Daigle were working the Johnny gun; Holbrook had set up the Browning and was rapidly running through his ammunition. It was now, as it was beginning to get light, that Crichlow noticed an attack developing from his left. He did not know it at the time, but it was Kaasch's 1st Platoon moving forward.[14]

Faced by at least two machine-gun nests, Kaasch ordered the bulk of his platoon to take up firing positions while he and two others worked their way forward. Lorin Waling spotted a German in the keyhole sight of his M1 and fired multiple shots: *Ping! Ping! Ping!* The man went down. "I got one, Sarge!" he blurted out to his section leader, Dick Boodleman. "I got one!"[15] Minutes later, Kaasch and his two men outflanked the first gun crew and forced them to surrender. They then moved on to the second position, which they took out with grenades, killing the crew.

This enabled Crichlow to move forward with Deyette and Daigle, an advance ordered by Captain Rothlin in support of Kaasch. "We managed to get into the depression between the strong points," noted Crichlow, "as [1st Platoon] was obviously getting control of the main area of resistance on the left. I recognized [Sergeant Benny] Bernstein throwing a grenade and running away." Bernstein—the butt of the practical joke at Blossburg—may have been one of the two men who went forward with Kaasch: it cost him his life.

As Crichlow entered the saucer, Deyette was right behind him. They were edging up the slope on the far side, heading for the summit, when Deyette called out, "They're below here!" A gunshot sounded and Deyette sank to the ground. Crichlow rolled him over to see a neat entry hole in the sergeant's forehead. He was still alive—just—"sucking in his breath with a loud snoring sound." Uncertain where the shot had come from, Crichlow scrambled back to the firing line and asked Staff Sergeant Bill Palmer of 1st Platoon if he could borrow a man to cover him. Palmer sent Ken Betts, and the pair recovered the dead Deyette's Johnny gun and ammunition. Of Dick Daigle, there was no sign.[16]

But the constant pressure the Forcemen were putting on the main German position was beginning to tell. At around the same time that Kaasch knocked out the two machine guns to the left of the saucer, Van Ausdale led an improvised section against two more strongpoints in caves, after first calling for the platoon mortar to drop high explosive and smoke rounds and for a nearby .30 Browning machine gun—possibly manned by Ray Holbrook—to lay down suppressing fire. "Grenades and bayonets got the first cave," recorded Burhans, "and the same instruments dispatched the second gun a bit further up."[17]

By now, almost all the strongpoints round the saucer had been taken and only a few pockets of resistance remained. Holding up the advance of Hugh McGinty's 5th Section to the right of the saucer, for example, was a particularly determined German with a machine pistol. Joe Glass got to within 20 feet of him. But having used all his grenades, his only option was to risk the occasional snap shot from his Garand, exposing himself between two rocks just long enough to fire, in the hope of getting lucky. Engrossed in this deadly game of cat and mouse, Glass suddenly saw a figure appear in his sights. He was about to shoot when he recognized Sergeant Jimmy Flack. "Get the hell out of the road, Jimmy!" shouted Glass.

Flack vanished as quickly as he had appeared, much to Glass's astonishment. "I don't know how he ever got out of there," said Glass, "because he was between me and the Kraut who was knocking our men off, one right after the other." With his field of fire now clear, Glass took aim. But the German shot first, and one of his burst of 9mm slugs hit the thumb of Glass's right hand and forced him to drop his rifle; others struck the rocks and sprayed chips of limestone in his face and right eye, temporarily blinding him. Glass rolled behind the rock to his left and waited for his vision to clear.

When it did, he could see a machine-gun crew surrendering and other white flags beginning to appear. "Jesus," he thought to himself, "we've got to get him now." But the German with the machine pistol would not give up, and any movement drew his fire. Also pinned down, immediately to Glass's left, were Private Syd Gath and Don MacKinnon. Eventually Captain Rothlin crawled up behind Glass's right shoulder and asked: "What's going on?"

Glass turned to Rothlin, his face dripping blood. "There's white flags going up all over the place, sir," he said, "but there's this one German who's not giving up. He's just the other side of this rock. Don't put your head up, whatever you do, because he has us zeroed in."[18]

At that moment, another German soldier walked toward 5th Section, his hands raised in surrender. Perhaps assuming he was the one who had been firing the machine pistol, both Gath and Rothlin lifted their heads a little so they could cover the German with their weapons. This prompted the first German to fire another burst, which hit both men in the face. Gath sank slowly to the ground and rolled onto MacKinnon's right arm and shoulder. Not aware his friend had been shot, MacKinnon pushed him away, saying: "For God's sake, Syd, you're leaning on me!"

Gath rolled over, recalled MacKinnon, "exposing the left side of his head, which had been torn open by several rounds from a machine pistol burst fired from a position behind the surrendering German, who had taken cover again." MacKinnon was stunned. Gath had been "a good friend from the beginning, a very likable guy," and now he was dead.[19] So too was Rothlin. Hit in the head by the same burst that killed Gath, his blood and brains were all over Glass. "God, it was terrible," remembered Glass. "I don't know why they did it. They had to have heard me." Glass then took some grenades from Rothlin's corpse and moved across to MacKinnon, who told him: "I'm scared, Joe."

"We're all scared, so have a cigarette."

And there, in the midst of battle, Glass lit two cigarettes and handed one to MacKinnon. Eventually the German with the machine pistol fled or was killed—possibly by Jimmy Flack, who had a better angle of fire. "I think he got him finally," said Glass, "but it was pretty confusing up there."[20]

Learning of Rothlin's death, Lieutenant Piette took over the company. His first priority was to spread the men out, because they were "bunching up" and "the fire was still pretty intense." He told them: "We're going to do this just like we always practiced in training. We're gonna clear them out of there."

And they did. "It worked like clockwork," remembered MacKinnon. "Before we knew it, we had a bag full of prisoners."[21]

One of the last strongpoints still holding out was manned by another German with a machine pistol. Losing patience, Private Sulo Suotaila of 2nd Platoon tried to rush the position but was shot in the stomach. As he lay there in the open, writhing in agony and gasping for breath, his comrades looked on helplessly. All, that is, except Private Gerald Dodson, a corpsman from Tulsa, Oklahoma. Already Dodson had "repeatedly exposed himself to withering fire to give immediate aid to the wounded." He now did so again, rushing to help the stricken Suotaila "while completely exposed." As well as dressing Suotaila's wounds, he pulled out his dentures to make it easier for him to breathe and then dragged him to safety. It was an extraordinary act of selfless heroism that, sadly, could not save Suotaila, who died from his wounds.[22] The German who shot Suotaila was himself killed soon after, when Sergeant Dennis George blasted his bunker with a rifle grenade. Rifle and machine-gun fire played their part, remembered Jack Callowhill, "but it was the grenades and rifle grenades that did the damage. Most of the posts were taken out by grenades, not bullets."[23]

Probably the last Forceman to die on Difensa was Sergeant Bill Kotenko of 1-2 Company HQ, the former leader of 5th Section. His body was spotted by Percy Crichlow as he climbed the last few feet to the summit of the mountain where other members of 3rd Platoon were digging in. "I took the unused Tommy gun magazines out of his pouches," recalled Crichlow, "and left my empty magazines. Just then mortars started to come and we heard a plane."[24] In fact, Kotenko was not yet dead. According to Don MacKinnon, he lay unconscious "for some time before he died, a medical man trying his best to keep him alive."[25]

32

"Medic! Medic!"

It was 7:00 a.m. and the two-hour battle for the summit of Difensa was over. But aware the Germans might counterattack, Piette ordered his men to dig in along the rim of the saucer that faced Remetanea and the saddle that led to Camino. "We took shelter," wrote Don MacKinnon, "in the well-prepared holes, fortifications and one large cave-like position at the high point."[1]

By now, 2-2 Company had deployed to the right of 1-2 Company and was busy clearing out the remaining pockets of German resistance in the ravine below the crest. But 1-2 Company alone had taken the hill—and paid the price. Rothlin and eight of his men had been killed, and a further 16 wounded. Four of the dead were from 3rd Platoon: Sergeants Harry Deyette and George Edwards, and Privates Syd Gath and Dick Daigle.[2] Daigle's bullet-riddled body was found just a few yards from Deyette's.

The number of wounded did not include minor and superficial injuries such as those suffered by Joe Glass and Percy Crichlow who, though he hardly noticed it at the time, had been hit in the knee by flying pieces of rock fragments and in his wrist and hand by mortar splinters. Even so, his section had taken a "real beating." He recorded: "Sergeant [Don] Fisher, my Browning Gun Squad Leader, was completely blind—struck by stone fragments; ["Pop"] Lewis had been sliced across the back by a bullet and then had been shot in the hand; Joe Dauphinais had a bullet through his arm; [Phil] Clark had a long gouge running back from the area just behind his eye; Deyette and Daigle were dead. During the day and night there were more casualties all the time."[3]

Crichlow forgot to mention one casualty: Ray Holbrook, who, like Lewis, had been shot in the back by a Schmeisser machine pistol. Other 1-2 men wounded in the attack were First Sergeant Harry Rayner (splinter wounds to the face and ear), Sergeant Dennis George (gunshot wound to the head), Sergeant Geoffrey Hart, Private Chester Galvas (both shot in the arm), and Private Walter Tompkins (shot in the cheek). Before the day was out, they would be joined at Major Evashwick's casualty station by Staff Sergeants Charles Seith and Hugh McGinty, both with serious wounds from mortar explosions.[4]

Yet during the assault, 1-2 Company alone had killed 35 Germans and captured a further 37,* most of them from the 115th's 2nd Company, though Leutnant Wolff, the company commander, lived to fight another day by withdrawing with his remaining men to the saddle between Difensa and Camino, from where they opened up on their former position with mortars.[5] His commander, Rittmeister Freiherr von der Borch, later wrote a brief and not entirely accurate account of the day's fighting. After an artillery bombardment, "the enemy attacked our two wings." At first repeated assaults were repulsed "in close-quarters fighting," wrote von der Borch, "in which our officers

---

* The regimental history gives the "first day's catch" of German POWs as 29 from the 115th Armored Reconnaissance Battalion, 13 from the III/104th Panzergrenadier Battalion, and a division artillery forward observer. A further 75 German dead were found on the hill, while "innumerable enemy wounded" had been evacuated (Burhans, p. 108).

and men performed magnificently." But eventually the enemy succeeded "in making penetrations on both wings" and, thanks to the lack of reserves, the "immediate counterattacks were unsuccessful."[6]

In reality, having reacted well to the initial shock of finding the enemy in their rear, Wolff's men had no answer to the speed and aggression of 1-2 Company's attack and, despite enjoying a numerical superiority,* were swept off the top of Difensa in just two hours. The much higher casualty rate suffered by defenders in well-fortified positions is testament to the ferocity of the Forcemen's assault. Lorin Waling put the success of his company's attack down to superior battle tactics, by which he meant "speed and firepower." He explained: "It was because of the speed we moved, and the fact that each Forceman was an excellent marksman, plus our mental attitude toward combat."[7]

The loss of close friends affected men in different ways. Working his way back to where the casualties were being gathered in a makeshift aid post, Joe Dauphinais passed some of his buddies "lying together in one area," their brains "knocked out" from head shots. "We had been together for over a year," he said, "so you would think that looking at those guys would shock us silly, but we accepted it immediately. We knew it was something that was bound to happen to any of us."[8] If anything, the sight of corpses was more of a shock for those Forcemen who arrived after the fighting was over. "Seeing our own dead up there," recalled a sergeant in 3-2 Company, "really was a rude awakening for me." Despite all his training, he had wondered if he could shoot someone when it came to it. Having seen "buddies who had been killed," he knew that he could. A private in 5-2 Company felt the same: "You think, 'These guys did this to us, so we gotta do something to them.' It was a gloomy thing to see."[9]

---

* The two companies of German defenders—about 175 strong—were defeated chiefly by a single company of 89 Forcemen (1-2), though 2-2 Company was deployed toward the end of the battle. MacWilliam's third company, 3-2, was held up on the ropes and played no part in the battle.

Joe Glass remembered "tempers were pretty hot" as the German prisoners were herded together. Still hyped from the battle, Lieutenant Piette was walking among them, yelling, "So these are the supermen we've been fighting! Boy, look what we have now! We have supermen! Boy, you'd better be careful!"[10]

Word had got around that some Forcemen, Captain Rothlin included, were shot after Germans had pretended to surrender. This was a distortion of the truth—there is no evidence that the German who shot Gath and Rothlin was trying to surrender or encouraged others to do so—but it was believed by some Forcemen, with lethal consequences for a few POWs. A few "of the guys" shot German prisoners, said a sergeant in 5-2 Company, "but, hey, that's the way it was." He added: "They all had to be taken down the mountain, and I guess some guys just didn't want to take them."[11]

First Platoon's Ken Betts claimed that some prisoners were shot in the heat of the battle after they ignored warnings to stay where they were. But murdering unarmed prisoners in cold blood, after the battle was over, is a different matter. Did it happen? Yes, according to one officer and three sergeants in the 2/2nd Battalion who arrived on the mountain after the crest had been captured. It was, they imply, revenge for the dastardly killing of Rothlin and others. Interestingly, apart from Betts no one else in 1-2 Company made such a claim. They had witnessed the Germans fighting hard and (mostly) fair, and when tempers cooled and the shock of their first battle had worn off, they felt a grudging respect for their tough opponents.[12]

How many prisoners were shot out of hand is impossible to say. What we do know is that 43 made it safely down to Frederick's advanced CP, where they were given a "stiff interrogation" by the German-speaking intelligence officer, Norwegian First Lieutenant Finn Roll. It was from these captives that Frederick's staff learned for the first time that Difensa's German garrison had recently been augmented by at least one company of the 115th. Three POWs—"young enough to be boy scouts" and "happy to be out of it"—were delivered by Don MacKinnon and two other Forcemen who also escorted a wounded comrade down the mountain. Descending by the easier eastern slope, MacKinnon was shocked to see yet more unrecovered bodies of GIs killed in earlier assaults, and to hear the "sporadic machine-pistol fire of German snipers who seemed to be hidden" in trees and brush to the south.

On the way back up, the young Canadian fell in with Frederick's command group—including Lieutenant Roll and Captain O'Neill—which was heading in the same direction. As they ascended, Frederick stopped and spoke to men coming down, "to get a better picture of what was happening on top." Near the summit they came across "a group of stretcher bearers, German prisoners carrying their wounded, with some walking wounded and Force men guarding them." One of those still on their feet was "refusing to walk and wanted a stretcher." Roll spoke to him in German, leaving the man in no doubt that if he did not walk, he would be left there. He moved off.

While Frederick and his staff made for the 2nd Regiment's CP "to take charge," MacKinnon looked for the 3rd Platoon survivors. He found them "sheltering in whatever holes they could find to avoid getting hit with incoming mortar shells, which the Germans were firing with deadly accuracy."[13] When one barrage started, MacKinnon, Herby Forester and Joe Glass jumped into the same foxhole. They were followed, soon after, by a mortar that landed between their legs but, incredibly, did not explode. It was a dud. "We were lucky," said Glass, "but that's how combat goes."[14]

Major Ed Thomas reached the summit of Difensa shortly after dawn to find "confusion": 1-2 Company had taken its objective but no one was defending the edge of the "elongated saucer" facing the enemy's positions. So he "commandeered" one of 2-2 Company's platoons and "posted it along this edge." Soon after, he met Tom MacWilliam, who told him that 1-2 Company had "taken many casualties, including its commander," Captain Rothlin. MacWilliam also said that as soon as Bob Moore's 2/2nd Battalion reached the top, they would gather 2-2 and 3-2 Companies for the assault on their second objective, Monte la Remetanea.[15]

A couple of hours later, by which time Moore's battalion had arrived* and taken over responsibility for repelling any German counterattack, the bulk of the 1/2nd Battalion was free to continue its mission. Despite being "dangerously low" on ammunition, MacWilliam was determined to keep the enemy off-balance by attacking at the earliest opportunity. Patrols had reported no sign of an enemy counterattack and only a limited enemy presence, chiefly snipers, on the saddle between Difensa and Remetanea. So leaving 1-2 Company to lick its wounds on Difensa, MacWilliam formed up his two largely intact companies in the ravine below the summit for the advance on Remetanea. MacWilliam was at the head of the column with his forward command group, while Thomas brought up the rear. As they moved off, recalled Thomas, the enemy was "blasting" the ravine "with mortar, artillery and a weapon new to us, the Nebelwerfer, a multi-barreled rocket launcher."[16]

A few minutes earlier, Private John O'Brien of 2-2 Company had been sent by his officer to ask MacWilliam if he wanted a "recce patrol sent out." He found the colonel sitting with two radiomen, trying to contact another regiment. "Although he was soaking wet," recalled O'Brien, "he didn't seem bothered at all. In fact his last words to me were, 'Don't look so worried, son. We'll soon be in Rome.'"

O'Brien was making his way back down the column when he heard "one hell of an explosion." He and everyone around him hit the dirt, waiting for more mortars to hit, "but none came." Instead they heard the shout: "Medic! Medic!" When O'Brien got to the site

---

* Moore would later insist that the 3-2 Company commander "froze" when he reached the top of the cliff, insisting his men were pinned down by enemy fire when the bullets were passing yards overhead. So Moore ordered him to step aside while he brought his battalion through (Bowlby, p. 113).

of the mortar strike, he could see four bodies lying on the ground, all from MacWilliam's command group. They included the colonel himself. He was lying on his back, "a large hole in his right temple and another in his neck." Someone said later that MacWilliam spoke before he died, but O'Brien thought that unlikely. Also killed was a sergeant on the battalion staff, while two more sergeants were badly wounded, with multiple shrapnel wounds to their legs and torsos.[17]

Aware that the column had stopped, but not why, Ed Thomas went forward to discover the "grimmest of situations." He wrote: "Tom MacWilliam and our operations sergeant had been killed and others in the [headquarters] group were wounded. I was now in command."

Soon after, Colonel Frederick appeared and Thomas reported the situation. "He suggested," recalled Thomas, "that we get an ammunition resupply before moving on to Remetanea, so I ordered the battalion to dig in as best it could in the rocky floor of the saucer." The pause was a mistake: if 1/2nd Battalion had pressed on during the morning of the 3rd, they would have captured the peak without too much resistance. So why did Frederick urge caution? It is hard to say. Earlier he had received a message that the British attack on Camino had been successful. This, as it happens, was inaccurate. The British had indeed captured Hills 727 and 819 but not the main peak, 963. Even so, Frederick was well aware that the advance of the US 142nd Infantry on Monte Maggiore was partly dependent upon him first capturing Remetanea. He had been told as much by Clark himself, and if he was in any doubt, he was reminded by Brigadier General Wilbur, who sent repeated messages asking for "his plans for cleaning up [Hill] 907 and continuing to end of ridge."[18]

In the end, the 142nd Infantry continued its assault on Maggiore without the Force's assistance and took its final objective at dusk. It was now that Wilbur offered to release the Force's 1st Regiment, then in divisional reserve, to assist in the capture of Remetanea.

Frederick was happy to accept. But as it was so late in the day, and the supply train had only recently arrived at the summit,* the attack was put off until the morning of the 4th. In his history of the Force, Burhans also insists that Frederick delayed the attack on Remetanea because 1/2nd Battalion's ammunition stocks were "dangerously low." Yet this had not deterred MacWilliam, who knew that any pause would expose the men on Difensa to a remorseless mortar and artillery bombardment. So something else must have been on Frederick's mind, and that was almost certainly the threat of a counterattack. Such was the tenor of the message he sent to Colonel Williamson, now back at the 2nd Regiment's CP on Difensa, during the afternoon of December 3. "Based on information from [Major] Grey [sic], understand you will attack 907 daylight 4 Dec," said Frederick. "Through your forward [Artillery] Observers call for such fire on positions to your W as needed to keep enemy pinned down during tonight and in preparation for your [attack]." Frederick also urged Williamson to send patrols toward the saddle between Difensa and Camino to protect his southern flank from attack "during night."[19]

Frederick kept himself busy, according to "Pat" O'Neill, moving "from unit to unit, sending out patrols and placing men in outposts to gradually widen the piece of territory we held." O'Neill was astonished by his boss's "casual indifference" to enemy fire, particularly when mortar barrages sent everyone "scurrying for cover, only to come back to find him sitting in the same position and place as we had vacated in a hurry."[20]

For the survivors of 1-2 Company in the saucer, however, the decision to postpone the attack on Remetanea was mystifying. They stayed "holed up on top of Difensa," wrote Don MacKinnon, "mostly in rotten wet and misty weather, expecting a German counter attack

---

* It took men with packboards at least six hours to ascend Difensa with ammunition, rations, water and stretchers.

at any time, and wondering why those in command did not order us to move out down the saddle to Remetanea to finish off the enemy and complete the victory." Anything would have been better "than sitting like ducks in this saucer which the German mortars had the exact range of."[21]

33

"Five yards! Five yards!"

Unlike Williamson's men, 1st Regiment had spent "an uneventful day" digging foxholes and "feeling miserable in the mud and rain" in woods near the 36th Division's Advanced CP, close to Ridge 368. At one point, Bill Becket noticed a brigadier general observing the Forcemen's activities. He did not appear to be "a happy man."

In the early afternoon of December 3, Becket and Jack Akehurst, commanding the 2/1st Battalion, received a message to meet their boss, "Cookie" Marshall, "on the bend of the mountain where we could get a look at the Liri Valley and fighting going on down there." When Becket got there, he found Marshall talking to the brigadier general he had noticed earlier. He was Bill Wilbur, assistant commander of the 36th Division and the holder of the Medal of Honor for leading an attack on a Vichy French artillery battery during Operation Torch. Addressing Marshall, Wilbur said that he wanted the 1st Regiment "to move immediately along the lower side of Mount la Difensa facing the Liri Valley, to the foot of Mount Maggiore just north of us."

Becket was horrified. The move would be "in full view of the enemy artillery observers in the valley and, probably, to whatever sniper positions there might be on the mountainside above us." Colonel Marshall must have felt the same, because he snapped sharply to attention and asked: "Excuse me, sir, but why?"

Wilbur could have given the real reason, which was that the 142nd Infantry was about to commence its final attack on Maggiore and he wanted the 1st Regiment on hand in case it was needed. But not used to having his orders questioned, he turned on Marshall and shouted: "To keep abreast of the situation, that's why!"

A short time later, Marshall's regiment was on the move, with Akehurst's 2/1st Battalion in the lead and Becket's 1/1st Battalion close behind. "It was a narrow trail with some scattered tree cover," recalled Becket, "but we were open to enemy observation and enemy fire." Within five or six minutes, as Becket had anticipated, the column was hit by a hail of artillery shells. "High explosive," noted the Force history, "air-burst, dead-head armor-piercing, white phosphorus—every type of round in the stockpile—fell on the regiment." This storm of steel landed most heavily on the companies in the center of the column—6-1 and 1-1—but no part of the 1/1st Battalion escaped. Spotting tree cover ahead, Becket urged his men to keep moving and not to bunch up. "Five yards! Five yards!" he kept shouting.[1]

But many were hit by flying shrapnel and, desperate to escape it, others went to ground. "We were trying to dig," noted a sergeant in 1-1 Company, "and there really was no way to dig, other than making a little scratch…They continued shelling right on down the line and then started walking them back."[2] Men were dropping "like flies," remembered a private in 6-1 Company. He and his section leader took cover behind a boulder, while two men crouched on the other side. The private made the right choice. When a phosphorus shell exploded nearby, he and the sergeant received only minor burns; the other two men were killed.[3]

Attached to 3-1 Company as a medic, Corporal Sam Boroditsky ran from one casualty to the next, injecting morphine and "putting on tourniquets." One sergeant said to him: "Stick close to me, Sam, I'm going to get it." He was right. Having patched up the sergeant, Boroditsky came to a man who said he had been hit in the leg. "I reached down to where his legs were," he recalled, "and there was no leg. He said, 'Move on, there is nothing you can do for me.' I don't know who he was." Struggling on, almost out of bandages and morphine, Boroditsky fell into a muddy stream, losing his helmet. A shell landed just a few feet away "and didn't explode but scattered mud" on him. As he lay there in the ice-cold water, he could hear cries of "Help! Help!"[4]

The greatest act of heroism during these 20 minutes of horror—which, in Becket's mind, "destroyed" the 1st Regiment before it even got into action—was performed by the most unlikely person: Lieutenant John H. Richardson. Since failing to secure a transfer from the Force in the autumn of 1942—a move that, in Frederick's opinion, was motivated by a desire to avoid dangerous duty—Richardson had become a valuable member of 5-1 Company. Now, as his platoon fell all around him, was his chance to prove Frederick wrong. "Hearing the cries of two wounded men," he "immediately left his own protected position and dragged one of the two soldiers to a foxhole." It was as he was moving the second man that he was hit by a shell fragment and killed instantly.[5]

Becket came upon this scene of carnage "in a small clearing, perhaps 20 yards long and five yards wide." Here he found more than 20 officers and men of the 2/1st Battalion wounded or dead, with just one medic to treat them. "A lad immediately in front of me was lying there still alive," he recorded, "with his intestines bulging out of his uniform on top of him."

Becket called for help and was soon joined by his XO, Major Ed Pearce, and Doc Neeseman, the regimental surgeon. Becket was telling Pearce to get the battalion into cover when he felt himself being "lifted slightly off the ground." Knowing instinctively it was a shell, he shouted, "Get down!"

When the smoke cleared, only Becket got to his feet. Pearce and Neeseman had both been wounded by shrapnel and were "out of action for the rest of the Difensa fight." As Becket wiped mud from his eyes and mouth, "Cookie" Marshall "came up and, under considerable stress," told him that he had just received orders to get the 1/1st Battalion to the top of Difensa "to support Colonel Williamson's 2nd Regiment in the expected counterattack up there." Becket was to leave at once; the 2/1st Battalion would look after his wounded.

It took a moment for Becket to gather his thoughts. Having just lost his XO, he had no idea how many men were left "or exactly where they were." Moments later, two of his three company commanders appeared. The third—commanding 1-1 Company—was a casualty, as were all his officers, and the first sergeant was now in charge. Becket instructed all three to gather their remaining men and return to their start point on Ridge 368, from where they would begin the climb.

The sun had set by the time Becket started up the slope with his companies in reverse order: 3-1, 2-1, 1-1. There was no trail and he had, in the dark, no idea where he was going. He trudged wearily on and, as it became light, had only reached the top of the tree line, where he shot at a German soldier who, he quickly discovered, was already dead. Noticing sheer cliffs directly above him, Becket angled to the left where the climb looked easier. He eventually came across some 2nd Regiment men who had been sent down to guide him in. By now, Becket was climbing with Captain Ed Borders,[*] commanding 3-1 Company, and two of his men. The rest of the battalion was farther down the hill. Sending one of Borders's men back to show the battalion the route, Becket and the others continued up the trail to near the summit, where they reported to the 2nd Regiment CP, "a

---

[*] Borders had polio as a child and fought off the disability by constant exercise. Before the war, he set a world long-distance ski record by trekking the 1,600 miles from Alaska to Washington State in 91 days, carrying a .22 rifle and accompanied by his dog, Butch. He was killed on Difensa by mortar fire on December 6, 1943, and never met his infant daughter.

hole in some rocks covered with German canvas." It was now the late morning of December 4, and the climb had taken hours longer than it should have.

A relieved Colonel Williamson told them how glad he was to see them because he expected a counterattack that night. Becket assured him that the battalion was on its way. He and Borders then tried to get some rest. But Becket could not sleep, and when he returned to Williamson's CP, there was still no sign of his men. Becket recalled: "I was frantic and tried desperately to reach 1st Regiment Headquarters and Force Headquarters on the field phone, but all wires were down." With no sleep and hardly any food for two days, Becket knew that neither he nor Borders "could go down that day and bring the Battalion up that night." Yet he also knew that Williamson needed his men "badly" and that made him "sick with concern."

That night—spent crouched in a "small rocky hole" with Williamson, his XO, Walter Gray, and several others—was the "worst" of Becket's life. It was cold, windy and wet. "Williamson kept expecting a counterattack which never came," recalled Becket. "I, on the other hand, could think of nothing but my missing Battalion and praying silently that it would arrive before the counterattack hit us."[6]

The failure of Becket's battalion to reinforce the troops on Difensa on December 4 was the final straw for Colonel Williamson. Earlier he had received debriefs from captured Germans that their comrades were massing for a counterattack, intelligence that seemed to be confirmed when night patrols reported "heavy pockets of Germans just south of the Remetanea ridge." Under the circumstances, Williamson further postponed the assault on Remetanea until the morning of the 5th. His staff, however, thought he was nervous and indecisive and only too willing to use the threat of a German counterstroke as an excuse not to take 2nd Regiment's final objective. According to Major Gray, Williamson's XO, it required Frederick's intervention "to push the attack and proceed with our mission." Even then, it needed Moore and Gray "to more or less take over and actually make decisions."[7]

Clearly, Williamson had not fully recovered from his earlier attack of nerves, and it is surprising that Frederick left him in charge on Difensa. According to Gray and Eino Olson, he rarely ventured out of the cave that housed his CP and never once inspected the 2/2nd Battalion's defensive positions.[8] "He even moved his bowels in there," claimed Bill Story, who by this time had been given a battlefield promotion by Williamson to first lieutenant. "He used an empty container that had held a mortar bomb. He then put the cover on it and gave it to his runner to take care of."[9]

While Williamson remained in his CP, and Remetanea and the Camino saddle were still in German hands, the men on Difensa continued to suffer. Reaching the summit on December 4, a sergeant in 1-3 Company noted that the 2nd Regiment men "were half frozen, as all they had were ground sheets to keep off the wet and no blankets."[10] Jack Callowhill and his buddy Clyde Spofford were sheltering from the rain under ponchos when a mortar exploded nearby. "Of course, you never hear the one that gets you," recalled Callowhill. "The next thing I remember, a medic was putting a pack on a huge hole in my thigh. I had other wounds but that was the worst. It had severed a tendon in my leg. Spofford got it too."[11]

A big piece of shrapnel had hit Spofford's right arm, fracturing his wrist. He also had minor head injuries. Once Callowhill and Spofford had been stabilized, they were carried to the makeshift aid post—described by Major Ed Thomas as "a shallow timber-covered bunker, the work of local Italian labor impressed by the Germans, with a capacity of about five or six prone bodies"—to await evacuation down the mountain. Thomas was already there. Earlier that day, he had jumped into a foxhole to escape a mortar barrage and skewered his left calf on a Forceman's bayonet. His fellow battalion commander, Bob Moore, extracted the bayonet by putting his foot on Thomas's shin and pulling on the blade. With blood cascading over Thomas's boot, the pair then argued over the correct location for a tourniquet: above the knee or below. "I do not remember," said Thomas, "who prevailed."

Thomas remained in the bunker for several days. "We lay on litters jammed together on the dirt floor," he recalled, "and prayed we would soon make the trip down the mountain. My companions had painful shrapnel or bullet wounds and there was constant moaning. Shelling, mortaring, and Nebelwerfering of the saucer never stopped, and that often brought the thought that the next round might come through our roof timbers. Rightly the most seriously wounded got evacuation priority, and since my wound was far from life threatening I quickly achieved seniority in that hole in the ground."

Occasionally aid men would come through the small entrance hole on the side of the bunker to treat the wounds and feed the casualties, a difficult task. They included a captured German medic who had volunteered to stay on Difensa and care for wounded Forcemen. He was, remembered Thomas, "a very cheerful and energetic individual and very helpful at ministering to us in the aid station hole. I wish he could have been recognized for what he did."[12]

With MacWilliam dead and Thomas wounded, the 1/2nd Battalion was taken over by Major Walter Gray, Williamson's XO. "He did a wonderful job for us," said Larry Piette. "He was a VMI [Virginia Military Institute] man. He was kind of a morale booster up there." So was Piette who, despite the scarcity of drinking water, insisted on shaving each morning on Difensa as an example to the men. At one point he jumped into a foxhole to avoid shellfire and found it occupied by a dead German. He ended up "munching on a D-bar ration, having a can of coffee while sitting on a dead man's chest, right there in the hole." It helped to have a sense of humor.[13]

That evening, as requested by Frederick, the supply column arrived with six cases of bourbon, condoms to stop rain getting into rifle barrels, and the first mail since the men's departure from Santa Maria. The whiskey was immediately shared out, two ounces per man, to warm the frozen soldiers and "raise their spirits." Even men who did not drink—like Lieutenant Wayne E. Boyce, a Mormon from Jerome, Idaho—took a slug. "Of all the supplies that came up the trail," wrote Burhans, "the whiskey was the biggest morale-raiser." The arrival of mail was also very welcome, though Frederick's only letter was from a concerned Quebec lady who informed him that one of his men—a private in 4-3 Company—had, on a recent furlough, got her maid pregnant. She was writing because the maid was "in an extremely depressed and nervous condition" and she hoped that Frederick would encourage the soldier to take his responsibilities seriously. She also explained that the couple were engaged, "had grown up together, and the families of both young people anticipate their marriage." Handing the letter to Lieutenant Roll, Frederick said he would deal with it later.[*] There was, he added, another piece of "offensive action" he needed to clear up first.[14]

Meanwhile, the new plan to attack Remetanea at first light on the 5th had been put in the balance by information from two German prisoners who were taken by a patrol during the afternoon of December 4. Questioned by Lieutenant Roll, they at first remained tight-lipped. But after being fed some K rations, they began to talk. Three companies of the III/104th Panzergrenadiers, they said, would counterattack Difensa at 3:00 a.m. the next morning. When asked why the German commanders had not attacked earlier, the prisoners said their casualties had been heavy, supplies were slow coming forward and the American shellfire was worse than anything they had seen on the Eastern Front. This was yet more evidence for Frederick and Williamson that a German counterattack was imminent and,

---

[*] Frederick replied to the Quebec lady on December 18, 1943, informing her that the soldier in question had no intention of evading his responsibilities and was "seriously concerned with making proper and adequate provisions" for the mother-to-be and her baby. They had "contemplated marriage for some time" and would marry as soon as possible. "We are endeavoring," wrote Frederick, "to arrange some means of accomplishing a marriage by proxy" (Frederick Papers, Box 2).

on top of the continued nonappearance of Becket's battalion, was enough to prompt yet another postponement of the assault on Remetanea—this time until the afternoon of the 5th.[15]

In fact, there is no evidence in contemporary German documents that a serious counterattack against Difensa was ever considered. This was partly because the rivers behind the front were flooded and it was difficult to move up reinforcements, and partly because they knew their defensive position on the Camino massif was still tenable as long as they kept hold of Camino itself, the saddle between Camino and Difensa, and Remetanea. It was for this reason that the main divisional reserve, II/104th Panzergrenadiers, was rushed not to Difensa but Camino, where its men retook the chapel on Monastery Hill from the British 56th Division "after a long, hard fight" on December 5. Meanwhile, von der Borch and his remaining men had repulsed all attacks on the saddle. "It was truly extraordinary," wrote von der Borch, "what the battalion demonstrated in terms of nerves, tenacity and bravery."[16]

The importance of Remetanea—Hill 907—was emphasized by Oberst Ens, commanding the 104th, when he sent a platoon of paratroopers, under Leutnant Walter Knaf, to "occupy and defend" it on December 5. The hill was, said Ens, of "decisive importance" for the future course of the battles around the massif: it could block an advance from Difensa, and, more important, it commanded "the only mule path, on which the supply of the 3 battalions deployed on Monte Camino relied." In other words, with Remetanea in Allied hands, the Camino massif was lost. According to Ens, Leutnant Knaf used great skill and determination to lead his platoon through heavy shellfire to the top of Remetanea, where the only cover was a few boulders and some overhanging rock. This left most of the men exposed to enemy fire, constant rain and plummeting temperatures.[17]

In fact, Knaf never got to the top of Hill 907, or if he did it was not for long. Perhaps realizing the impossibility of remaining on Remetanea's summit under constant shellfire, he set up his defensive position a little farther to the west, on the spur that led to Rocca d'Evandro. Yet what Ens's account makes clear is that the summit of 907 was not held in any strength prior to December 5, and even after that date its defense was chiefly reliant upon artillery observation and long-distance machine-gun and mortar fire. This makes the re-peated postponements of the Force's attack on Remetanea even more inexplicable.

34

"I don't know how we did it"

Bill Becket's 1/1st Battalion finally reached the summit of Difensa at midday on Sunday, December 5. Arriving with Colonel Marshall and the rest of the 1st Regiment, it promptly took over the defense of the hill from the 2nd Regiment, which set out to capture Remetanea and the saddle between Difensa and Camino that afternoon. The two attacks had mixed results. Gray's 1/2nd Battalion was halfway along the ridgeline to Remetanea when it came under machine-gun and mortar fire from the German-held village of Rocca d'Evandro in the valley below. Taking heavy casualties, Gray ordered the men to dig in where they could.

Moore's 2/2nd Battalion, meanwhile, had been ordered to capture two strongpoints held by von der Borch's 115th Reconnaissance Battalion on the Camino saddle. The assaulting 1st Platoon of 5-2 Company was met by "fierce machine gun, machine pistol, and mortar fire which halted the advance." But inspired by Lieutenant Wayne Boyce, the Mormon from Idaho who led from the front, the platoon moved forward and rushed the position from three sides with bayonets and grenades. Boyce then reorganized his men for an attack on the second position, 200 yards down the slope. "Here the scrub cover ceased," noted the Force history, "[and] it was slow advancing between the bare rock clumps." With his platoon now down to half strength, Boyce was hit by three bullets. Yet "he remained in command" long enough to direct his sections "working the flanks" and lead "the final charge onto the hump." He died soon after. "His determined courage and aggressive leadership," read his gallantry citation, "are an everlasting inspiration to those who followed him in his heroic assaults against the enemy."[1]

A report by XIV Panzer Korps described this "incursion" on "the ridge between 963 and 960 into our previously firmly held main line of resistance" as "particularly nasty."[2] It also marked the beginning of the end for the defense of the Camino massif. German strength there was now down to 23 officers and 650 men. The 115th Reconnaissance Battalion alone numbered just 180 men, having lost 5 officers and 200 men killed, wounded and missing, and a further 100 to sickness thanks to "the extreme demands of fighting in the mountains and the terrible weather conditions."[3]

Early next morning, a worried Kesselring phoned Lemelsen, commanding the Tenth Army, and asked how the battle was going. "Everything is fine along the entire front," said Lemelsen, "apart from the matter at Camino; it is looking pretty bad there."

Describing enemy gains on both sides of Hill 963, Lemelsen added: "I am gravely concerned about how we are going to keep Camino on account of the number of incursions."[4]

He was right to be concerned. By noon, Gray's battalion had taken Remetanea and sent patrols farther west toward Rocca d'Evandro. That evening, the summit of Monte Camino finally fell to the British 56th Division. Bowing to the inevitable, Generalleutnant Rodt ordered von der Borch to withdraw his remaining men from the massif under cover of darkness. The 115th had put up a remarkable defense, said Rodt, but it was better to live to fight another day.[5]

The German withdrawal was not a moment too soon for the

shattered Forcemen. At noon that day, Frederick had sent an an-
guished message to General Walker, begging for his men to be relieved. They were, said Frederick, "getting in bad shape from fatigue,
exposure and cold," and many had got sick from a "bad batch of
K-ration." He added: "German snipers are giving us hell and it is extremely difficult to catch them." He wanted his men taken off the hill
because "every additional day here will mean two more days necessary
for recuperation before next mission." They were "willing and eager"
but "becoming exhausted." His final suggestion was for the Force to attack Camino from the north if the British had not taken it "before dark
today." Fortunately for the spent Forcemen, the British did just that.[6]

The 7th was spent clearing the massif of the last pockets of German
snipers and pushing patrols toward Rocco d'Evandro. One bumped
into the strongpoint manned by Leutnant Knaf's platoon and withdrew with two dead. It estimated the German strength at 50 men
"well supplied with machine guns and mortars."[7] The 7th also saw
the end of Major Thomas's torment when, finally, after three days'
waiting, it was his turn to be stretchered down the mountain. Five
men from 3rd Regiment made up the litter team: one on each handle
and one holding a rope attached to the upper end. It was, remembered Thomas, "an arduous and difficult physical task for these men
to carry a loaded litter down a trail descending over 2,000 vertical
feet in only a mile-and-a-quarter horizontally." When it got particularly steep, the man on the rope "helped belay the litter down."
He added: "Wounded were strapped down securely and released during rest breaks. During one stop some shells landed nearby and this
motivated me to crawl off of the litter for better cover. After several
hours we finally reached a waiting ambulance that already held several other wounded men and in a short time were deposited at the
38th Evacuation Hospital."[8]

More seriously injured, Callowhill and Spofford had gone down
a couple of days earlier, both heavily sedated with morphine. "They
tied me in the stretcher and lowered me down the steep bits," said

Callowhill. "It took eight hours. I kept drifting in and out of consciousness. At one point I came to, and one of the guys carrying me said he needed water. I told him to drink mine." He was unlucky enough to be put in an ambulance that got into a rut and "flipped on its side." But "nobody was hurt" and they were eventually transferred to another one and taken to a hospital in Caserta.

Also carried down and hospitalized was Sergeant Johnny Walter, the Montana cowboy, who had shrapnel wounds in his shoulder and face, and Private Ray Kushi, the budding entrepreneur from Pittsfield, Massachusetts, with mortar fragments in his right arm and both legs.[9] By now, not many of the 1-2 originals were still on Difensa. Joe Glass, Percy Crichlow and Walter Wolf had all gone down to the casualty station on the 5th, suffering from minor wounds and exhaustion. They were followed on the 6th by Ken Betts, Tom Fenton and Don MacKinnon, the latter unable to get his boots "on and laced up over swollen feet."[10]

In a neat touch of symmetry, the battalion that had assaulted Difensa was also the last to see action on the massif when Gray's men attacked the remaining pocket of German resistance—the strongpoint held by Knaf's platoon—in the morning of December 8. Supported by accurate artillery fire, the 1/2nd Battalion made short work of the opposition, killing 25 and taking seven prisoners. Having defended heroically for three days, wrote Oberst Ens, "the last fighters of the platoon, filled with the highest sense of duty and true to the oath of allegiance, died in battle. Leutnant Knaf, who had led his men into battle in such an exemplary fashion, went with them to their deaths."[11]

In the early hours of December 9, having handed their forward positions over to the 142nd Infantry, the Forcemen began the long trek down the mountain to waiting trucks in the valley below. Of the Force's total casualties of 511 officers and men—73 killed, 9 missing, 313 wounded or injured and 116 exhaustion cases—the vast majority were suffered by the 1st and 2nd Regiments, which had both lost around 40 percent of their combat strength.[12] The company hardest hit was, not surprisingly, 1-2, which, having made the initial assault, was forced to endure five more days of cold, rain and constant shell-fire. It was, stated 1-2's war diary, "an ordeal since unequalled," with many more men wounded by mortar fire and hospitalized with "exhaustion, trench feet, etc." The diary added: "The men were soaking wet, with no change of clothing and no bed rolls. Rations had to be dropped by plane and water obtained from muddy shell holes." Small wonder that only Lieutenant Piette and 21 of the original 89 men were still on duty by December 9. Of Crichlow's 6th Section, just one of the original 14 men—Private Clarence DeCamp—walked back down the hill without a scratch.[13]

The descent was the first time that Larry Piette had seen the side of the mountain in daylight. Astonished at how steep it was, he could not imagine how they had managed the climb at night. He remembered places where they had had to walk with their backs to the precipice so they "wouldn't fall off." He thought: "It was amazing. I don't know how we did it."[14]

Later that day, returning to the barracks at Santa Maria after a brief stay in the hospital, Don MacKinnon and Tom Fenton found the rest of 3rd Platoon, or "what was left of them, sprawled out on top of their sleeping bags, clothes on most of them, asleep." It was, for MacKinnon, a particularly moving sight. "More than half our number had been killed or wounded," he wrote, "leaving some 15 or 16 empty sleeping bags on the floor."[15]

35

"KIA, return to sender"

At 10:00 a.m. on Sunday, December 12, a bugle sounded and more than 1,500 Forcemen snapped to attention as a jeep with a three-star flag swept into the western compound of the Santa Maria barracks. It contained the tall, gaunt figure of Lieutenant General Mark Clark, just back from Sicily, where he had received the Distinguished Service Cross for gallantry during the Salerno landings from President Franklin D. Roosevelt himself. Clark had come to Santa Maria to pay homage to the memory of the Forcemen killed on Difensa.

The day was cold and wet, to match the Forcemen's somber mood, and Clark kept his address brief. He welcomed the Forcemen to the Fifth Army—particularly the Canadians who were the first of that nationality to come under his command—and congratulated them on the accomplishment of a very difficult mission. "You were given," he said, "the task of capturing la Difensa, an extremely difficult piece of high ground in the Mt. Maggiore hill mass, the possession of which was vital to our further advance in that sector. The mission was carried out at night in spite of adverse weather conditions and heavy enemy rifle, machine-gun, mortar, and artillery fires on precipitous slopes over which it was necessary to attack. Furthermore, the position was maintained despite counterattacks and difficulties of communication and supply. The fact that you have acquitted yourself well in your first action under enemy fire is a tribute to fine leadership and a splendid reward for time spent in arduous training."

There would be, Clark explained, more battles to be fought and more lives lost. But he could promise the Force one thing: it would always fight as a single unit. A new mission would not be long coming. "Remember," said Clark, "you are now marked men and must dress and act the part at all times, especially on leave or when in contact with other military personnel."[1]

With Clark's address over, the roster of the 73 dead was read out in order of regiments and rank. From the 1st Regiment: "Captain Elden C. Borders, First Lieutenant Frank W. Eiwen, First Lieutenant John H. Richardson..." and on for another 31 names. Then the 36 dead of the 2nd Regiment: "Lieutenant Colonel T. C. MacWilliam, Captain William T. Rothlin...Sergeant George M. Edwards...Technician Grade 4 Ben Z. Bernstein, Technician Grade 4 Harry N. Deyette...Private Richard E. Daigle, Private S. Gath, Private S. R. Suotaila..." Two from the 3rd Regiment and one from the Service Battalion: "Private George J. Davis."[2]

After the memorial prayer and the sounding of "Taps," Clark departed, leaving Frederick to say a few final words: "I've been thinking about how we can best spend the more than five thousand dollars we raised on the way to the Aleutians as a fund to replace the sunk cruiser *Helena*. It has, as you know, been converted into war bonds and held for the Force. But given the sad events of the last few days, what better use for the money than the construction of a memorial in Helena for all the members of the Force killed in battle. All those in favor, raise your hand."

The response was unanimous.[3]

Clark was not the only general to congratulate the Force on its success. In the early afternoon of December 3, with the 36th Division's initial objectives secured, General Keyes wired General Walker: "Congratulations to you, Frederick, and Lynch, and all your officers and men for a fine job promptly done."[4]

Once the Force had taken Remetanea, Keyes wrote to Colonel Frederick to commend his troops for carrying out "a very successful operation under most adverse conditions." He was well aware of "the stubbornness of the enemy and the difficulties of weather and terrain encountered in the seizure of Mt. Difensa and Hill 907, and of the bravery, fortitude, and resourcefulness with which your command overcame them." He looked forward to the Force's next mission under his command "with genuine anticipation."[5] If the Forcemen were hoping for an apology from Keyes after his insensitive comments of December 1 ("War isn't Hollywood glamor stuff"), this was as good as it got.

Even General Eisenhower was told the story of Difensa during a brief tour of the front. Ike had come to Italy to discuss future plans with Clark—notably Operation Shingle, the amphibious landing at Anzio, just south of Rome, that was designed to outflank the Gustav Line. On December 19, after lunch at General Walker's CP, Ike, Clark and Keyes were driven up Highway 6 to look at the remaining German positions in the Mignano Gap, including those on Monte Sammucro, the Force's next objective. "We took only two jeeps," noted Clark, "leaving the rest of our party at a point a little beyond Mignano in order not to attract the attention of enemy artillery in the hills ahead of us."[6]

On the way, Walker stopped opposite the cliffs on the northern slope of Difensa and explained how the Forcemen had scaled them at night and captured the peak. Eisenhower was flabbergasted. "In order to outflank one of these mountain strongpoints," he wrote later, "a small detachment had put on a remarkable exhibition of mountain climbing. With the aid of ropes a few of them climbed steep cliffs of great height." Yet he could never understand how, "encumbered by their equipment," they were able to accomplish a feat that any

Alpine climber would have thought twice about. Once on top, according to Eisenhower, the Forcemen "ferreted out the location of the German company headquarters" and "seized the captain," who spluttered: "You can't be here. It is impossible to come up those rocks."[7]

Ike's anecdote about the captured company commander is not repeated in any other source and is probably apocryphal. Yet he almost certainly got it from one of the other senior officers, possibly Clark, and it could be partly true. Some German officers were taken prisoner on Difensa and, when questioned, may well have expressed their surprise at the direction and timing of the attack.

The large press corps in Italy—many of whom lunched at General Walker's CP on the day the mission was launched—were just as impressed by the Force's achievement. "This feat captured the imagination of the entire Fifth Army," wrote Clark Lee, war correspondent for the International News Service, whose stories were syndicated all over the United States, "and overnight [Colonel] Frederick and his soldiers became almost legendary figures in a battle area where heroism was commonplace." The Difensa attack, added Lee, would long be remembered "because of the endurance, daring and fighting skill it involved."[8]

Two days after the Forcemen paid their last respects to their 73 fallen comrades, the families of the dead began to receive the news they had been dreading since their loved ones went abroad. Bobby MacWilliam was still waiting to hear Tom's response to her letter informing him she was pregnant when the Canadian Pacific telegram, with its distinctive blue-and-yellow livery, was delivered to 27 Bromley Avenue in Moncton, where she was living with her parents. She knew, as did all service wives, that an official telegram was bad news. They were only sent in the event of death or a serviceman going missing. She must have prayed, as she tore open the envelope, that it was the latter. But the simple, formulaic wording confirmed her worst fears:

Regret deeply Lieutenant Colonel Thomas Cail MacWilliam officially reported killed in action 3rd December 1943. Further information follows when received.[9]

She had lost her husband, her unborn child its father. Prostrate with grief, she clung to the hope that at least Tom had known she was pregnant before he died. But was that the case? To find out for certain, she wrote to his XO, Major Ed Thomas, who was recovering from his bayonet wound in the 300th General Hospital in Naples. Bobby "wanted to know," recalled Thomas, "whether Tom had received her letter telling him that he was to become a father." The answer, sadly, was no. The American Forcemen had received their mail just before Difensa, but not the Canadians. His letter telling her this was "one of the toughest" he ever had to write.[10]

Bobby also received a letter of condolence from Colonel Frederick. Her husband, wrote the Force commander, was killed "leading his battalion in battle." He and his men had "behaved bravely and well in the face of danger and acquitted themselves proudly." His death had been "deeply felt" by his fellow Forcemen. Frederick added: "He shall live in our memory and his sacrifice for the nation he served in the cause of liberty and justice shall inspire us in the fight against a ruthless and dangerous enemy."[11]

A couple of months later, Tom's personal effects were returned to his widow. They included his gold wedding ring, collar insignia, three keys and his identity disc, all taken from his corpse. By the time a service of remembrance was held for MacWilliam and the other "Fallen Heroes" of Moncton in St. John's Church on the last day of 1944, Bobby had given birth to a baby son. She named him Tom.[12]

The families of the dead American Forcemen were, thanks to the inefficiencies of the US Army postal system, spared the bad news for a few days longer. It was, for example, not until December 22 that a Western Union telegram boy arrived at the front door of No. 71, a "festively decorated" timber-framed house on Fay's Avenue, Lynn, Massachusetts. It was a bitterly cold day, and two inches of freshly fallen snow lay on the ground. The boy rapped on the door, but there was no response. In cases such as this, he was supposed to keep the telegram until there was somebody available to sign for it. But for some reason—perhaps because he suspected the content of the telegram—he pushed it under the closed door.

Fifty-four-year-old Placide Daigle was the first to arrive home, from his job as a shoe patternmaker. Picking up the telegram, he saw it was addressed to his wife and knew at once what it would say. "Noooo!!" he screamed as he tore it open:

> The Secretary of War desires me to express his deep regret that your son Private Richard E. Daigle was killed in action in defense of his country on 3 December in Italy. Letter follows. The Adjutant General.*

Dick Daigle had died just 17 days short of his 22nd birthday. When his 16-year-old sister, Phyllis, returned home later that day from a basketball game, she found the crumpled telegram lying in the hall and could hear her father howling with grief in the laundry room. It was the first and only time she heard him cry. Two days later, as the whole grief-stricken Daigle clan gathered at the house for a somber Christmas, Dick's mother, Martha, replaced one of the three blue stars in the front window with a gold one, to indicate that one of her three servicemen sons had made the ultimate sacrifice.

When Dick's personal effects were returned to his family a few months later, they included the photo of his young nephew Ken that was in his helmet when he died, and also the Buck folding knife, Winooski Park money belt and Fanny Allen Hospital coin that

---

* Ida Deyette, Harry's wife, would have received an identical telegram. Their daughter Henrietta was just five months old when Harry died and would grow up with no memory of her father.

his sweetheart, Rae Bourgeois, had given him before he left for the Aleutians. These latter items were returned to the heartbroken Rae, who probably first heard of Dick's death when her Christmas card came back with the envelope marked: "KIA, return to sender." Rae graduated from nursing school in 1945, married the same year and had a daughter two years later. She died in February 2013.[13]

Originally buried on Difensa by the Graves Registration unit, Dick and the other dead were later disinterred and taken to separate US and Canadian military cemeteries in southern Italy. Dick was placed beside his buddy Harry Deyette in the US cemetery. But in 1948, at the request of his parents, Dick's body was repatriated to the United States. Before this third and final burial, the embalmer noted that Dick's "badly decomposed" body had multiple gunshot wounds to his upper chest. This was consistent with the story told to Dick's parents in early 1945 by a couple of fellow 3rd Platoon soldiers that "Dick and Harry Deyette had taken out a machine gun nest, but a second machine gun shot them before they could return fire." Dick was finally laid to rest in the Second World War section of Lynn's Pine Grove Cemetery on September 20, 1948. He was given a funeral with full military honors, at the close of which the Stars and Stripes draped on his coffin was folded 13 times by two representatives of the Veterans of Foreign Wars organization and handed to his tearful mother.[14]

36

"The best god-damned fighters in the world"

The distribution of gallantry awards is an imprecise business, and the medals given for Difensa are a case in point. The situation was further complicated by the fact that Canadian servicemen, at this stage of the war, were only eligible for British and not American medals. Yet, at the same time, they could not be given British awards while under US command. This would change. But in the immediate aftermath of the battle, it was mainly American Forcemen who were honored. The recipients included Lieutenant Wayne Boyce (posthumous Distinguished Service Cross), Lieutenant John Richardson (posthumous Silver Star), Lieutenant Larry Piette and Private Gerald Dodson (both Silver Stars). Piette's citation reads:

> Lt. Piette commanded the leading platoon in an assault on a vital crest. The final advance was made through a narrow defile up almost vertical cliffs...Within a few moments after the company, of which Lt. Piette's platoon was a part, had reached the crest, it suffered heavy casualties, including the company commander who was killed. Lt. Piette instantly assumed command

of the company and, while exposed to intense fire, went from one group to another encouraging the men, consolidating the company's gains, and organizing assault teams. When new enemy positions opened fire, he sent small units to attack them. [His] grasp of a critical situation and his calm courage and great energy during the initial phase of this attack were a valuable contribution to the success of a most difficult operation.[1]

In early January, the Canadian government finally agreed that its servicemen could be given US awards. Among the Canadians honored for bravery at Difensa was the scout Tom Fenton, who was given the newly instituted Bronze Star—awarded for acts of valor and "meritorious service" that did not quite qualify for the Silver Star or Legion of Merit—for leading his company "in an advance up the precipitous slopes of Mount la Difensa," and then helping to destroy "six machine gun positions" and capture "more than thirty prisoners." Fenton's fellow scout, Howard Van Ausdale, was also awarded the Bronze Star.[2]

But not all the heroes of Difensa got their just deserts. Second Lieutenant Karl Kaasch, commanding 1st Platoon, was quite rightly recommended for a Bronze Star for clearing the "left ridge of the saucer of 2 machine guns and several snipers."[3] This was the least he deserved. For some reason, perhaps because there were not enough living witnesses to his gallantry, the award was never confirmed and he got nothing. Another surprising omission was Captain Bill Rothlin, who had played such a key role in planning and executing the assault. The reason might be that many accounts of the battle record him dying at the start of the firefight, when in truth he was killed shortly before it ended.

Nor, at first, was any posthumous award made to Lieutenant-Colonel Tom MacWilliam, despite the obvious heroism he had displayed on Difensa. Finally, in 1945, Bobby MacWilliam was told that her husband had been given the minor British honor of a Mention in Despatches. But the wording of the citation, alone, is proof that a more substantial medal—either the American Distinguished Service Cross or the British Distinguished Service Order—was deserved. Part of it reads: "It was…Lt.-Col. MacWilliam's thorough planning, calm and efficient execution, and unswerving determination to accomplish his mission that led to the capture of a mountain mass that had held up the advance of the 5th Army for four weeks."[4]

Incredibly, Colonel Don Williamson was for a short time in line for an award after Frederick recommended him for the Legion of Merit. Williamson's regiment had, wrote Frederick, "led the attack on the Mount la Difensa portion of the hill mass, overcoming severe difficulties arising from precipitous mountains, adverse weather and stubborn enemy resistance." It had then "successfully destroyed" all German troops on the hill, held it "against numerous counterattacks" and, by the "prompt accomplishment of its mission," contributed to the success of adjacent Allied attacks "on other portions of the hill mass." It was to be, in effect, an award for leadership.[5]

Frederick, of course, made no mention of Williamson's erratic behavior during the assault. He must have assumed this was a minor aberration and that, thereafter, Williamson had performed creditably on Difensa. He was disabused of this notion—and withdrew his recommendation for Williamson's Legion of Merit—after speaking to Lieutenant Colonel Bob Moore and other senior 2nd Regiment officers just before Christmas. With Williamson's career at stake, Frederick asked for signed affidavits and got them from Moore and five members of the 2nd Regiment's HQ staff, including Gray, Olson and Story. Though their versions of events were all slightly different, they agreed on one thing: that Williamson was extremely jittery during the climb and had returned down the trail to report to Frederick, effectively abandoning his command, against their advice. On Difensa, moreover, Williamson had appeared nervous and indecisive, rarely ventured out of his cave, and it was left to Moore and Gray to make decisions.

Armed with these revelations, Frederick now made a very different recommendation: that Colonel Williamson be relieved of his command. "As a result of his performance during recent combat operations," wrote Frederick, his subordinates had "lost confidence in him and do not regard him with the respect which a senior officer and combat commander must hold." Williamson was, in Frederick's opinion, "emotionally and temperamentally unfitted for combat duty." Frederick's recommendation was approved and on January 1, 1944, he called Williamson to his command post, showed him the affidavits and sacked him. By that afternoon he was back at the Force's base camp in Santa Maria.[6]

Some of Williamson's fellow Canadian officers were shocked. "Not one [regimental] officer said a word to him about it," noted paymaster Major Jack Biscoe in the Canadians' war diary, "and he was given no intimation that they lacked confidence in his leadership until he was handed the declarations...He had no opportunity to defend himself, a most unfair way to handle the case and especially to treat the man who had helped to create the Force and who has been at the helm through its many turbulent and trying times."[7]

On January 14, Biscoe and Lieutenant-Colonel Tom Gilday, the new temporary commander of the Force's Canadian contingent, went to see Williamson at the 14th Canadian General Hospital in Caserta, where he had been sent for a psychological evaluation. Having promised to help exonerate him, they gathered a number of affidavits and statements in his support, including one from "Cookie" Marshall, his fellow regimental commander, which stated that Williamson "was directly responsible for bringing his regiment up to the high state of training it attained when it went into its first combat operation." Marshall added: "I am firmly convinced that he did a competent job, that he handled his subordinate units well and that there was no doubt as to the ultimate success of the operation." Colonel Ed Walker, commanding 3rd Regiment, was just as complimentary. "You did a lot for this organization, whether it was appreciated or not—your conscience can be clear—and you can be glad to be clear of a one-man unappreciative show."[8]

What is telling about these letters of support is that they were not written by people who were close to Williamson and in a position to know the truth about his behavior on Difensa. Those who did know were in no doubt that his sacking was deserved. Ed Thomas, for example, was in hospital when he heard that Williamson "had been relieved and transferred, due apparently to his performance during the Difensa operation." He added pointedly: "I could well understand that."[9]

The psychiatric evaluation was just as damning: Williamson had admitted to being "jittery" at the start of the Difensa battle, and thereafter displayed behavioral problems brought on by combat stress. Williamson hoped to clear his name in a court of inquiry. But that request, perhaps unfairly, was denied. He was shipped back to Canada, via the UK, and never again commanded troops in battle.[10]

Loyal to the last, Biscoe wrote in the Canadians' war diary: "It is sincerely regretted that he should be leaving the Force and certainly under conditions which he did not deserve."[11] It was a sentiment that not all Forcemen shared.

The capture of Difensa was the first—and arguably toughest—Force mission of the war. But there were many more. By the time the Force was disbanded in December 1944, its men had been in combat for an unprecedented eight of the previous 12 months. That included a 99-day unbroken stretch in the Anzio beachhead, where 1,500 Forcemen held an eight-mile sector of the defensive perimeter (a quarter of the total). "Defense of this long line with the limited number of troops available to the First Special Service Force," wrote Robert Frederick, "was possible by maintaining an alert outpost line, a highly mobile, centrally located reserve, and by extremely aggressive patrolling."[12]

So aggressive, in fact, with blacked-up Force patrols ranging well behind enemy lines, leaving red spearhead stickers with the words

"*Das dicke Ende kommt noch*" ("the worst is yet to come") on their victims, that the enemy dubbed them the "Black Devils."[13] It was during this time that the Force came to the attention of 22-year-old Bill Mauldin, the ex-GI who had become famous for his cartoons in the US Army publication *Stars and Stripes*, particularly the "Willie and Joe" series that so accurately depicted the trials and tribulations of the frontline soldier. Mauldin later described the Force as his "favorite outfit at Anzio." As men who had volunteered for a suicide mission, they "did not make good spit-and-polish soldiers." Instead they "called their officers by their first names," wore what they pleased and "carried the weapons that suited them best." Their sector on the "southern rim of the Anzio perimeter" was, wrote Mauldin, "the only quiet place on the whole beachhead." This was because the "monster patrols" they sent out every night "had the Germans terrorized." To escape the Force, "the enemy lines grew farther and farther away—as much as five miles," while the rest of the beachhead resembled the trench warfare of the First World War. This enabled the Forcemen "to live comparatively well," and "nowhere else on the beachhead could you find men sunbathing" beside their foxholes. Many of the stories Mauldin heard "while hanging around" the Force he was unable to use. "It was so wild," he wrote, "it defied caricature."[14]

The Forcemen may have been unorthodox but, as Mauldin recognized, they were also highly effective during their time at Anzio, taking no fewer than 603 German prisoners and inflicting thousands of casualties. They lost, in turn, 114 dead, 65 missing and 702 wounded.

On May 23, they spearheaded the breakout from Anzio and led the drive into the city of Rome, seizing the important bridges over the Tiber on the night of June 4. Six weeks later, as part of the 1st Airborne Task Force, they made successful amphibious landings on the enemy-held islands of Port Cros and Le Levant as the US Seventh Army invaded southern France in Operation Dragoon. Shipped to mainland France on August 22, they were continuously in combat, helping to drive German forces back to the Franco-Italian border,

until finally relieved by the Japanese-American 100th Battalion on
November 28.[15]

A week later, in an emotional ceremony on the banks of the River
Loup, near the town of Villeneuve-Loubet, the Force was formally
deactivated. The Canadian military was no longer prepared to send
its best troops to an American-dominated unit, and with Eisenhower's
armies advancing into Germany on a broad front with armor and
air support, there was no longer the need for a specialist commando
force. Once the dead had been honored and the red Force flag, with
its black dagger on a white shield, wound to its staff, the remaining
620 Canadian Forcemen fell out of the ranks and formed their own
battalion (for the first and only time). With many from both nationalities shedding tears, the Canadians left in trucks for Marseille, where
they were shipped to Normandy and reassigned to Canadian units.[16]

That left around 1,450 American Forcemen, 350 of whom volunteered for the US 82nd and 101st Airborne Divisions, while the
remaining 1,100 fought on with the independent 474th Infantry Regiment, working in the rear of the advancing US Twelfth Army Group
"in an anti-sabotage and anti-espionage role." On April 12, 1945,
shortly before the end of the war, the men of the 474th moved
gold bullion (a third of Germany's gold reserves) and art treasures,
captured a few days previously, from a salt mine to the Reichsbank
in Frankfurt. The regiment then followed General George Patton's
Third Army as it advanced into Bavaria and Austria, where it was
assumed the Germans would make a final stand. Numerous Nazi
officials and SS men were ferreted out of hiding by the 474th and
handed over to US counterintelligence. After VE Day, May 7, 1945,
the 474th Regiment was sent to Norway—the site of its original canceled mission—to help disarm and repatriate the German garrison of
300,000 men. It finally sailed from Norway to the United States on
October 15, 1945, and was disbanded in New York 12 days later.[17]

The Force had fought for just over a year, losing 401 killed and
1,803 wounded. Yet in that time its men had won 21 Distinguished

Service Crosses, 5 Legions of Merit, 104 Silver Stars, 105 Bronze Stars and 1 Soldier's Medal. They had also received 1,214 Purple Hearts and oak-leaf clusters (awarded to soldiers wounded in action), and 916 Good Conduct Medals. Foreign awards included one Military Cross, one Distinguished Conduct Medal and two Military Medals from the British government and, from the French and Italian governments, 10 Croix de Guerre and one Italian War Cross respectively.[18]

Sholto Watt, a *Montreal Star* reporter who got to know the Force well, always regretted that "this North American 'corps d'elite' could not have been employed in the lightning, staggering blow for which it had been trained." Even so, the impact it *did* make in just a year of combat was nothing short of extraordinary. "I can testify," wrote Watt, "to their spectacular power and efficiency, their marvelous morale and their never-failing spirit of attack. They were exactly what one would expect from North America's best—an inspiration to see and a terror to their enemy."[19]

In the opinion of one veteran of the US 3rd Infantry Division— no slouches themselves—the Forcemen were "the best god-damned fighters in the world." Watt felt the same. But for him, the Force's real importance was much greater than even its "outstanding military contribution." It was the fact that "it was the first joint force of its kind, drawn from two neighbor democracies, and that it was a brilliant success throughout." It is this "example of international brotherhood," wrote Watt, "which deserves enduring honor."[20]

37

"They were best friends for the rest of their lives"

"Hi Sis," wrote Corporal Ray Holbrook to his sister Gladys on March 26, 1944.

> *Just a line to let you know that I am still kicking and in good health in spite of the weather here. It rains about two out of every three days but that one day is a honey…Don't worry about me not getting those Lucky Strikes as I have plenty to smoke even if they are Old Golds, Twenty Grand, etc. Well, here is hoping that we will be marching through Rome and we can come home. Tell Dad hello for me if you see him.*
>
> *Heaps of love, Ray.*[1]

What Holbrook could not say was that he was writing from the Anzio beachhead where, having recovered from his bullet wound, he had rejoined the remnants of the old 3rd Platoon in a new amalgamated company under Lieutenant Tom Gordon. His platoon leader, as before, was Larry Piette. Four days after penning the letter, he was on a night patrol with Piette and part of his platoon when one of the new men—a "big, tough macho guy" who was "a bundle of nerves"—accidentally triggered an antipersonnel mine known as a Bouncing Betty. Without hesitating, Holbrook "deliberately threw himself" onto the exploding mine, sacrificing himself to save "the lives of three buddies." He was killed instantly. For this outstanding act of courage, he was awarded a posthumous Silver Star. His comrades felt it should have been more—and they had good reason to think so. Corporal Richard Bush of the US Marine Corps did something similar during the Okinawa campaign in 1945 and, having survived, was decorated with the Medal of Honor. But Holbrook's battalion commander, Colonel Akehurst, "did not believe in awarding medals because we had all volunteered for duty above and beyond the call—to serve in the Force was reward enough." By the time the Silver Star was presented to Holbrook's mother, Etta, at her home in Colville, Washington, the family had received not only the telegram notifying them of his death but also the last letter that Gladys had sent to him, stamped "Deceased."[2]

Gladys had just started her first office job after completing a business course when her mother phoned to tell her Ray was gone. Though distraught, she was so afraid of losing her new job that she said nothing and "stayed at work the rest of the day, accomplishing absolutely nothing." The death of her brother was a "real disaster" for the Holbrooks. "Everyone depended on Ray," wrote his niece Janice. "He was a kind, loving and supportive man and was the glue that held the family together, even from wherever he was with the Force. I often wonder how differently our lives would have turned out if Ray had lived."[3]

Of the remaining 3rd Platoon men, all would survive the war—but in varying states of mental and physical fitness. Don MacKinnon, for example, lost a leg to shellfire during the Force's assault on Monte Majo, north of Difensa, on January 6, 1944. He returned to Canada in July 1944 after lengthy hospital treatment and, despite his disability, enjoyed a successful career as a management consultant and member of the Canadian Senate. He died in 2002.[4]

Joe Dauphinais's wounds were still healing when he rejoined the Force in late December, so for a time he was given the job of leading pack mules, which he hated. At Anzio, by now reunited with his former comrades, he volunteered as a scout and would often go out with Howard Van Ausdale before a raid. The pair were leading the night patrol when Holbrook was killed, and were 150 yards ahead of the rest when they heard the explosion. "We never even found a button off Holbrook," he recalled. "Of course that was the end of the patrol." Dauphinais was wounded again—in the right arm this time—during the breakout from Anzio, but had recovered in time to take part in the assault on the Ile du Levant and the invasion of southern France. He remembered the disbandment of the Force on December 5, 1944, as the "saddest day" of his life. As he and the other Canadians were ordered to "fall out in a column of threes" while the American Forcemen stood fast, tears were "falling all over the bloody place, among all of these tough bastards." One American comrade, Jimmy Flack, ran behind the trucks carrying the Canadians to Marseille. Not, said Dauphinais, "because he was an American and we were Canadians; he was running after us because we were all First Special Service Force."[5]

Clarence "D" DeCamp, the lanky Californian, had the almost unique distinction of coming through Difensa, Anzio and the rest of the war unscathed. The only time he visited a field hospital was when his appendix burst. Shortly after returning to Los Angeles in 1945, he walked into a Thrifty drugstore where the young woman at the counter, spotting the red spearhead on his shoulder, asked if he was in the First Special Service Force. When he said yes, she asked him if he knew Art Schumm. He nodded. "He was my first sergeant." Schumm had been killed at Anzio in February 1944 and the young woman, it turned out, was his widow. She and DeCamp started dating and were married in 1946. DeCamp later worked for a cabinet and fixture company, "traveling all over the country" putting cabinets in stores. "He bore no scars from wounds," recalled his daughter Sharyn, "but he had a lot of mental scars. He had anger issues and drank a lot. He would kick out a lot in his sleep. Of course, they didn't treat for PTSD back then. I wonder sometimes what it would've been like for him to have had some treatment."[6]

Percy Crichlow was shot in the leg during a big raid in Anzio and, after recovering, was promoted to first lieutenant and given a platoon in Gordon's company. He took part in the Anzio breakout and was one of the first Allied soldiers to enter Rome on June 4. "We went among the houses, up a deserted main street where a couple of German tanks were burning," he remembered. "Some girls rushed out as I moved the platoon cautiously up the street. They kissed us and stuck flowers in our belts and equipment, but when a shot went off they disappeared completely." He was wounded again near Castillon, in southern France, and evacuated back to Italy and eventually the UK. After the war he returned to his job as a teacher at the Lodge School in St. John, Barbados, and served as headmaster from 1965 until 1972.[7]

Larry Piette commanded a platoon at Anzio that contained many of the Helena originals—including Dauphinais, Holbrook, Van Ausdale, Fenton, Glass and Waling—and led many night patrols. He later recalled that one officer would carry a baseball bat at night because it was a "lot easier to handle than a rifle." Promoted to captain in charge of 6-2 Company, Piette was given a "nice pistol" by a captured Waffen-SS officer during the Anzio breakout. "I want you to have it," the officer told him. "You are a combat man." A couple of days later he was wounded for the first time—in the left arm and elbow—at Artena and never made it as far as Rome. His main gripe about the month he spent in hospital was the theft of his jump boots, and he was still "hot about that" 40 years later. He rejoined the Force for Operation Dragoon and was hit again, not seriously, at Grasse in southern France. In his pocket was a small bottle of the perfume

Chanel No. 5, made at Grasse, that he intended to give to his fiancée, Marin deGravelles (she had accepted his proposal of marriage). But the bottle broke when he was wounded, drenching him in perfume and making him the "best-smelling patient in the hospital."[8]

Soon after he recovered, Piette's company spearheaded a battalion attack on the town of Villeneuve-Loubet. "Time and again" he "exposed himself to the intense small arms fire to encourage and deploy his men." Following his "inspirational example of fearlessness and courage, the men quickly stormed and seized the enemy positions, capturing 40 POWs and killing or wounding 25 others." For this second act of outstanding gallantry, Piette was awarded a Bronze Star to add to his Silver Star. After the Force was disbanded, he joined the 474th and accompanied it as far as Oslo, where he helped to repatriate German POWs (who called him the "Big Dog") and look after Norwegian orphans. One submarine commander told him he knew the war was lost when the Allies landed in North Africa and were able to maintain a supply line across the Atlantic. "We realized," said the German, "we could never beat a country that could do that." It was during Piette's time in Norway that he was presented with the Croix de Guerre at the French Embassy for his gallant service in France.

In June 1946, Piette married Marin deGravelles at the Church of the Assumption in Franklin, Louisiana, and the couple honeymooned in New Orleans. They lived in Larry's hometown of Appleton, Wisconsin, where they brought up four sons and three daughters. Larry worked as a research chemist for the Kimberly-Clark Corporation until his retirement in 1978. After Marin's early death in 1969, he married her sister Jeannette. He died in 2004 at the age of 88.[9]

Joe Glass was seriously wounded by shrapnel from an 88mm shell during one of his company's last raids at Anzio in May 1944. It hit him underneath the arm, went right through his chest—collapsing his lung—and came out his back. As he lay there, coughing up blood, unable to move from the waist down, he was convinced he was dying. "You tell my wife and kid goodbye from me," he told a friend.

But Percy Crichlow, the platoon leader, would not leave him. He and Johnny Walter grabbed Glass and dragged him to safety, though both Walter and Glass were hit by more shrapnel. When Glass's good buddy Lorin Waling saw the extent of his friend's injuries, he cried.[10] But Glass survived and, a day later, dictated a letter to his wife from the beachhead hospital:

Dearest Dot

Just a few lines to tell you that no doubt you will receive a notice from the War Department saying I've been wounded in action. I want to get this off to you right away to tell you not to worry as it isn't anything serious. How is the baby and everyone at home…

Best to you all, your loving husband Joe.[11]

Glass returned to the Force shortly before its invasion of southern France in August 1944—but was never fit enough to rejoin the combat echelon. Instead he was sent back to Canada in early 1945, gambling away the last of his army pay en route, and made his way to Sarnia, Ontario, where Dot and their 18-month-old son, Chuck, were living with Glass's parents. It was the first meeting between father and son, a moving if awkward ritual that was replicated in many thousands of homes across North America that year. Unfortunately Glass's own homecoming was slightly marred by the fact that he had been drinking heavily on the train to Sarnia and, much to Dot's fury, spent most of that first afternoon sleeping off the effects. He and Dot had three more children. By the birth of the third, Dottie, in 1947, they had moved back to Helena, Montana, where Joe worked for a sand and gravel company and later ran a bar, a speedway track and a casino. He also had a lengthy spell as a salesman for a food company, missing out on a number of promotions because he refused to leave Helena. He was a strict father who sometimes found it hard to show affection. "I think he was affected by PTSD," says his daughter Dottie. "He had a lot of demons and the war played its part. But I always knew and felt that he loved me and his family very much. He was a really good and honest man."[12]

Glass died at the age of 92 in 2012, outliving his best friend, Lorin Waling, by four years. Waling had almost died on the Ile du Levant in August 1944 when he was hit by multiple pieces of mortar shrapnel that nearly severed his right arm. But he survived, informing his mother from a hospital bed in Italy with typical understatement: "Just a line to tell you that I am well...I received a slight injury in my right arm which explains why I'm not writing this letter." When Steffie received the telegram informing her of Lorin's injury, she was "never so upset," and remained so for some time.[13] But the worst of her worries were over because Lorin's "slight injury" was enough to end his war. He was invalided back to Canada in late 1944 and Steffie came to live with him in Edmonton. After Lorin had trained as an electrician, he and Steffie moved back to Helena, where they had four children and spent all their spare time with the Glasses. "They were best friends for the rest of their lives," remembered Lorin's son Jerry. "For a long time we thought we were all related." Though Lorin was prone to "terrible nightmares," his happy-go-lucky nature was unaffected by his experiences of war. He ran a successful electrical business and died in 2008, 12 years after Steffie.[14]

What of the other men who fought on Difensa? Jack Callowhill returned to the Force after his serious leg wound had healed; but too lame to see frontline action, he remained with the rear echelon at Avellino near Naples until he was reunited with the Canadian originals on their way back to the UK in December 1944. After returning to Hamilton a year later, Callowhill got a job at the American Can Company—where his father was manager of purchases—and worked for the business until he retired. In 1946 he married Donna, a local girl he had known since childhood, and they had two children. Donna died in 2016, a week before their 70th wedding anniversary.

Callowhill is, at the time of writing, the last survivor of the men who scaled and fought on Difensa. He is 95.

Geoffrey Hart was wounded twice more in action: near Rome and on the Isle du Levant. On the former occasion, "despite severe pain he refused treatment and remained in command of his [rocket launcher] crew until his company was relieved the following day." His "determination to remain in the fight despite his wound was an inspiration to his men" and "contributed materially to the effectiveness of his section." He was awarded the Bronze Star.[15] He returned to the Peace Country in British Columbia and married Mary Chamberlain in 1952. They had one son, John, who today is a prominent member of the First Special Service Force Association. Hart was tragically killed in a work accident at the W. A. C. Bennett Dam in 1966.

Captain Tom Gordon won the Silver Star for his "courage under fire and aggressive leadership" during the breakout from Anzio on May 21, 1944, when he "personally destroyed several of the enemy with his carbine and grenades." He was wounded in the chest on the outskirts of Rome on June 4 and returned to the Force, after a long spell in hospital, for the last few weeks of the southern France campaign. Gordon then saw out the war with the 1st Canadian Parachute Battalion, returning home in 1945. He married in 1945 and had three children. He worked as an investment counselor and died in 1979.[16]

Recovered from his bayonet wound, Ed Thomas rejoined the Force in January 1944 before it was shipped to Anzio. His new job was XO for the 1/3rd Battalion, commanded by Tom Gilday, which was holding the left flank of the Force position in the beachhead. The battalion CP was in a house set back from the Mussolini Canal—the front line—where Thomas lived with Gilday and the rest of the command group. "We had," recalled Thomas, "domestic animals and fowl left by the former residents—chickens, ducks, a crook-necked goose, a couple of dogs and a cat or two. The chickens occasionally supplied eggs." Shortly before the Anzio breakout, Thomas took command of his old 1/2nd Battalion and fought at Rome, on the Ile du Levant and on through southern France. The departure of the Canadians on December 5 left Thomas and the other Americans with "many sad and empty feelings." He noted: "For us, an era had ended." Thomas served first with the 474th Infantry, the lowlight being a march near Weimar, southern Germany, when they came across Buchenwald concentration camp, which had been liberated the day before. "I had seen the horrors of war," wrote Thomas, "but nothing in combat approached what I saw at Buchenwald. This charnel house was an unbelievably horrible example of man's inhumanity to man, the most horrific example of this in my life. I saw it, it was real and it remains an indelible memory."

In late April 1945, Thomas rejoined his old airborne regiment, the 505th Parachute Infantry (part of the 82nd Airborne Division). After a spell with the occupying forces in Berlin, he returned to the United States in January 1946. He settled in Charlotte, North Carolina, where he became a successful property developer. In 1956 he married Ann Davis, a graduate from the University of Texas, and they had two daughters. He remained in the Army Reserve and eventually made the rank of brigadier general with responsibility for Unconventional Warfare. He died in 2010.[17]

Bill Becket paid the price for losing contact with his battalion on the climb up Difensa when, shortly after the battle, he was relieved of his command and assigned to Force HQ. It was, he recalled, "the most serious and emotional personal experience" of his six years of war service. He was shocked when "Cookie" Marshall,[*] a man he considered a close friend, gave him the bad news, but he later acknowledged that he would probably have done the same thing to a battalion commander who had "failed to properly accomplish an order." Grateful that Frederick had given him the opportunity to restore his reputation, he vowed he would not let him down a second

---

[*] Colonel Marshall was later killed by sniper fire as the Force entered Rome on June 4, 1944. He was the senior Forceman to be KIA.

time—nor did he. After a six-week spell in a Santa Maria hospital with amebic dysentery and hepatitis—where he briefly met Brigadier General Wilbur, who was being sent home with "bad feet" (though in reality he had been sacked by Clark)—Becket rejoined the Force at Anzio and served as Frederick's assistant operations officer, planning patrols and arranging raids, and even going on a couple himself. Becket's rehabilitation was complete when, following the capture of Rome and Frederick's appointment to head the 1st Airborne Task Force, he was given command of the 3rd Regiment by the Force's new leader, Colonel Fred Walker. "Here at last," recalled Becket, "was the end of my tribulation of having lost command of my original battalion. I could scarcely speak."[18]

The icing on the cake for Becket came on September 3, near Castillon in southern France, when, after a personal reconnaissance in a jeep in "enemy held territory, over mined roads," he "led his troops in a boldly devised and vigorously executed plan of attack which quickly overcame enemy resistance and resulted in the capture of Mount Ours, a terrain feature of critical importance." For his part, Becket was awarded the Silver Star.[19] After the Force was deactivated, he was shipped to the UK, where, for the rest of the war, he commanded the 1st Canadian Parachute Training Battalion. He returned to Charlottetown, Prince Edward Island, in the summer of 1945 for an emotional reunion at the train station with his wife, Evelyn. They drove home and there, playing in front of the house with some other children, was his daughter Heather. He had not seen her for more than three years. Walking up to the unfamiliar four-year-old wearing a "Black Watch plaid coat, skirt and tam [o'shanter]," Becket smiled and said: "Heather dear, I am your father."

She smiled back and let Becket take her in his arms. "It was as if," he wrote, "she had known me all along."[20]

Epilogue

"They helped save a continent in chaos"

When Bob Frederick said goodbye to his beloved Force at Lake Albano, near Rome, on June 23, 1944, he already possessed two Distinguished Service Crosses, a Silver Star, a Bronze Star and a Purple Heart with six oak leaves. Hobbling up to the microphone, his right leg still splinted after a recent wound, he said: "One of a general's pleasant jobs is to decorate soldiers with medals they richly earned and"—he paused briefly—"one of the toughest jobs is to tell an outfit he loves goodbye, which I am telling you now."

There was an audible gasp. Not even Frederick's senior commanders knew he was leaving. Some of the bolder Forcemen asked where he was going so they could put in for a transfer. He shook his head. "I can't tell you. But I expect you to go on fighting, not as Yanks or Canadians, but as North Americans, upholding the tradition of the best damned combat outfit in existence."

He then turned to salute the Force flag, climbed into his staff car and, "with one last proud look at his Force," drove away.[1]

The announcement "really shook us," recalled Bill Becket. "The General had taken a place in the heart of every man in the Force.

[He] had always been 'up-front'—and he had been wounded eight times."[2]

Promoted to major general at the age of 37 (the second youngest US officer to reach that rank during the Second World War), Frederick was given command of the 1st Airborne Task Force for Operation Dragoon. After the 1st ATF was deactivated in southern France in late 1944, he took over the 45th Infantry Division and led it into southern Germany. Following postwar stints in Austria and Greece, he retired on health grounds in March 1952. He explained later: "I was exhausted." He settled with his family in California and died in 1970 at the age of 63.[3]

Today both the US Army's Special Forces ("Green Berets") and the Canadian Special Operations Regiment (CSOR) trace their heritage back to the First Special Service Force. In 1960, the link between the Force and the Green Berets was formalized when General Frederick handed the Force colors and streamers to the colonel of the 7th Special Forces Group during a formal ceremony at Fort Bragg. These close ties were confirmed in 1992 when the 3rd Special Forces Group (Airborne) named their new headquarters building at Fort Bragg after the late Lieutenant-Colonel Tom MacWilliam. His widow and son, Tom Junior, attended the dedication ceremony as guests of honor.

In 2013, to commemorate the 70th anniversary of the battle for Monte la Difensa, the CSOR completed a daytime reenactment of the famous climb up the north cliffs. Arriving at the summit, Chief Warrant Officer Tom Verner said he and his men were "truly in awe of the accomplishment of the [Force] veterans." Having just climbed with "top-of-the-line equipment, during the day" and "in optimal conditions," Werner could "only imagine what it was like for them—in imminent presence of the enemy, in darkness, the fear of the unknown." Werner added: "We can only hope to honor that as we move forward with our history, and we will endeavor to do that."[4]

The most recent mark of appreciation was by the United States

Congress. In February 2015, it formally recognized the Force's extraordinary wartime feats by awarding its surviving members the Congressional Gold Medal, given to persons "who have performed an achievement that has an impact on American history and culture." More than 40 former Forcemen traveled to Washington to hear Senate Majority Leader Mitch McConnell declare: "Some of their more daring mission plans would have made James Bond blush... But this isn't just some Hollywood script. It's a true story about a fearless group of young Canadians and Americans...who were willing to put their lives on the line in the truest sense of the term...Through it all, they helped save a continent in chaos."[5]

Acknowledgments

This book could not have been written without the help of the few surviving Forcemen and the families of those who are no longer with us. I would particularly like to thank Jack Callowhill, the last remaining member of 1-2 Company, the unit that led the assault on Monte la Difensa on that cold and wet night in December 1943, for generously sharing his memories with me. I also spoke at length with two other Force veterans, S. E. "Cy" Mermelstein and Eugene Gutierrez.

I'm grateful to family members who shared stories of their Forcemen relatives, and sent me photos, letters, diaries, and memoirs: Ken Beaton, Wilson Becket, Manny Boroditsky, Darrell Boyd, Nathan Gordon, Janice Harshbarger, John Hart, Casey Hilton, Tricia Hofeld, Sharyn DeCamp Jones, Raymond T. Kushi Jr., Shirley Long, Madge Wilson, Cheryl Waling Hysell, Cliff Maclean, Tom MacWilliam Jr., Dee Matthews, Dottie Glass Maxted, Dan J. Piette, Cathy Rachui, Raymond Sanders, Bobby Sanders, Ann Thomas, Kelly Turnbull, Dave Waling, Jerry Waling, and Valerie Waling.

I'd also like to thank the leading lights of the First Special Service Force Association—the then President John Woon, President Elect Don Shelton, Secretary Bill Woon and Assistant Secretary Tricia Hofeld—who let me attend the 2017 reunion in Sacramento where I met veterans and family members. The latter included Sharyn DeCamp Jones, daughter of Clarence E. DeCamp, who sadly passed away before the completion of this book; and John Hart, Canadian vice president of the FSSF Assocation and son of the late Geoffrey

Hart, who gave me invaluable help with contact details, documents, and photos, and I'm extremely grateful.

Others who assisted in various ways include: Tom MacWilliam Jr., who accompanied me on my research trip to Italy in the spring of 2018, climbing Monte la Difensa and visiting his father's grave at Monte Cassino; Andrew Seys Llewellyn, my translator and drinking companion on the same trip; Tristan Horx, who played much the same role in Germany; Dorothy Volpe, owner of the wonderful Dimora del Prete di Belmonte guesthouse in Venafro (www.dimoradelprete.it); Luciano Bucci, cofounder of the extraordinary Winterline Museum in Venafro (www.winterlinevenafro.it), who guided us up Monte la Difensa and its surrounding peaks; Giani Blasi; Helen Nurse, my daughter Tamar's German teacher, who expertly translated documents from the Militärarchiv in Freiburg; my mother, Cherry, who acted as an unpaid, and often unthanked, research assistant; and Louis Freiherr von der Borch who gave me invaluable insight into the upbringing and character of his late father Rittmeister Alhard Freiherr von der Borch, commander of the German 115th Armored Reconnaissance Battalion on Difensa. I salute you all.

I'm grateful to the staff of the following libraries and archives for assisting with my research and, in some cases, granting permission for me to quote from documents in their possession: the Canadian Airborne Forces Museum, Petawawa; the Department of National Defence Directorate of History and Heritage, Ottawa; the Hoover Institution Archives, Stanford, CA; the Library and Archives of Canada, Ottawa; the Militärarchiv in Freiburg, Germany; the UK National Archives, Kew, London; and the US National Archives and Records Administration, College Park, MD.

Wilson Becket gave me permission to quote from his father's unpublished manuscript, *The Stars and Jack*, and Ann Thomas did the same for her husband Ed's unpublished account *Auburn to Berlin*. Thank you. I have endeavored to contact other copyright holders for permission to include material in the book. I would urge those who did not respond to get in touch.

Lastly, I'm indebted to Caroline Michel, my wonderful literary agent, for instantly knowing the best way to tell this incredible story; to Nelle Andrew, also of PFD, for her expert handling of the US contract; to Mauro DiPreta, former publisher at Hachette Books in New York, for his unwavering faith in the project and perceptive edits; to David Lamb, who inherited the book from Mauro and expertly saw it through to publication; to Michael Barrs, Mike Giarratano, Melanie Gold, and Richard Ljoenes and Amanda Kain on the design side, and the rest of the excellent publishing team at Hachette Books; and to my wife, Louise, and daughters Nell, Tamar, and Tashie, who are tired of hearing me say, "I've got a good feeling about this book." Truth is: I really do.

Bibliography

PRIMARY SOURCES, UNPUBLISHED

Archives

Canadian Airborne Forces Museum (CAFM), Petawawa, Ontario

FSSF First Hand Accounts and Memoirs (Sims Fonds): "Memories of the Battle of Mount la Difensa," by Donald MacKinnon, 1st Co. 2nd Regiment, FSSF.

Department of National Defence Directorate of History and Heritage (DHH), Ottawa, Ontario

145.3009 (D2). "List of Citations for Awards, 1st Canadian Special Service Battalion."
145.3009 (D4). "Monthly Reports of 1st Canadian Special Service Battalion, August 1942–January 1945."
Robert H. Adleman Papers. Boxes 7, 8, 12.
Robert D. Burhans Papers. Boxes 2, 5, 7, 15, 18, 19, 21, 28, 30.
Robert T. Frederick Papers. Boxes 1, 2, 5, 8.

Library and Archives Canada (LAC), Ottawa, Ontario

RG 24/6921. "Major G. W. L. Nicholson, 'Report No. 5: 1st Canadian Special Service Battalion,' Historical Section (G.S.), Department of National Defence."
RG 24/15301. "Secret War Diary of 2nd Canadian Parachute Battalion (AF) within 1st Special Service Force."

Bundesarchiv-Militärarchiv (BMA), Freiburg, Germany

MSG 2/5724. "Darmstädter Reiter und Aufklärer: Festschrift anlässlich des Treffens am 15.–16. Mai 1954."

RH/20/10/71-75. "Armeeoberkommando 10: November 6–Dezember 7, 1943."

RH/26/1023. "15. Panzergrenadier-Division."

RH/82/156. "Pz. Gren. Regt. 104: 5. Kompanie.- Antrag auf Verleihung einer Nahkampfspange."

RH/82/226. "Pz. Gren. Regt. 104: Gefechtsbericht über den Einsatz bei Monte Camino im Dez. 1943."

Private Papers

R. W. Becket Papers
Sam Boroditsky Papers
Richard Daigle Papers
Sharyn DeCamp Jones Papers
Joe Glass Papers
Tom Gordon Papers
Geoffrey Hart Papers
Ray Holbrook Papers
Tom MacWilliam Papers
Lawrence Piette Papers
Ed Thomas Papers
Lorin Waling Papers

The National Archives (TNA), Kew, London

Cabinet Office Papers:

CAB 120/416. Minister of Defence Secretariat, "'Plough' Force (snow warfare brigade)."

CAB 121/179. "Combined Operations, 'Plough' Force: development of special vehicles and training of troops for use in snow."

CAB 122/659. "War Cabinet and Cabinet Office: British Joint Staff Mission and British Joint Services Mission: Washington Office Records. 'Plough' Force."

Records of the Combined Operations Headquarters:

DEFE 2/883. "Armoured fighting vehicles to operate in snow (Plough Scheme): the Plough Mission to Washington and scheme planning reports etc."

DEFE 2/884. "Armoured fighting vehicles to operate in snow (Plough Scheme): equipment."

DEFE 2/885. "Armoured fighting vehicles to operate in snow (Plough Scheme): trials and progress reports."

DEFE 2/886. "Armoured fighting vehicles to operate in snow (Plough Scheme): correspondence, minutes and reports."

DEFE 2/887. "Armoured fighting vehicles to operate in snow (Plough Scheme): correspondence, minutes and reports."

War Office Papers:

WO 106/1974. "'Plough'; special Force for reconquest of Norway."
WO 204/1532. "First Special Service Force (trained for operations in snow): proposed employment: movements. Movement of Ranger battalions."

US National Archives and Records Administration (USNARA), College Park, Maryland

NND/730029. Boxes 65 and 135. HQ Army Ground Forces: G-3 Section, Correspondence File, 1942–49.
NND/735017. Boxes 18483–89. Records of the Adjutant General's Office: Operations Reports, 1941–48, Special Services.
NND/740106. Boxes 968 and 969. General Correspondence of the 1st Special Service Force, 1941–1943.
NND/750114. Box 30. Allied Operation and Occupation HQ: HQ Twelfth Army Gp, Admin. Branch, 1943–45.
NND/760209. Box 41. SHAEF, Special Staff, Adjutant General's Division, 1944: FSSF Disbandment.
NND/803119. Boxes 663, 672 and 689. Adjutant General Section: General Correspondence, 1992–94.

PRIMARY SOURCES, PUBLISHED

Published Documents, Diaries, Letters and Memoirs

Churchill, Winston S. *The Second World War*, 6 vols. London: Cassell, 1948–54.
Clark, Mark W. *Calculated Risk: His Personal Story of the War in North Africa and Italy*. London: Harrap, 1951.
Danchev, Alex, and Daniel Todman, eds. *War Diaries 1939–1945: Field Marshal Lord Alanbrooke*. London: Weidenfeld & Nicolson, 2001.
Eisenhower, Dwight D. *Crusade in Europe*. 1948. Reprint, Baltimore: Johns Hopkins University Press, 1997.
Kesselring, Albert. *The Memoirs of Field-Marshal Kesselring*. London: William Kimber, 1953.
Lewis, William R. *GI Blue: An MP's Journey Through WWII*. Bloomington, IN: iUniverse, 2010.
Liddell Hart, B. H., ed. *The Rommel Papers*. 1953. Reprint, London: Collins, 1987.
Mauldin, Bill. *The Brass Ring: A Sort of Memoir*. New York: W. W. Norton, 1972.
Nelson, Mark J. *With the Black Devils: A Soldier's World War II Account with the First Special Service Force and the 82nd Airborne*. Atglen, PA: Schiffer, 2004.
Nichols, David, ed. *Ernie's War: The Best of Ernie Pyle's World War II Dispatches*. New York: Random House, 1986.
Peppard, Herb. *The LightHearted Soldier: A Canadian's Exploits with the Black Devils in WWII*. Halifax, NS: Nimbus, 1994.
Senger und Etterlin, General F. von. *Neither Fear nor Hope: The Wartime Career*

of General Frido von Senger und Etterlin, *Defender of Cassino*. Translated by George Malcolm. London: Macdonald, 1963.

Sherwood, Robert E. *The White House Papers of Harry L. Hopkins: An Intimate History*, 2 vols. London: Eyre & Spottiswoode, 1948–49.

Walker, Fred L. *From Texas to Rome with General Fred L. Walker: Fighting World War II and the Italian Campaign with the 36th Infantry Division, as Seen Through the Eyes of its Commanding General*. Dallas: Taylor Publishing, 1969.

Wedemeyer, Albert C. *Wedemeyer Reports!* New York: Devin-Adair, 1958.

Westphal, General Siegfried. *The German Army in the West*. London: Cassell, 1951.

Newspapers and Journals

Globe and Mail, Toronto
Independent Record, Helena, MT
London Gazette
Los Angeles Times

SECONDARY SOURCES

Books and Articles

Adleman, Robert H., and George Walton. *The Devil's Brigade*. 1966. Reprint, Annapolis, MD: Naval Institute Press, 1968.

Ambrose, Stephen E. *Band of Brothers: E Company, 506th Regiment, 101st Airborne from Normandy to Hitler's Eagle's Nest*. 2001. Reprint, London: Simon & Schuster, 2016.

——. *Eisenhower: Soldier and President*. 1990. Reprint, New York: Simon & Schuster, 2003.

——. *The Supreme Commander: The War Years of Dwight D. Eisenhower*. 1970. Reprint, New York: Doubleday, 2012.

Atkinson, Rick. *The Day of Battle: The War in Sicily and Italy 1943–1944*. London: Little, Brown, 2007.

Blumenson, Martin. *United States Army in World War II: The Mediterranean Theater of Operations; Salerno to Cassino*. Washington, DC: Office of the Chief of Military History, 1969.

Bowlby, Alex. *Countdown to Cassino: The Battle of Mignano Gap, 1943*. London: Leo Cooper, 1995.

Burhans, Robert D. *The First Special Service Force: A War History of the North Americans 1942–1944*. 1947. Reprint, Nashville, TN: Battery Press, 1978.

David, Saul. *Military Blunders: The How and Why of Military Failure*. London: Robinson, 1997.

——. *Mutiny at Salerno 1943: An Injustice Exposed*. 1995. Reprint, London: Conway Maritime, 2005.

Edward Smith, Jean. *FDR*. New York: Random House, 2007.

Bibliography

Edwards, Robert J. *Tip of the Spear: German Armored Reconnaissance in Action in World War II.* Mechanicsburg, PA: Stackpole Books, 2015.

Fraser, David. *Knight's Cross: A Life of Field Marshal Erwin Rommel.* London: HarperCollins, 1993.

Gilbert, Martin. *Winston S. Churchill: Road to Victory, 1941–1945.* London: Heinemann, 1986.

Hastings, Max. *Finest Years: Churchill as Warlord 1940–1945.* London: HarperPress, 2009.

Hemming, Henry. *Churchill's Iceman: The True Story of Geoffrey Pyke: Genius, Fugitive, Spy.* London: Preface, 2014.

Hicks, Anne. *The Last Fighting General: The Biography of Robert Tryon Frederick.* Atglen, PA: Schiffer, 2006.

Horn, Colonel Bernd, and Michel Wyczynski. *Of Courage and Determination: The First Special Service Force, "The Devil's Brigade," 1942–44.* Toronto: Dundurn, 2013.

Jenkins, Roy. *Churchill.* London: Macmillan, 2001.

Jordan, Jonathan W. *American Warlords: How Roosevelt's High Command Led America to Victory in World War II.* New York: Dutton Caliber, 2015.

Joyce, Kenneth H. *Snow Plough and the Jupiter Deception: The True Story of the 1st Special Service Force and the 1st Canadian Special Service Battalion, 1942–1945.* St. Catharines, Ontario: Vanwell, 2006.

Kershaw, Ian. *Hitler: A Biography,* 2 vols. London: Allen Lane, 1998–2000.

McGeer, Eric. *The Canadian Battlefields in Italy: Ortona & the Liri Valley.* Waterloo, Ontario: Laurier Centre, 2007.

Mortimer, Gavin. *The Daring Dozen: 12 Special Forces Legends of World War II.* Oxford, UK: Osprey, 2012.

Nadler, John. *A Perfect Hell: The True Story of the Black Devils, the Forefathers of the Special Forces.* Toronto: Doubleday, 2005.

Oxford Dictionary of National Biography. Oxford, UK: Oxford University Press, 2018.

Roberts, Andrew. *Masters and Commanders: How Roosevelt, Churchill, Marshall and Alanbrooke Won the War in the West.* London: Allen Lane, 2008.

Shakespeare, Nicholas. *Six Minutes in May: How Churchill Unexpectedly Became Prime Minister.* London: Harvill Secker, 2017.

Springer, Joseph A. *The Black Devil Brigade: The True Story of the First Special Service Force; An Oral History.* Pacifica, CA: Pacifica Military History, 2001.

Werner, Bret. *Storming Monte La Difensa: The First Special Service Force at the Winter Line, Italy 1943.* Oxford, UK: Osprey, 2015.

Ziegler, Philip. *Mountbatten: The Official Biography.* London: Collins, 1985.

Websites

https://www.tracesofwar.com/persons/5084/Gienanth-Freiherr-von-Walter.htm. Accessed January 24, 2019.

https://www.britannica.com/biography/Geoffrey-Keyes. Accessed July 26, 2018.

www.cmohs.org/recipient-detail/2653/britt-maurice-I.php. Accessed July 8, 2018.

https://www.sac.on.ca/page/upper-school/cadet-corps/corps-history/awards-for-best-upper-school-cadet. Accessed January 24, 2019.

https://history.army.mil/brochures/aleut/aleut.htm. Accessed May 28, 2018.

https://www.irishcentral.com/roots/history/americas-deadliest-irishman-the-irish-james-bond.

http://www.liverpoolships.org/empress_of_scotland_canadian_pacific.html. Accessed June 6, 2018.

https://nebula.wsimg.com/c87ccca6603034a6951f7e6974439b7a?AccessKeyId=BC21553 F553BBD27F066&disposition=0&alloworigin=1. Accessed August 9, 2018.

https://www.pbs.org/newshour/nation/congress-awards-first-special-service-force-gold-medal. Accessed August 24, 2018.

https://rohnasurvivors.org/history/. Accessed June 12, 2018.

www.specialforcesroh.com/showthread.php?3252-Deyette-Harry-N.

www.specialforcesroh.com/showthread.php?29287-Van-Ausdale-Howard-Clifford.

http://www.thedropzone.org/training/story.html.

https://www.youtube.com/watch?v=cKLG4F4eqkA. Accessed August 24, 2018.

http://apps.westpointaog.org/Memorials/Article/8349/.

Notes

Prologue. "It seemed like the mountain was on fire"

1   College Park, MD, US National Archives and Records Administration (USNARA), NND/740106, "Identification of Especially Qualified Personnel," 2nd Lt. Earl R. Williams, Fort Ord, California, July 1942.

2   Petawawa, Canadian Airborne Forces Museum (CAFM), FSSF First Hand Accounts and Memoirs (Sims Fonds), "Memories of the Battle of Mount La Difensa," by Donald MacKinnon, 1st Co. 2nd Regiment, FSSF, p. 4.

3   Bob Davis, in Alex Bowlby, *Countdown to Cassino: The Battle for the Mignano Gap, 1943* (London: Leo Cooper, 1995), p. 111.

4   Private Papers (PP), Ed Thomas Papers, Ed Thomas, "Auburn to Berlin: A World War II Memoir, 1936–1946," p. 47.

5   MacKinnon, "Memories of the Battle," p. 5.

6   Stanford, CA, Hoover Institution Archives (HIA), Adleman Papers, Box 7, Percy McDonald Crichlow, "Questionnaire About Military Service with the FSSF," November 2, 1963.

Chapter 1. Forcemen

1   Ottawa, Library and Archives of Canada (LAC), RG 24/15301, "Secret War Diary of 2nd Canadian Parachute Battalion (AF) within 1st Special Service Force," August 3–6, 1942; William Story,

"The Early Days of the Force," http://www.thedropzone.org/training/story.html.

2 LAC, RG 24/15301, "Secret War Diary of 2nd Canadian Parachute Battalion," August 5, 1942.

3 LAC, RG 24/6921, Major G. W. L. Nicholson, "Report No. 5: 1st Canadian Special Service Battalion," Historical Section (G.S.), Department of National Defense, pp. 3–4.

4 Author interview with Tom MacWilliam Jr., Ottawa, January 9, 2018; PP, Tom MacWilliam Papers, RMC Company Commanders' Course (Qualifying), May 10 to July 31, 1942.

5 Crichlow, "Questionnaire About Military Service."

6 Pvt. Joe Dauphinais, in Joseph A. Springer, *The Black Devil Brigade: The True Story of the First Special Service Force; An Oral History* (Pacifica, CA: Pacifica Military History, 2001), pp. 10–13.

7 Author interview with Jack Callowhill, Stoney Creek, Ontario, January 11, 2018.

8 Pvt. Donald MacKinnon, in Springer, *Black Devil Brigade*, p. 15; Bill Halewood and Bill Harris, "Don MacKinnon," *Toronto Globe and Mail*, February 11, 2003; MacKinnon, "Memories of the Battle," p. 11.

9 USNARA, NND/740106, "Declaration to Be Signed by All Officers and Other Ranks Posted to the 2nd Canadian Parachute Battalion," August 1942.

10 Special Forces Roll of Honour, "Thread: Rothlin, William T. (Bill)," http://www.specialforcesroh.com/showthread.php?3502–Rothlin-William-T-(Bill)&highlight=rothlin; HIA, Burhans Papers, Box 7, Lt. Col. K. J. Wickham, Adjutant, FSSF, "Memorandum for the Commanding General, Army Ground Forces, July 13, 1942."

11 2nd Lt. T. Mark Radcliffe, in Springer, *Black Devil Brigade*, p. 4.

12 2nd Lt. Radcliffe, in Springer, *Black Devil Brigade*, p. 4.

13 HIA, Burhans Papers, Box 7, Lt. Col. Ken Wickham to the Commanding General, 7th Motorized Division, Camp San Luis Obispo, CA, June 26, 1942.

14 USNARA, NND/740106, "Especially Qualified Personnel" from Fort Ord California, July 1942.

15 Special Forces Roll of Honour, "Thread: Van Ausdale, Howard Clifford," www.specialforcesroh.com/showthread.php?29287-Van -Ausdale-Howard-Clifford.

16 Emails to author from Janice Harshbarger (Ray Holbrook's niece), September 26 and 28, 2017.

17 Bowlby, *Countdown to Cassino*, p. 99.

Chapter 2. "Where you from, soldier?"

1   Story, "Early Days," p. 3.

2   2nd Lt. T. Mark Radcliffe, in Springer, *Black Devil Brigade*, p. 17.

3   Story, "Early Days," p. 1.

4   Story, "Early Days," p. 3.

5   Author interview with Jack Callowhill.

6   Story, "Early Days," p. 3.

7   Sergeant Bill Story, in Springer, *Black Devil Brigade*, p. 18.

8   MacKinnon in Springer, *Black Devil Brigade*, p. 17; Mac-Kinnon, "Memories of the Battle," p. 11.

9   PP, R. W. Becket Papers, Lieutenant Colonel R. W. "Bill" Becket, "The Stars and Jack" (unpublished memoir), pp. 1–24.

10 Becket, "Stars and Jack," p. 24.

11 Anne Hicks, *The Last Fighting General: The Biography of Robert Tryon Frederick* (Atglen, PA: Schiffer Military History, 2006), p. 72.

12 Becket, "Stars and Jack," p. 24; Lieutenant Colonel Robert D. Burhans, *The First Special Service Force: A War History of the North Americans, 1942–1944* (1947; repr., Washington, DC: Battery Press, 1978), p. 15.

13 Becket, "Stars and Jack," pp. 25–6; LAC, RG 24/15301, "Secret War Diary of 2nd Canadian Parachute Battalion," October 29, 1942.

14 HIA, Adleman Papers, Box 8, Press Release by War Department's Bureau of Public Relations, August 6, 1942.

Chapter 3. "Germany First"

1   General Albert C. Wedemeyer, *Wedemeyer Reports!* (New York: Devin-Adair, 1958), pp. 16–17, 97–99.

2   Wedemeyer, *Wedemeyer Reports!*, pp. 15–21, 63–76; Jonathan W. Jordan, *American Warlords: How Roosevelt's High Command Led America to Victory in World War II* (New York: NAL Caliber, 2015), p. 97.

3   Andrew Roberts, *Masters and Commanders: How Roosevelt, Churchill, Marshall and Alanbrooke Won the War in the West* (London: Allen Lane, 2008), pp. 69–70.

4   Max Hastings, *Finest Years: Churchill as Warlord 1940–1945* (2009; repr., London: HarperPress, 2010), p. 239.

5   Roberts, *Masters and Commanders*, pp. 129–30; Stephen E. Ambrose, *Eisenhower: Soldier and President* (1990; repr., New York: Simon & Schuster, 2003), p. 68; "Operations in Western Europe" [Marshall] Memorandum, April 1942, quoted in Winston S. Churchill, *The Second World War*, vol. 4, *The Hinge of Fate* (London: Cassell, 1950), pp. 281–2.

6   Wedemeyer, *Wedemeyer Reports!*, pp. 98–103.

7   Eric Seal, quoted in Hastings, *Finest Years*, p. 182.

8   Wedemeyer, *Wedemeyer Reports!*, p. 103; Roberts, *Masters and Commanders*, p. 141; Churchill, p. 281.

9   Robert E. Sherwood, *White House Papers of Harry L. Hopkins*, vol. 2 (London: Eyre & Spottiswoode, 1949), p. 528.

10 Churchill, *Second World War*, vol. 4, p. 283.

11 Sherwood, *White House Papers*, vol. 2, p. 528.

12 Wedemeyer, *Wedemeyer Reports!*, pp. 104–8.

Chapter 4. The Plough Project

1   Wedemeyer, *Wedemeyer Reports!*, pp. 109–10.

2   London, The National Archives (TNA), CAB 121/179, Mountbatten to the Secretary of the COS Committee, Q/485, April 3,

1942, with enclosures "Mr Pyke's Project" and "Draft of Proposed Telegram to Field Marshal Dill"; TNA, DEFE 2/883, "'Snow Plough'—Résumé of Mr Pyke's Scheme and Action Taken up to This Date," by Brigadier Wildman-Lushington, 21 April 1942.

3   Wedemeyer, *Wedemeyer Reports!*, pp. 111, 116.

4   TNA, DEFE 2/883, Mountbatten to Field Marshal Dill, April 24, 1942.

5   Henry Hemming, *Churchill's Iceman: The True Story of Geoffrey Pyke: Genius, Fugitive, Spy* (London: Preface, 2014), p. 243.

6   TNA, CAB 121/179, "Minutes of a Meeting Held on April 11, 1942, to Consider the SNOW PLOUGH Scheme," drafted by Mountbatten and initialed W.S.C. (Churchill), April 12, 1942.

7   Alex Danchev and Daniel Todman, eds., *War Diaries 1939–1945: Field Marshal Lord Alanbrooke* (London: Weidenfeld & Nicolson, 2001), p. 248.

8   Sherwood, *White House Papers*, vol. 2, p. 547.

Chapter 5. "Push ahead with all possible speed"

1   Marshall, quoted in Hicks, *Last Fighting General*, pp. 62–63.

2   TNA, DEFE 2/883, Mountbatten to Marshall, April 24, 1942; Hemming, *Churchill's Iceman*, pp. 295–6.

3   TNA, DEFE 2/885, "Progress Report—Week Ending May 2, 1942" by Brigadier Duncan; TNA, DEFE 2/883, "Signals April 24th–May 20th, 1942."

4   Duncan, "Progress Report—Week Ending May 2nd, 1942."

5   USNARA, NND/740106, "Memorandum for the Assistant Chief of Staff, Operations Division" by Brig. Gen. R. G. Moses, May 3, 1942.

6   Ambrose, *Eisenhower: Soldier and President*, pp. 15–61.

7   Stephen E. Ambrose, *The Supreme Commander: The War Years of General Dwight D. Eisenhower* (1970; repr., New York: Anchor, 2012), pp. 318–19.

8 USNARA, NND/740106, "Memorandum for the Assistant Chief of Staff, Operations Division" by Col. J. E. Hull, May 7, 1942.

9 USNARA, NND/740106, "Memorandum for the Chief, Future Operations Section" (Col. Hull) by Col. Thomas D. Davis, May 12, 1942.

10 TNA, DEFE 2/886, Pyke to Mountbatten, May 12, 1942; Hemming, *Churchill's Iceman*, pp. 300–301.

11 USNARA, NND/740106, "Memorandum for the Chief of Staff" by Maj. Gen. D. D. Eisenhower, Davis, May 17, 1942.

12 HIA, Frederick Papers, Box 1, "Plough Project Diary: 22 May–20 July 1942" by Lieut. Col. R. T. Frederick; Hicks, *Last Fighting General*, p. 63.

13 Hicks, *Last Fighting General*, pp. 11–31; West Point Association of Graduates (website), http://apps.westpointaog.org/Memorials/Article/8349/.

14 Hicks, *Last Fighting General*, pp. 31–62.

15 TNA, DEFE 2/886, Pyke to Mountbatten, May 14, 1942.

16 Wedemeyer, *Wedemeyer Reports!*, p. 135.

17 "Plough Project Diary: 22 May–20 July 1942" by Frederick; Hicks, *Last Fighting General*, pp. 63–64; Burhans, *First Special Service Force*, p. 9.

Chapter 6. "Frederick, you are now in charge"

1 "Plough Project Diary: 22 May–20 July 1942" by Frederick; Hicks, *Last Fighting General*, p. 64.

2 TNA, DEFE 2/883, "Memorandum by Chief of Combined Operations on the Snow Plough Scheme," undated [early June 1942].

3 "Plough Project Diary: 22 May–20 July 1942" by Frederick.

4 "Plough Project Diary: 22 May–20 July 1942" by Frederick.

5 Hicks, *Last Fighting General*, pp. 65–66.

6 TNA, DEFE 2/886, Pyke to Mountbatten, June 9, 1942.

7 TNA, DEFE 2/886, Pyke to Mountbatten, June 7, 1942.

8   "Plough Project Diary: 22 May–20 July 1942" by Frederick.

9   "Plough Project" directive, June 16, 1942, reproduced in Burhans, *First Special Service Force*, p. 10.

10 USNARA, NND/803119, "Plough Project," order by General Marshall, June 16, 1942.

11 "Plough Project Diary: 22 May–20 July 1942" by Frederick.

12 Hicks, *Last Fighting General*, p. 69.

13 "Plough Project Diary: 22 May–20 July 1942" by Frederick.

14 USNARA, NND/803119, "Constitution and Activation of 1st Special Service Force," July 5, 1942; Hicks, *Last Fighting General*, p. 68.

15 "Plough Project Diary: 22 May–20 July 1942" by Frederick.

Chapter 7. 1-2 Company

1   Author interview with Jack Callowhill.

2   HIA, Frederick Papers, Box 2, "2nd Canadian Parachute Battalion Interim Report," August 15, 1942.

3   "Plough Project Diary: 22 May–20 July 1942" by Frederick.

4   Thomas, "Auburn to Berlin," p. 10.

5   HIA, Frederick Papers, Box 2, "2nd Canadian Parachute Battalion Interim Report," August 15, 1942.

6   Author interview with Jack Callowhill.

7   Thomas, "Auburn to Berlin," p. 11; PP, Sam Boroditsky Papers, "Sam Boroditsky's War" (unpublished manuscript), p. 5.

8   Crichlow, "Questionnaire About Military Service."

9   Author interview with Jack Callowhill.

10 HIA, Frederick Papers, "2nd Canadian Parachute Battalion Interim Report," August 15, 1942.

11 PP, Ray Holbrook Papers, Pvt. Ray Holbrook to his sister Gladys, August 23, 1942.

12 Walter Lewis, in Springer, *Black Devil Brigade*, p. 22.

13 Joe Dauphinais, in Springer, *Black Devil Brigade*, p. 23.

14 Author interview with Jack Callowhill.

15 Nicholson, "Report No. 5," pp. 9–10.

16 Author interview with Shirley Long (Lorin Waling's younger sister), October 19, 2017.

17 PP, Lorin Waling Papers, Lorin Waling to his mother, July 5, 1942.

18 Pvt. Lorin Waling, in Springer, *Black Devil Brigade*, p. 10.

19 PP, Lorin Waling Papers, Lorin Waling to his mother, August 30, 1942.

20 Ken Joyce, "A Case of Differentiation: The Story of Colonel Donald Dobie Williamson, Officer Commanding the First Canadian Special Service Battalion/1st Special Service Force, 1942–1944," pp. 1–5, accessed August 9, 2018, https://nebula.wsimg.com /c87ccca6603034a6951f7e6974439b7a?AccessKeyId= BC21553F553BBD27F066&disposition=0&alloworigin=1.

21 Author interviews with Nathan Gordon (Tom's grandson), September 10, 2017, and January 9, 2018; https://www.sac.on.ca /page/upper-school/cadet-corps/corps-history/awards-for-best-upper-school-cadet.

22 Pvt. Ken Betts, in Springer, *Black Devil Brigade*, p. 7.

23 Crichlow, "Questionnaire About Military Service."

24 PP, Sharyn DeCamp Jones Papers, "1-2 Company History" (unpublished), p. 1.

25 Author interview with Jack Callowhill.

26 Burhans, *First Special Service Force*, pp. 23–24.

27 Nicholson, "Report No. 5," p. 12.

28 Lorin Waling and Walter Lewis, in Springer, *Black Devil Brigade*, pp. 25–26.

29 HIA, Burhans Papers, Box 19, "Monthly Report of 2nd Cdn Parachute Bn," September 30, 1942.

Chapter 8. "Everybody fought somebody"

1 PP, Ray Holbrook Papers, Pvt. Ray Holbrook to his sister Gladys, August 23, 1942.

2 Ottawa, Department of National Defence Directorate of History and Heritage (DHH), 145.3009 (D4), "Monthly Reports of Canadian Special Service Battalion, August 1942–January 1945," October 31, 1942; Author interview with Jack Callowhill.

3 Story, "Early Days," p. 11.

4 HIA, Frederick Papers, Box 1, "Plough Project Diary: August 9th–October 13th, 1942" by Colonel R. T. Frederick; Story, "Early Days," p. 11.

5 HIA, Burhans Papers, Box 21, "Principal German Infantry Weapons," undated.

6 PP, Ray Holbrook Papers, Pvt. Ray Holbrook to his sister Gladys, August 23, 1942.

7 Joe Dauphinais, in Springer, *Black Devil Brigade*, p. 32.

8 USNARA, NND/740106, "Memorandum for Major Baldwin: Production of Poisonous Darts" by Major Burhans, August 6, 1942.

9 Patrick Ryan, "America's Deadliest Irishman—the Irish James Bond," IrishCentral, October 14, 2016, https://www.irish-central.com/roots/history/americas-deadliest-irishman-the-irish-james-bond; "Plough Project Diary: 22 May–20 July 1942" by Frederick.

10 Bill Story, in Springer, *Black Devil Brigade*, p. 35; Ryan, "America's Deadliest Irishman."

11 Bill Story, in Springer, *Black Devil Brigade*, p. 35.

12 Adams, quoted in Hicks, *Last Fighting General*, p. 72.

13 Joe Glass, in Springer, *Black Devil Brigade*, p. 36.

14 PP, Lorin Waling Papers, Lorin Waling to his mother, August 30, 1942.

15 PP, Lorin Waling Papers, Lorin Waling to his mother, August 30, 1942.

16 Joe Dauphinais, in Springer, *Black Devil Brigade*, p. 27.

17 PP, Lorin Waling Papers, Lorin Waling to his mother, August 30, 1942.

18 Story, "Early Days," p. 6.

19 Kenneth Betts, in Springer, *Black Devil Brigade*, p. 44.

20 Bill Story, in Springer, *Black Devil Brigade*, p. 45.

21 Lorin Waling, in Springer, *Black Devil Brigade*, p. 45; Author interview with Jack Callowhill.

22 Joe Dauphinais, in Springer, *Black Devil Brigade*, pp. 45–46.

23 Joe Dauphinais, in Springer, *Black Devil Brigade*, pp. 41–42.

24 Author interview with Jack Callowhill.

25 Crichlow, "Questionnaire About Military Service."

26 Crichlow, "Questionnaire About Military Service."

27 Thomas, "Auburn to Berlin," p. 33.

Chapter 9. Waling and Glass

1 PP, Lorin Waling Papers, Waling to his mother, September 24, 1942; John Nadler, *A Perfect Hell: The True Story of the Black Devils, the Forefathers of the Special Forces* (2005; repr., New York: Ballantine/Presidio, 2006), p. 64.

2 PP, Joe Glass Papers, "From Joe Glass to His Children, October 14, 1991," pp. 1–5; Cpl. Joe Glass, in Springer, *Black Devil Brigade*, p. 13.

3 Author interview with Shirley Long, younger sister of Lorin Waling; Nadler, *A Perfect Hell*, p. 64.

4 Author interview with Cheryl, Jerry, Dave and Valerie Waling, Sacramento, CA, August 13, 2017.

5 PP, Lorin Waling Papers, Waling to his mother, August 30, 1942.

6 Thomas, "Auburn to Berlin," pp. 5–32.

7 USNARA, NND/740106, "Captain Touchette to the Commanding General, SOS," September 14, 1942 and SO No. 149, HQ Engr. Sch., September 15, 1942; PP, Lawrence Piette Papers, Dan Piette, "Biography of Lawrence J. Piette, Captain, First Special Service Force"; Larry Piette, in Springer, *Black Devil Brigade*, p. 5.

Chapter 10. "Suspend effort on present line"

1   HIA, Frederick Papers, Box 1, "Plough Project Diary: August 9th to October 13th, 1942" by Col. R. T. Frederick; Hicks, *Last Fighting General*, pp. 77–78.

2   "Plough Project Diary: August 9th to October 13th, 1942" by Col. R. T. Frederick; Kenneth H. Joyce, *Snow Plough and the Jupiter Deception: The True Story of the 1st Special Service Force and the 1st Canadian Special Service Battalion, 1942–1945* (St. Catharines, Ont.: Vanwell, 2006), p. 88; TNA, CAB 121/179, "Plough Scheme," Extract from COS (42), 130th Meeting, September 28, 1942.

3   "Plough Project Diary: August 9th to October 13th, 1942" by Col. R. T. Frederick; HIA, Frederick Papers, Box 8, General Hansteen to Colonel Frederick, September 18, 1942.

4   TNA, CAB 122/659, Gubbins to Brig. Vivian Dykes, January 4, 1943.

5   TNA, CAB 122/659, Commander R. D. Coleridge, RN, to Gubbins, January 30, 1943.

6   TNA, DEFE 2/887, Wildman-Lushington to Wedderburn, September 28, 1942; TNA, CAB 121/179, "Plough Scheme," Extract from COS (42), 130th Meeting, September 28, 1942.

7   HIA, Frederick Papers, Box 1, Priority Message from Frederick to Burhans, September 26, 1942.

8   Hicks, *Last Fighting General*, p. 79.

9   TNA, CAB 122/659, Gubbins to Brigadier Vivian Dykes, January 4, 1943.

10 Hicks, *Last Fighting General*, pp. 79–80.

11 USNARA, NND/803119, "McNarney to the Commanding General, Army Ground Forces, October 15, 1942."

12 USNARA, NND/740106, "Marshall to Major-General Pope, Canadian Army Staff, Washington DC, October 17, 1942."

13 Joyce, *Snow Plough*, p. 90.

Chapter 11. "They blew up bridges, culverts and everything"

1   PP, Thomas Papers, Thomas, "Auburn to Berlin," p. 33.

2   Crichlow, "Questionnaire About Military Service."

3   Burhans, *First Special Service Force*, p. 23.

4   HIA, Burhans Papers, Box 19, "Monthly Report of 2nd Cdn Parachute Bn," September 30, 1942.

5   Joe Dauphinais and Joe Glass, in Springer, *Black Devil Brigade*, pp. 30–31.

6   Becket, "Stars and Jack," pp. 38–39.

7   LAC, RG 24/15301, "Secret War Diary of 2nd Canadian Parachute Battalion," October 5–9, 1942; Nadler, *A Perfect Hell*, pp. 65–66; Hicks, *Last Fighting General*, p. 75.

8   Walter Lewis, in Springer, *Black Devil Brigade*, p. 31.

9   LAC, RG 24/15301, "Secret War Diary of 2nd Canadian Parachute Battalion," October 7–12, 1942.

10 Crichlow, "Questionnaire About Military Service."

11 Author interview with Jack Callowhill.

12 LAC, RG 24/15301, "Secret War Diary of 2nd Canadian Parachute Battalion," October 13, 1942.

13 Ken Beaton, *A Toddler's Picture in his Uncle's Helmet* (ebook, 2018), Chapter 9; Special Forces Roll of Honour, "Thread: Deyette, Harry N.", www.specialforcesroh.com/showthread.php?3252-DeyetteHarry-N.

14 Author interview with Sharyn DeCamp Jones (Clarence DeCamp's daughter), August 11, 2017.

15 Crichlow, "Questionnaire About Military Service."

16 HIA, Burhans Papers, Box 19, "Monthly Report of 2nd Cdn Parachute Bn," September 30, 1942.

17 LAC, RG 24/15301, "Secret War Diary of 2nd Canadian Parachute Battalion," September 29–30, 1942.

18 LAC, RG 24/15301, "Secret War Diary of 2nd Canadian Parachute Battalion," October 15 and 30, 1942.

Chapter 12. "A very special Force"

1 USNARA, NND/803119, "Memorandum for the Chief of Staff, Army Ground Forces" by Lt. Col. Ridgely Gaither, Special Projects Branch, AGF, September 24, 1942.

2 Colonel Bernd Horn and Michel Wyczynski, *Of Courage and Determination: The First Special Service Force, "The Devil's Brigade," 1942–44* (Toronto: Dundurn, 2013), p. 132.

3 LAC, RG 24/15301, "Secret War Diary of 2nd Canadian Parachute Battalion," October 21, 1942.

4 Horn and Wyczynski, *Of Courage and Determination*, p. 132.

5 HIA, Burhans Papers, Box 7, 2nd Lt. John H. Richardson to Adjutant General, US Army, "Request for Transfer to Military Intelligence Service," October 24, 1942.

6 HIA, Burhans Papers, Box 7, Col. R. T. Frederick to the Adjutant General, US Army, October 27, 1942.

7 TNA, CAB 120/416, Secret Cypher Telegram from Dill to the Chiefs of Staff, JSM 437, October 23, 1942.

8 TNA, CAB 120/416, Prime Minister's Personal Minute for the Chiefs of Staff, M493/2, October 26, 1942.

9 TNA, CAB 120/416, Most Secret and Personal Cypher Telegram from Churchill to Roosevelt, No. 177, October 30, 1942.

10 TNA, CAB 120/416, Most Secret and Personal Cypher Telegram from Roosevelt to Churchill, No. 223, December 2, 1942.

11 USNARA, NND/803119, "Conference with Col. Frederick, First Special Service Force," HQ Army Ground Forces Memo, October 31, 1942.

12 TNA, CAB 122/659, Lt. Gen. Joseph T. McNarney to Dill, November 13, 1942.

13 TNA, CAB 120/416, Secret Cypher Telegram from Dill to Chiefs of Staff, November 16, 1942.

14 TNA, CAB 121/179, Extract from COS (42) 184th Meeting, November 17, 1942.

15 TNA, CAB 120/416, Secret Cypher Telegram from Chiefs of Staff to Dill, November 18, 1942.

16 TNA, CAB 122/659, Dill to McNarney, November 18, 1942, and McNarney to Dill, November 20, 1942.

17 TNA, CAB 122/659, Dill to McNarney, November 21, 1942.

18 TNA, CAB 121/179, Extract from COS (42) 326th Meeting, November 24, 1942; TNA, CAB 120/416, Personal and Most Secret Cypher Telegram from Churchill to Dill, T1599/2, November 26, 1942.

19 TNA, CAB 120/416, Secret Cypher Telegram from Dill to Chiefs of Staff, JSM 567, December 15, 1942.

20 TNA, WO 106/1974, Most Secret Cypher Telegram from Chiefs of Staff to Dill, COW (W) 398, December 21, 1942, and Most Secret Cypher Telegram from Dill to Chiefs of Staff, JSM 601, December 22, 1942.

Chapter 13. "The battle of the slabs"

1 USNARA, NND/803119, Col. R. T. Frederick to Commanding General, Army Ground Forces, November 24, 1942.

2 LAC, RG 24/15301, "Secret War Diary of 2nd Canadian Parachute Battalion," November 28–29, 1942.

3 LAC, RG 24/15301, "Secret War Diary of 2nd Canadian Parachute Battalion," December 2, 1942.

4 Becket, "Stars and Jack," p. 29.

5 DHH, 145.3009 (D4), "Monthly Reports of 1st Canadian Special Service Battalion, August 1942–January 1945," January, 1943.

6 HIA, Frederick Papers, Box 2, Frederick's "Christmas Greetings" to the men, December 24, 1942.

7 Thomas, "Auburn to Berlin," p. 35.

8 Crichlow, "Questionnaire About Military Service."

9 LAC, RG 24/15301, "Secret War Diary of 2nd Canadian Parachute Battalion," November 28–29, 1942; 2nd Lt. Walford Michaelson, in Springer, *Black Devil Brigade*, p. 38.

10 Larry Piette, in Springer, *Black Devil Brigade*, p. 38.

11 Joe Dauphinais, in Springer, *Black Devil Brigade*, p. 38.

12 Crichlow, "Questionnaire About Military Service."

13 Joe Dauphinais, in Springer, *Black Devil Brigade*, p. 38.

14 Burhans, *First Special Service Force*, p. 49.

15 Hicks, *Last Fighting General*, p. 83.

16 Crichlow, "Questionnaire About Military Service."

17 Nadler, *A Perfect Hell*, pp. 88–89; PP, Tom MacWilliam Papers, Letter from Sgt. J. K. O'Brien, 2-2 Company, undated.

18 Nadler, *A Perfect Hell*, p. 89.

19 Burhans, *First Special Service Force*, p. 49.

20 PP, Richard Daigle Papers, Ken Beaton, "A Tale of Two Uncles," pp. 5–14.

21 Stephen E. Ambrose, *Band of Brothers: E Company, 506th Regiment, 101st Airborne from Normandy to Hitler's Eagle's Nest* (2001; repr., London: Simon & Schuster, 2016), pp. 23–33.

22 Beaton, "A Tale of Two Uncles," pp. 13–14.

23 Burhans, *First Special Service Force*, p. 47.

Chapter 14. "Their chance will come"

1 Joe Dauphinais and Donald MacKinnon, in Springer, *Black Devil Brigade*, p. 40.

2 Author interview with Jack Callowhill.

3 TNA, DEFE 2/885, Captain Knox, RN, to Mountbatten, January 19, 1943.

4 Roberts, *Masters and Commanders*, pp. 316–34; Rick Atkinson, *The Day of Battle: The War in Sicily and Italy, 1943–1944* (London: Little, Brown, 2007), pp. 6–7.

5 Roberts, *Masters and Commanders*, pp. 334–35.

6 HIA, Frederick Papers, Box 2, Major General Handy's Memorandum for the Deputy Chief of Staff, February 8th, 1943; TNA, CAB 122/659, Classified Incoming Message from Algiers to Agwar, No. 8532, February 2, 1943.

7 TNA, CAB 122/659, Classified Cipher from Marshall to Lieutenant General Andrews, R-5754, February 10, 1943.

8 TNA, CAB 122/659, Classified Cipher from Andrews to Marshall, No. 7202, February 12, 1943.

9 TNA, CAB 122/659, Classified Cipher from Marshall to Andrews, R-5887, February 15, 1943.

10 TNA, CAB 122/659, Classified Cipher from Andrews to Marshall, No. 7396, February 20, 1943.

11 TNA, WO 106/1974, Most Secret Cipher Telegram from Marshall to Mountbatten, R-6066, February 21, 1943.

12 TNA, WO 106/1974, Most Secret Cipher Telegram from Mountbatten to Marshall, No. 7568, February 27, 1943.

13 Text of Eisenhower's February 27 cable in TNA, WO 106/1974, Most Secret Cipher Telegram from Dill to the Chiefs of Staff, JSM 781, March 4, 1943.

14 TNA, WO 106/1974, Most Secret Cipher Telegram from Dill to the Chiefs of Staff, JSM 774, March 3, 1943.

15 TNA, WO 120/416, Most Secret Cipher Telegram from Churchill to Dill, OZ. 659, March 5, 1943.

16 TNA, WO 120/416, Secret Cipher Telegram from Chiefs of Staff to Dill, OZ. 660, March 5, 1943.

17 TNA, WO 120/416, Most Secret Cipher Telegram from Dill to Churchill, IZ. 933, March 6, 1943.

18 TNA, WO 120/416, Personal Telegram from Churchill to Dill, T. 275/3, March 7, 1943.

19 DHH, 145.3009 (D4), "Monthly Reports of 1st Canadian Special Service Battalion, August 1942–January 1945," March 4, 1943.

20 Author interview with Jack Callowhill.

21 Story, "Early Days," p. 12.

22 Sam Byrne to his father, February 28, 1943, in Mark J. Nelson, *With the Black Devils: A Soldier's World War II Account with the First Special Service Force and the 82nd Airborne* (Atglen, PA: Schiffer Military History, 2004), p. 23.

23 Sam Byrne to his family, March 28, 1943, in Nelson, *With the Black Devils*, p. 24.

24 HIA, Frederick Papers, Box 2, Lt. Col. Alfred F. Biles, Post Commander, to Governor, Mayor and Commissioners, February 18, 1943.

25 HIA, Frederick Papers, Box 2, Paul T. Keller, Police Judge in Helena, to Lt. Col. Alfred F. Biles, February 24, 1943.

26 LAC, RG 24/15301, "Secret War Diary of 2nd Canadian Parachute Battalion," February 12, 1943.

27 Nadler, *A Perfect Hell*, p. 90; PP, Joe Glass Papers, "From Joe Glass to His Children, October 14, 1991," p. 5.

28 Nadler, *A Perfect Hell*, p. 90.

29 Burhans, *First Special Service Force*, p. 52.

30 DHH, 145.3009 (D4), "Monthly Reports of 1st Canadian Special Service Battalion, August 1942–January 1945," April 8, 1943; LAC, RG 24/15301, "Secret War Diary of 2nd Canadian Parachute Battalion," April 5, 1943.

31 PP, Ray Holbrook Papers, Holbrook to his sister Gladys, March 29, 1943.

Chapter 15. "We had a crazy bunch of guys"

1 LAC, RG 24/15301, "Secret War Diary of 2nd Canadian Parachute Battalion," April 6, 1943; Burhans, *First Special Service Force*, pp. 52–53.

2 HIA, Frederick Papers, Box 2, John Haytin (and Committee) to Frederick, April 7, 1942.

3 LAC, RG 24/15301, "Secret War Diary of 2nd Canadian Parachute Battalion," April 11–15, 1943; Nadler, *A Perfect Hell*, p. 92.

4 Burhans, *First Special Service Force*, p. 53.

5 Author interview with Jack Callowhill.

6 Burhans, *First Special Service Force*, p. 55.

7 LAC, RG 24/15301, "Secret War Diary of 2nd Canadian Parachute Battalion," April 25, 1943; DeCamp Jones Papers, "1-2 Company History," p. 3; Burhans, *First Special Service Force*, pp. 55–56.

8   Kenneth Betts, in Springer, *Black Devil Brigade*, pp. 49–50.

9   HIA, Frederick Papers, Box 2, Report of Training of 1st Special Service Force by Col. Louis. B. Ely, May 7, 1943; HIA, Frederick Papers, Box 2, Col. Elbert W. Martin, officer in charge of amphibious training, to Col. Louis B. Ely, May 3, 1943.

10   DeCamp Jones Papers, "1-2 Company History," p. 3.

11   Crichlow, "Questionnaire About Military Service."

12   PP, Tom Gordon Papers, Nathan Gordon interview with Joe Glass, undated.

Chapter 16. "The objective now was perfection"

1   Burhans, *First Special Service Force*, p. 56.

2   LAC, RG 24/15301, "Secret War Diary of 2nd Canadian Parachute Battalion," May 22–23, 1943.

3   Burhans, *First Special Service Force*, p. 56.

4   Nelson, *With the Black Devils*, p. 29.

5   Boroditsky Papers, "Sam Boroditsky's War," p. 9.

6   USNARA, NND/740106, Baldwin to the Assistant Chief of Staff, S-4, February 15, 1943; NND/740106, Chief of the Bureau of Ordnance to the QM, US Marine Corps, April 20, 1943; Crichlow, "Questionnaire About Military Service."

7   Beaton, "A Tale of Two Uncles," p. 20.

8   Crichlow, "Questionnaire About Military Service."

9   Nadler, *A Perfect Hell*, p. 92; PP, Tom MacWilliam Papers, Last Will of Thomas Cail MacWilliam, February 9, 1943.

10   TNA, CAB 121/179, Churchill's Minute to the COS Committee on "Future Strategy," April 18, 1943.

11   TNA, CAB 121/179, "Snow Plough—Progress Report" by Brigadier Wildman-Lushington, April 22, 1943.

12   HIA, Frederick Papers, Box 2, "Memorandum for General Wedemeyer," May 12, 1943.

13   HIA, Frederick Papers, Box 2, "Memorandum for the Chief of Staff" by Brigadier General Wedemeyer, May 20, 1943.

14 TNA, WO 106/1974, "Extract from 6th Meeting at the White House, Washington," May 25, 1943, COS (43) 281 (0), Trident, 6th Meeting, Item 8.

15 Burhans, *First Special Service Force*, p. 57.

16 TNA, CAB 122/659, "Message to British Chiefs of Staff re Operation Against Kiska," June 8, 1943.

17 TNA, CAB 120/416, Copy of Minute by the Prime Minister, June 9, 1943.

18 TNA, WO 106/1974, Extract from the minutes of the COS(43)101 meeting held on June 9, 1943.

19 TNA, CAB 120/416, Most Secret Cypher Telegram from Chiefs of Staff to Dill, OZ 1620, June 9, 1943.

20 Burhans, *First Special Service Force*, p. 57; Hicks, *Last Fighting General*, p. 88.

21 Burhans, *First Special Service Force*, p. 57.

22 Hicks, *Last Fighting General*, p. 88.

23 Burhans, *First Special Service Force*, p. 58; Author interview with Jack Callowhill.

24 Burhans, *First Special Service Force*, p. 58.

25 Beaton, "A Tale of Two Uncles," p. 20.

26 Burhans, *First Special Service Force*, p. 58.

27 Becket, "Stars and Jack," p. 40.

Chapter 17. "We want to take as many prisoners as possible"

1 Burhans, *First Special Service Force*, p. 59; LAC, RG 24/15301, "Secret War Diary of 2nd Canadian Parachute Battalion," July 1–4, 1943.

2 Burhans, *First Special Service Force*, p. 59.

3 LAC, RG 24/15301, "Secret War Diary of 2nd Canadian Parachute Battalion," July 4–9, 1943; Burhans, *First Special Service Force*, p. 59.

4 Burhans, *First Special Service Force*, pp. 59–60; LAC, RG 24/15301, "Secret War Diary of 2nd Canadian Parachute Battalion," July 9–11, 1943; Thomas, "Auburn to Berlin," p. 37.

5 Thomas, "Auburn to Berlin," p. 37.

6   Walter Lewis and Joe Dauphinais, in Springer, *Black Devil Brigade*, p. 54.

7   Author interview with Jack Callowhill; Thomas, "Auburn to Berlin," p. 37; LAC, RG 24/15301, "Secret War Diary of 2nd Canadian Parachute Battalion," July 13, 1943.

8   LAC, RG 24/15301, "Secret War Diary of 2nd Canadian Parachute Battalion," July 14, 1943; Walter Lewis, in Springer, *Black Devil Brigade*, p. 53.

9   Burhans, *First Special Service Force*, pp. 64–65; Hicks, *Last Fighting General*, p. 89; Horn and Wyczynski, pp. 145–46.

10 Burhans, *First Special Service Force*, p. 65; DeCamp Jones Papers, "1-2 Company History," p. 4.

11 Burhans, *First Special Service Force*, p. 65; Boroditsky Papers, "Sam Boroditsky's War," p. 13; Thomas, "Auburn to Berlin," p. 40.

12 Thomas, "Auburn to Berlin," p. 38.

13 DeCamp Jones Papers, "1-2 Company History," p. 4.

14 Horn & Wyczynski, Chapter 9, "Kiska: The Battle That Never Was"; Nicholson, "Report: No. 5," pp. 24–25.

15 Thomas, "Auburn to Berlin," p. 39.

16 Becket, "Stars and Jack," pp. 43–44.

Chapter 18. Kiska

1   Becket, "Stars and Jack," pp. 45–48.

2   Thomas, "Auburn to Berlin," p. 39; Crichlow, "Questionnaire About Military Service."

3   Thomas, "Auburn to Berlin," p. 39; Burhans, *First Special Service Force*, p. 76.

4   DeCamp Jones Papers, "1-2 Company History," p. 5; Piette, "Biography of Lawrence J. Piette," p. 6; Thomas, "Auburn to Berlin," p. 39; Author interview with Jack Callowhill.

5   Thomas, "Auburn to Berlin," pp. 39–40.

6   Hicks, *Last Fighting General*, pp. 90–91; Burhans, *First Special Service Force*, p. 74.

7   Becket, "Stars and Jack," pp. 48–49.

8   Nicholson, "Report No. 5," pp. 26–27; HIA, Burhans Papers, Box 1, S-1 Journal, August 15, 1943.

9   HIA, Adleman Papers, Box 12, "Diary of Sergeant A. W. Ovenden," 3-1 Company.

10 Burhans, *First Special Service Force*, pp. 76–78, 69.

11 George L. MacGarrigle, "Aleutian Islands: The US Army Campaign of World War II," accessed May 28, 2018, https://history.army.mil/brochures/aleut/aleut.htm.

12 Nicholson, "Report No. 5," pp. 27–28.

13 Burhans, *First Special Service Force*, p. 82.

Chapter 19. "Picked men of first-class physique"

1   Martin Gilbert, *Winston S. Churchill: Road to Victory, 1941–1945* (London: Heinemann, 1986), p. 462; Ziegler, *Mountbatten*, p. 216.

2   Winston S. Churchill, *The Second World War*, vol. 5, *Closing the Ring* (London: Cassell, 1952), p. 67; Hastings Ismay, quoted in Gilbert, *Winston S. Churchill*, p. 463.

3   Churchill, *Second World War*, vol. 5, p. 69.

4   Ziegler, *Mountbatten*, p. 217.

5   TNA, CAB 120/416, "Use of the Plough Force: Memorandum by the Chief of Combined Operations," August 8, 1943.

6   Gilbert, *Winston S. Churchill*, pp. 470–71.

7   TNA, CAB 120/416, "Use of the Plough Force," COS Committee meeting, August 13, 1943.

8   Churchill, *Second World War*, vol. 5, p. 74.

9   TNA, CAB 120/416, "Use of the Plough Force," JPS Report, August 18, 1943; TNA, CAB 120/416, "The Plough Force," Memorandum by the British Chiefs of Staff, August 18, 1943.

10 TNA, CAB 120/416, "Use of 'Plough' Force," Item 5 of the 112th meeting of the Combined Chiefs of Staff, August 19,

1943; TNA, CAB 120/416, Secret Cipher Telegram from the Combined Chiefs of Staff to Eisenhower and Morgan, August 24, 1943.

11 Ziegler, *Mountbatten*, pp. 217, 220–22.

12 Churchill, *Second World War*, vol. 5, p. 81.

13 Ziegler, *Mountbatten*, pp. 210–11.

Chapter 20. "We had a swell 3 decker cake"

1   Burhans, *First Special Service Force*, p. 80.

2   DeCamp Jones Papers, "1-2 Company History," p. 5.

3   Hicks, *Last Fighting General*, p. 94.

4   HIA, Frederick Papers, Box 2, Major General Charles H. Corlett to the Adjutant General, August 24, 1943.

5   Ken Beaton, "The Devil's Brigade in Vermont," *Burlington Free Press*, December 3, 2018, https://eu.burlingtonfreepress.com /story/news/local/2018/12/03/history-space-devils-brigade-vermont/38653579/ [accessed December 6, 2018].

6   PP, Ray Holbrook Papers, Holbrook to his sister Gladys, August 23, 1942.

7   Author interview with Shirley Long.

8   PP, Lorin Waling Papers, Waling to his mother and siblings, September 21, 1942.

9   Author interview with Dave Waling, Sacramento, CA, August 13, 2017.

10 PP, Lorin Waling Papers, Waling to his mother and siblings, September 21, 1942.

11 Author interviews with John Hart (Geoffrey's son), Sacramento, CA, August 11 and 13, 2017; PP, Geoffrey Hart Papers, Geoffrey Arthur William Hart, "Canadian Army World War II Service Records," pp. 2–4, 9, 11.

12 Joe Dauphinais, in Springer, *Black Devil Brigade*, p. 63.

13 Thomas, "Auburn to Berlin," p. 41.

14 Hicks, *Last Fighting General*, p. 94.

15 USNARA, NND/803119, Adjutant General to Commanding Officer, Fort Ethan Allen, October 6, 1943.

16 Gilbert, *Winston S. Churchill*, p. 496.

Chapter 21. "This excellent and specially trained force"

1 TNA, WO 106/1974, Secret Cipher Telegram from Eisenhower to the Combined Chiefs of Staff, September 8, 1943.

2 TNA, WO 106/1974, Secret Cipher Telegram from Wilson to Eisenhower, September 10, 1943.

3 Gilbert, *Winston S. Churchill*, p. 491.

4 TNA, CAB 122/659, "Use of Plough Force," Agenda 8 of the Meeting in the White House, September 11, 1943.

5 TNA, WO 204/1532, Secret Cipher Telegram from Maj. Gen. Lowell W. Rooks, Assistant Chief of Staff, AFHQ, to Marshall, September 13, 1943.

6 TNA, WO 106/1974, "'Plough' Force," Minutes of the Chiefs of Staff Committee, No. 217th, September 16, 1943.

7 TNA, CAB 121/179, Secret Cipher Cable from Morgan to the Combined Chiefs of Staff, September 16, 1943.

8 TNA, WO 106/1974, Secret Cipher Telegram from the Combined Chiefs of Staff to Eisenhower, September 17, 1943.

9 PP, Lorin Waling Papers, Waling to his mother and siblings, October 13, 1943.

10 Thomas, "Auburn to Berlin," p. 41.

11 PP, Tom MacWilliam Papers, Tom MacWilliam to Mr. Robinson (father-in-law), October 26, 1943.

12 Beaton, "A Tale of Two Uncles," pp. 20–26.

13 Boroditsky Papers, "Sam Boroditsky's War," p. 2.

14 Nicholson, "Report No. 5," p. 33.

15 PP, Lorin Waling Papers, Waling to his mother and siblings, October 22, 1943.

Chapter 22. The *Empress of Scotland*

1   Becket, "Stars and Jack," p. 54; HIA, Frederick Papers, Box 2, "Troops Embarked on MR-632 Empress of Scotland," October 29, 1943; Author interview with Jack Callowhill.

2   DHH, 145.3009 (D4), "Monthly Reports of Canadian Special Service Battalion, August 1942–January 1945," October 27, 1943.

3   HIA, Frederick Papers, Box 2, "Troops Embarked on MR-632 Empress of Scotland," October 29, 1943; HIA Frederick Papers, Box 2, "Embarkation Uniform, Equipment," October 23, 1943.

4   William R. Lewis, *GI Blue: An MP's Journey Through WWII* (Bloomington, IN: iUniverse, 2010), pp. 15–16.

5   "The Canadian Pacific Liner 'Empress of Scotland' (ex 'Empress of Japan')," accessed June 6, 2018, http://www.liverpoolships.org /empress_of_scotland_canadian_pacific.html; Lewis, *GI Blue*, p. 16.

6   Adleman Papers, "Diary of Sergeant A. W. Ovenden."

7   Crichlow, "Questionnaire About Military Service"; Thomas, "Auburn to Berlin," p. 41; Becket, "Stars and Jack," p. 55.

8   Thomas, "Auburn to Berlin," p. 41; Author interview with Jack Callowhill.

9   Boroditsky Papers, "Sam Boroditsky's War," p. 3.

10 Lewis, *GI Blue*, p. 18; Boroditsky Papers, "Sam Boroditsky's War," pp. 3–4.

11 Lewis, *GI Blue*, p. 18.

12 DeCamp Jones Papers, "1-2 Company History," p. 5; Thomas, "Auburn to Berlin," p. 41; LAC, RG 24/15301, "Secret War Diary of 2nd Canadian Parachute Battalion," November 1, 1943.

13 Becket, "Stars and Jack," p. 55.

14 LAC, RG 24/15301, "Secret War Diary of 2nd Canadian Parachute Battalion," November 3, 1943.

15 LAC, RG 24/15301, "Secret War Diary of 2nd Canadian Parachute Battalion," November 4–5, 1943; Author interview with Jack Callowhill; Boroditsky Papers, "Sam Boroditsky's War," p. 6.

16   Author interview with Jack Callowhill; Boroditsky Papers, "Sam Boroditsky's War," p. 6; Piette, "Biography of Lawrence J. Piette."

17   TNA, WO 204/1532, Memorandum by Major General Lowell W. Rooks, G-3, AFHQ, on "Arrival of 1st Special Service Force (Plough Force)," November 2, 1943.

18   TNA, WO 204/1532, Memorandum by Lt. Col. T. J. Conway, G-3 (Plans), AFHQ, on "Movement of Plough Force," October 4, 1943; General Mark W. Clark, *Calculated Risk: His Personal Story of the War in North Africa and Italy* (London: Harrap, 1951), pp. 227–28.

19   Author interview with Jack Callowhill.

20   Author interview with Jack Callowhill.

21   Nelson, *With the Black Devils*, p. 44; Hicks, *Last Fighting General*, p. 95; Piette, "Biography of Lawrence J. Piette."

22   Becket, "Stars and Jack," p. 56.

23   Becket, "Stars and Jack," p. 57.

24   Crichlow, "Questionnaire About Military Service."

Chapter 23. "There was utter destruction"

1   HIA, Burhans Papers, Box 2, 1st Special Service Force Field Order No. 13, November 11, 1943; Nelson, *With the Black Devils*, p. 44; Becket, "Stars and Jack," p. 58.

2   HIA, Burhans Papers, Box 2, 1st Special Service Force Field Order No. 13, November 11, 1943; Nelson, *With the Black Devils*, p. 44; Becket, "Stars and Jack," p. 58; The Rohna Survivors Memorial Association, "History," accessed June 12, 2018, https://rohnasurvivors.org/history/.

3   Clark, *Calculated Risk*, pp. 207, 210.

4   Crichlow, "Questionnaire About Military Service"; Nelson, *With the Black Devils*, p. 45.

5   Author interview with Jack Callowhill.

6   Burhans, *First Special Service Force*, p. 88; Boroditsky Papers, "Sam Boroditsky's War," p. 16.

7   Burhans, *First Special Service Force*, pp. 87–8; Author interview with Jack Callowhill.

8   Atkinson, *Day of Battle*, p. 373.

9   Clark, *Calculated Risk*, p. 221.

10   Martin Blumenson, *The Patton Papers: 1940–1945* (Boston: Houghton Mifflin, 1974), p. 258.

11   Atkinson, *Day of Battle*, p. 183.

12   Atkinson, *Day of Battle*, p. 226; Ambrose, *Supreme Commander*, pp. 270–7.

13   Saul David, *Mutiny at Salerno 1943: An Injustice Exposed*, (1995: repr., London: Brassey's, 2005), pp. 7–8.

14   Clark, *Calculated Risk*, p. 201.

15   Ambrose, *Eisenhower: Soldier and President*, p. 109.

16   Clark, *Calculated Risk*, pp. 202–3.

17   Dwight D. Eisenhower, *Crusade in Europe* (1948; repr., Baltimore: Johns Hopkins University Press, 1997), pp. 202–3.

18   Clark, *Calculated Risk*, pp. 204, 220.

19   David Nichols, ed., *Ernie's War: The Best of Ernie Pyle's World War II Dispatches* (New York: Random House, 1986), pp. 172–73.

Chapter 24. The Winter Line

1   B. H. Liddell Hart, ed., *The Rommel Papers* (1953; repr., London: Arrow, 1987), pp. 427–32.

2   Ian Kershaw, *Hitler: A Biography*, vol. 2 (London: Allen Lane, 2000), pp. 395–96.

3   Liddell Hart, *Rommel Papers*, pp. 431–32.

4   Kershaw, *Hitler*, vol. 2, pp. 595–96; Liddell Hart, *Rommel Papers*, pp. 431–32; David Fraser, *Knight's Cross: A Life of Field Marshal Erwin Rommel* (1993; repr., London: HarperCollins, 1994), p. 441.

5   Liddell Hart, *Rommel Papers*, p. 432.

6   Fraser, *Knight's Cross*, p. 442.

7   Liddell Hart, *The Rommel Papers*, pp. 438–40.

8   Fraser, *Knight's Cross*, p. 446.

9   General Siegfried Westphal, *The German Army in the West* (London: Cassell, 1951), pp. 149–52.

10   Albert Kesselring, *The Memoirs of Field-Marshal Kesselring* (London: William Kimber, 1953), pp. 186—87.

11   Westphal, *German Army in the West*, pp. 153–54; Kesselring, *Memoirs*, pp. 190–91.

12   Frido von Senger und Etterlin, *Neither Fear nor Hope: The Wartime Career of General Frido von Senger und Etterlin, Defender of Cassino*, trans. George Malcolm (London: Macdonald, 1963), pp. 181–82.

13   Martin Blumenson, *United States Army in World War II: The Mediterranean Theatre of Operations; Salerno to Cassino* (Washington, DC: Office of the Chief of Military History, 1969), p. 228.

14   Von Senger, *Neither Fear Nor Hope*, pp. 179–81.

15   Blumenson, *Salerno to Cassino*, p. 224.

16   Von Senger, *Neither Fear Nor Hope*, pp. 181–84; Bowlby, *Countdown to Cassino*, p. 48.

17   Von Senger, *Neither Fear Nor Hope*, pp. 182–83.

18   Mary Williams Walsh, "Ex-Nazi in War Crimes Case Freed on Technicality," *Los Angeles Times*, March 2, 1995.

19   Von Senger, *Neither Fear Nor Hope*, pp. 182–83.

20   Von Senger, *Neither Fear Nor Hope*, pp. 181–83.

Chapter 25. "Met at every turn by rifle and machine-gun fire"

1   Clark, *Calculated Risk*, p. 221.

2   Bowlby, *Countdown to Cassino*, pp. 42–43.

3   Blumenson, *Salerno to Cassino*, p. 224.

4   Bowlby, *Countdown to Cassino*, pp. 48–50.

5   Kesselring, *The Memoirs of Field Marshal Kesselring*, p. 188.

6   Von Senger, *Neither Fear Nor Hope*, p. 185; Bowlby, *Countdown to Cassino*, pp. 51–52.

7   Blumenson, *Salerno to Cassino*, p. 224.

8   Bowlby, *Countdown to Cassino*, pp. 43–45.

9   HIA, Burhans Papers, Box 15, *Fifth Army History*, II, pp. 50–51; Bowlby, *Countdown to Cassino*, pp. 57–71.

10   Clark, *Calculated Risk*, pp. 225–26.

11   HIA, Burhans Papers, Box 15, *Fifth Army History*, II, pp. 52–53.

12   Bowlby, *Countdown to Cassino*, p. 72.

13   Bowlby, *Countdown to Cassino*, pp. 54–55.

14   Congressional Medal of Honor Society, "Britt, Maurice L.," accessed July 8, 2018, www.cmohs.org/recipient-detail/2653/britt-maurice-I.php.

15   Bowlby, *Countdown to Cassino*, pp. 80–81; Kurt Albert Rust, *Der Weg der 15 Panzer Grenadier Division von Sizilien Nach Wesermünde* (Berlin: privately printed, 1990), p. 64.

16   Clark, *Calculated Risk*, pp. 226–27.

Chapter 26. A "Herculean" Task

1   Clark, *Calculated Risk*, pp. 227–28, 230.

2   HIA, Burhans Papers, Box 15, *Fifth Army History*, II, pp. 13–14.

3   HIA, Burhans Papers, Box 30, Field Order by Major General Walker, HQ US 36th Division, November 27, 1943; HIA, Burhans Papers, Box 2, Field Order No. 14, HQ First Special Service Force, November 29, 1943; Burhans, *First Special Service Force*, pp. 88–89.

4   Fred L. Walker, *From Texas to Rome with General Fred L. Walker: Fighting World War II and the Italian Campaign with the 36th Infantry Division, as Seen Through the Eyes of its Commanding General* (Dallas: Taylor Publishing, 1969), Chapter 11, diary entry for November 18, 1943.

5   HIA, Burhans Papers, Box 2, Field Order No. 14, HQ First Special Service Force, November 29, 1943.

6   Joe Dauphinais, in Springer, *Black Devil Brigade*, p. 70.

7   Thomas, "Auburn to Berlin," pp. 43–45.

Chapter 27. "Difensa or Bust"

1 Hicks, *Last Fighting General*, pp. 97–98.
2 Thomas, "Auburn to Berlin," pp. 42–43; DeCamp Jones Papers, "1-2 Company History," p. 7.
3 Nelson, *With the Black Devils*, pp. 47–48.
4 Becket, "Stars and Jack," pp. 59–60.
5 Email from John Hart, August 18, 2017, citing George Wright's recollection of the Bazooka incident on November 28, 1943.
6 Becket, "Stars and Jack," pp. 60–61.
7 Email from John Hart, citing George Wright's recollection of the Bazooka incident.
8 PP, Lorin Waling Papers, Waling to his mother and siblings, November 28, 1943.
9 DeCamp Jones Papers, "1-2 Company History," p. 7; HIA, Burhans Papers, Box 2, "Field Order No. 14" by order of Colonel Frederick, November 29, 1943.
10 Nelson, *With the Black Devils*, p. 49.
11 DeCamp Jones Papers, "1-2 Company History," p. 7.
12 Joe Dauphinais, in Springer, *Black Devil Brigade*, p. 78.
13 MacKinnon, "Memories of the Battle," p. 4.
14 Piette, "Biography of Lawrence J. Piette," p. 9.
15 LAC, RG 24/15301, "Secret War Diary of 2nd Canadian Parachute Battalion," November 29–December 1, 1943.
16 Burhans, *First Special Service Force*, p. 97; HIA, Burhans Papers, Box 21, Force HQ Journal, December 1, 1943; MacKinnon, "Memories of the Battle," p. 1.
17 Piette, "Biography of Lawrence J. Piette," p. 9.
18 HIA, Frederick Papers, Box 5, "First Special Service Force" by Robert Burhans (pre-publication typescript), p. 133.
19 LAC, RG 24/15301, "Secret War Diary of 2nd Canadian Parachute Battalion," December 1, 1943; Encyclopaedia Brittanica, "Geoffrey Keyes: American Army Officer," accessed July 26, 2018, https://www.britannica.com/biography/Geoffrey-Keyes; Atkinson, *Day of Battle*, p. 334.

20   Atkinson, *Day of Battle*, p. 334.
21   HIA, Frederick Papers, Box 5, "First Special Service Force" by Robert Burhans, pp. 133–34.

Chapter 28. The Defenders

1   Burhans, *First Special Service Force*, p. 96.
2   Walker, *From Texas to Rome*, Chapter 11, diary entry for November 18, 1943.
3   HIA, Burhans Papers, Box 18, G-2 Report (No. 78), HQ Fifth Army, November 23, 1943.
4   HIA, Burhans Papers, Box 18, G-2 Report (No. 79), HQ Fifth Army, November 24, 1943.
5   HIA, Burhans Papers, Box 18, G-2 Report (No. 85), HQ Fifth Army, November 29, 1943.
6   Rust, *Der Weg*, p. 68.
7   Freiburg, Bundesarchiv: Militärarchiv (BMA), MSG 2/5724, A. von Gaudecker, "Panzer-Aufklärungs-Abteilung 115," *Darmstädter Reiter und Aufklärer: Festschrift anlässlich des Treffens am 15./16. Mai 1954*, p. 22; Robert J. Edwards, *Tip of the Spear: German Armored Reconnaissance in Action in World War II* (Mechanicsburg, PA: Stackpole Books, 2015), pp. 33–34; Rust, *Der Weg*, p. 60.
8   https://www.tracesofwar.com/persons/5084/Gienanth-Freiherr-von-Walter.htm [accessed July 28, 2018].
9   Edwards, *Tip of the Spear*, p. 334.
10   Emails to author from Louis Freiherr von der Borch (son of Rittmeister Alhard Freiherr von der Borch), May 26 and July 4, 2017; BMA, MSG 2/5724, A. von Gaudecker, "Panzer-Aufklärungs-Abteilung 115," p. 22.
11   Emails to author from Louis Freiherr von der Borch.
12   BMA, MSG 2/5724, A. von Gaudecker, "Panzer-Aufklärungs-Abteilung 115," p. 22.
13   Report by Rittmeister Freiherr von der Borch on the fighting on

the Camino massif, December 12, 1943, in Edwards, *Tip of the Spear*, p. 335; BMA, MSG 2/5724, A. von Gaudecker, "Panzer-Aufklärungs-Abteilung 115," p. 22.

14 BMA, MSG 2/5724, A. von Gaudecker, "Panzer-Aufklärungs-Abteilung 115," p. 22.

15 BMA, RH20/10/73, Highest Priority Radio Message from Kesselring to Lemelsen, No. 843/43, 0255hrs, November 27, 1943.

16 Rust, *Der Weg*, p. 71.

Chapter 29. "A wet and forbidding mountain"

1 HIA, Burhans Papers, Box 30, "Details for the Movement of Personnel to Forward Assembly Area, Wednesday, 1 December 1943," First Special Service Force HQ, November 30, 1943; Thomas, "Auburn to Berlin," p. 45.

2 MacKinnon, "Memories of the Battle," p. 2.

3 Burhans Papers, "Details for the Movement of Personnel to Forward Assembly Area, Wednesday, 1 December 1943."

4 Thomas, "Auburn to Berlin," p. 46.

5 MacKinnon, "Memories of the Battle," pp. 2–3.

6 Thomas, "Auburn to Berlin," p. 46.

7 MacKinnon, "Memories of the Battle," p. 3.

8 Author interview with Jack Callowhill.

9 Thomas, "Auburn to Berlin," p. 46; PP, Tom Gordon Papers, Nathan Gordon interview with Bill Story, August 2008.

10 MacKinnon, "Memories of the Battle," p. 3.

11 PP, Joe Glass Papers, V-Mail from Glass to his wife Dorothy, January 20, 1944; Author interview with Tom MacWilliam Jr.

12 Author interview with Ken Beaton (Dick Daigle's nephew).

13 Thomas, "Auburn to Berlin," p. 46.

14 Burhans, *First Special Service Force*, pp. 101–2.

15 Hicks, *Last Fighting General*, p. 98.

16 Burhans, *First Special Service Force*, p. 99.

17 Joe Dauphinais, in Springer, *Black Devil Brigade*, p. 75;

Thomas, "Auburn to Berlin," p. 47; Crichlow, "Questionnaire About Military Service."

18 Bowlby, *Countdown to Cassino*, p. 110.

19 Thomas, "Auburn to Berlin," p. 47.

20 Burhans, *First Special Service Force*, p. 103; HIA, Burhans Papers, Box 2, "Annex No. 1 to Field Order No. 14," November 28, 1943.

Chapter 30. The Climb

1 Author interview with Jack Callowhill.

2 Burhans, *First Special Service Force*, pp. 102–3; HIA, Burhans Papers, Box 30, 36th Division's Plan of Attack, November 27, 1943; MacKinnon, "Memories of the Battle," p. 4.

3 Burhans, *First Special Service Force*, p. 103.

4 Bob Davis, in Bowlby, *Countdown to Cassino*, p. 111; Joe Glass, in Springer, *Black Devil Brigade*, p. 76.

5 *Neither Fear Nor Hope*, p. 186.

6 Von der Borch, in Edwards, *Tip of the Spear*, p. 335.

7 Thomas, "Auburn to Berlin," pp. 47–48.

8 PP, Tom MacWilliam Papers, Letter from Sgt. J. K. O'Brien, 2-2 Company, undated.

9 Thomas, "Auburn to Berlin," p. 47; DeCamp Jones Papers, "1-2 Company History," p. 7.

10 Crichlow, "Questionnaire About Military Service."

11 MacKinnon, "Memories of the Battle," p. 5.

12 Crichlow, "Questionnaire About Military Service"; Walter Lewis and Larry Piette, in Springer, *Black Devil Brigade*, p. 77.

13 Author interview with Jack Callowhill.

Chapter 31. "All hell broke loose"

1 MacKinnon, "Memories of the Battle," p. 5.

2 Crichlow, "Questionnaire About Military Service"; MacKinnon,

"Memories of the Battle," p. 5; Lorin Waling, in Springer, *Black Devil Brigade*, p. 78.

3   Crichlow, "Questionnaire About Military Service."

4   Walter Lewis, in Springer, *Black Devil Brigade*, p. 79.

5   Joe Dauphinais, in Springer, *Black Devil Brigade*, pp. 79–80.

6   Author interview with Jack Callowhill.

7   Thomas, "Auburn to Berlin," p. 48.

8   PP, Gordon Papers, Nathan Gordon interview with Bill Story, August 2008.

9   Joyce, *Snow Plough*, pp. 174–75; Joyce, "A Case of Differentiation," p. 14.

10 Joyce, *Snow Plough*, pp. 174–75; Horn and Wyczynski, *Of Courage and Determination*, pp. 175, 190–92; Nathan Gordon interview with Bill Story, August 2008.

11 Author interview with Jack Callowhill; DHH, 145.3009 (D2), "List of Citations for Awards, 1st Canadian Special Service Battalion," A/Lt.-Col. Thomas MacWilliam, Mention in Dispatches.

12 Ken Betts, in Springer, *Black Devil Brigade*, p. 80.

13 Joe Dauphinais, in Springer, *Black Devil Brigade*, pp. 81–82, 85.

14 Crichlow, "Questionnaire About Military Service."

15 Nadler, *A Perfect Hell*, p. 115.

16 Crichlow, "Questionnaire About Military Service."

17 Burhans, *First Special Service Force*, p. 106.

18 Joe Glass, in Springer, *Black Devil Brigade*, pp. 82–83.

19 MacKinnon, "Memories of the Battle," pp. 5–6; Don MacKinnon, in Springer, *Black Devil Brigade*, p. 83.

20 Joe Glass, in Springer, *Black Devil Brigade*, pp. 83–84.

21 Larry Piette and Don MacKinnon, in Springer, *Black Devil Brigade*, p. 84.

22 HIA, Burhans Papers, Box 28, Awards for Monte la Difensa, Pvt. Gerald L. Dodson, Silver Star.

23 Author interview with Jack Callowhill.

24 Crichlow, "Questionnaire About Military Service."

25 MacKinnon, "Memories of the Battle," p. 6.

Chapter 32. "Medic! Medic!"

1 MacKinnon, "Memories of the Battle," p. 6.

2 DeCamp Jones Papers, "1-2 Company History," p. 7.

3 Crichlow, "Questionnaire About Military Service."

4 HIA, Burhans Papers, Box 19, "Consolidation of Surgeons' Reports on the Activity of the Force Clearing Station During Action at Mount La Difensa, Italy, 3-9 December 1943."

5 DeCamp Jones Papers, "1-2 Company History," p. 7.

6 Von der Borch, in Edwards, *Tip of the Spear*, p. 335.

7 Lorin Waling, in Springer, *Black Devil Brigade*, p. 84.

8 Joe Dauphinais, in Springer, *Black Devil Brigade*, p. 85.

9 Norval Riggs and Thomas O'Brien, in Springer, *Black Devil Brigade*, p. 87.

10 Larry Piette, in Springer, *Black Devil Brigade*, p. 86.

11 Del Stonehouse, in Springer, *Black Devil Brigade*, p. 88.

12 Ken Betts, Lt. Walford Michaelson, Sgts. Gil McNeese, John Dawson and Del Stonehouse, in Springer, *Black Devil Brigade*, pp. 88–89.

13 MacKinnon, "Memories of the Battle," pp. 7–8.

14 Joe Glass, in Springer, *Black Devil Brigade*, p. 93.

15 Thomas, "Auburn to Berlin," p. 48.

16 Burhans, *First Special Service Force*, p. 107; Thomas, "Auburn to Berlin," p. 48.

17 PP, MacWilliam Papers, Letter from Sgt. J. K. O'Brien, 2-2 Company, undated.

18 Thomas, "Auburn to Berlin," p. 48; Burhans, *First Special Service Force*, p. 110; Joyce, *Snow Plough*, p. 158.

19 Joyce, *Snow Plough*, pp. 158–9; Joyce, "A Case of Differentiation" p. 17.

20 Hicks, *Last Fighting General*, p. 101.

21 MacKinnon, "Memories of the Battle," p. 8.

Chapter 33. "Five yards! Five yards!"

1 Becket, "Stars and Jack," pp. 66–68; Burhans, *First Special Service Force*, p. 111.

2 George Wright, in Springer, *Black Devil Brigade*, pp. 98–99.

3 HIA, Adleman Papers, Box 12, Interview with Wilson K. Wheatley Jr., September 28, 1963.

4 Boroditsky Papers, "Sam Boroditsky's War," p. 18.

5 Becket, "Stars and Jack," p. 67; HIA, Burhans Papers, Box 28, Awards for Monte la Difensa, 1st Lt. John H. Richardson, Silver Star.

6 Becket, "Stars and Jack," pp. 68–73.

7 Burhans, *First Special Service Force*, pp. 112–13; Joyce, *Snow Plough*, p. 175.

8 Joyce, *Snow Plough*, p. 175.

9 PP, Tom Gordon Papers, Nathan Gordon interview with Bill Story, August 2008.

10 Adleman Papers, "Diary of Sergeant A. W. Ovenden."

11 Author interview with Jack Callowhill.

12 Burhans Papers, "Consolidation of Surgeons' Reports"; Thomas, "Auburn to Berlin," pp. 48–49.

13 Larry Piette, in Springer, *Black Devil Brigade*, pp. 101–2; Piette, "Biography of Lawrence J. Piette," p. 10.

14 Burhans, *First Special Service Force*, p. 116; Hicks, *Last Fighting General*, p. 104; Donald Rowe, in Springer, *Black Devil Brigade*, p. 111; HIA, Frederick Papers, Box 2, Mrs. Ben Alexander to Frederick, undated.

15 Burhans, *First Special Service Force*, pp. 114–15; Joyce, *Snow Plough*, pp. 161.

16 Rust, *Der Weg*, p. 67; Von der Borch, in Edwards, *Tip of the Spear*, p. 335.

17 BMA, RH/82/226, Oberst Karl Ens, "*Gefechtsbericht über den Kampf des Zuges Leutnant Knaf*," January 17, 1944.

Chapter 34. "I don't know how we did it"

1   Burhans, *First Special Service Force*, pp. 117–18; HIA, Burhans Papers, Box 28, Awards for Monte la Difensa, Wayne E. Boyce, Distinguished Service Cross.

2   BMA, RH/20/10/75, Morning Report of XIV Panzer Korps to Tenth Army HQ, No. 4188/43, December 6, 1943.

3   BMA, RH/20/10/75, Interim Report of XIV Panzer Korps to Tenth Army HQ, No. 4295/43, December 6, 1943; Von der Borch, in Edwards, *Tip of the Spear*, p. 335.

4   BMA, RH/20/10/75, Telephone conversation between von Vietinghoff and Kesselring, 0855hrs, December 6, 1943.

5   Burhans, *First Special Service Force*, p. 119; Rust, *Der Weg*, p. 68; Borch, in Edwards, *Tip of the Spear*, p. 335.

6   Burhans, *First Special Service Force*, p. 119; Joyce, *Snow Plough*, p. 163.

7   Burhans, *First Special Service Force*, p. 120.

8   Thomas, "Auburn to Berlin," pp. 49–50.

9   Author interview with Jack Callowhill.

10 Burhans Papers, "Consolidation of Surgeons' Reports"; MacKinnon, "Memories of the Battle," p. 8.

11 Ens, *"Gefechsberticht über den Kampf,"* January 17, 1944; Burhans, *First Special Service Force*, p. 122.

12 Burhans Papers, "Consolidation of Surgeons' Reports."

13 DeCamp Jones Papers, "1-2 Company History," p. 7; Crichlow, "Questionnaire About Military Service."

14 Larry Piette, in Springer, *Black Devil Brigade*, p. 116.

15 MacKinnon, "Memories of the Battle," pp. 9–10.

Chapter 35. "KIA, return to sender"

1   HIA, Burhans Papers, Box 19, Schedule of Events, Sunday, December 12, 1943; Clark, *Calculated Risk*, pp. 235–36; LAC, RG 24/15301, "Secret War Diary of the 2nd Canadian Parachute

Battalion," December 12, 1943; Burhans, *First Special Service Force*, pp. 124–26.

2   HIA, Burhans Papers, Box 19, "Members of the Force Who Gave Their Lives, December 3rd to December 7th, 1943."

3   LAC, RG 24/15301, "Secret War Diary of the 2nd Canadian Parachute Battalion," December 12, 1943.

4   HIA, Burhans Papers, Box 19, Keyes to Walker, 1320hrs, December 3, 1943.

5   Burhans, *First Special Service Force*, pp. 124–25.

6   Clark, *Calculated Risk*, pp. 240–41; Walker, *From Texas to Rome*, Chapter 11, diary entry for December 19, 1943.

7   Eisenhower, *Crusade in Europe*, p. 203.

8   Clark Lee, "American-Canadian Troops Are Crack Mountain Fighters," *Independent Record* (Helena, Montana), February 13, 1944.

9   PP, Tom MacWilliam Papers, Telegram from Director of Army Records to Mrs. Harriet MacWilliam, December 14, 1943.

10 Ed Thomas, in Springer, *Black Devil Brigade*, p. 120; Thomas, "Auburn to Berlin," p. 50.

11 PP, Tom MacWilliam Papers, Frederick to Mrs. H. N. MacWilliam, December 18, 1943.

12 PP, Tom MacWilliam Papers, "Inventory of Effects," April 22, 1944.

13 PP, Richard Daigle Papers, Ken Beaton, "A Blue Christmas Without You" and "A Tale of Two Uncles."

14 Beaton, "A Tale of Two Uncles."

Chapter 36. "The best god-damned fighters in the world"

1   Piette, "Biography of Lawrence J. Piette," p. 10.

2   DHH, 145.3009 (D2), "List of Citations for Awards, 1st Canadian Special Service Battalion," S.Sgt. Thomas E. Fenton.

3   HIA, Burhans Papers, Box 19, "Citations on Difensa."

4   HIA, Burhans Papers, Box 28, "Awards to the First Special Service Force."

5   Joyce, *Snow Plough*, p. 170.

6   Joyce, *Snow Plough*, pp. 174–77.

7   LAC, RG 24/15301, "Secret War Diary of 2nd Canadian Parachute Battalion," January 1, 1944.

8   Joyce, *Snow Plough*, pp. 178–79.

9   Thomas, "Auburn to Berlin," p. 50.

10 Joyce, *Snow Plough*, p. 177.

11 LAC, RG 24/15301, "Secret War Diary of 2nd Canadian Parachute Battalion," January 25, 1944.

12 USNARA, NND/760209, Col. Edwin A. Walker, Commanding 1st SSF, to Commanding General, US Sixth Army Group, November 15, 1944.

13 Burhans, *First Special Service Force*, p. 194; HIA, Adleman Papers, Box 8, Major-General Robert T. Frederick to Commanding General, US Sixth Army Group, November 20, 1944.

14 Bill Mauldin, *The Brass Ring: A Sort of Memoir* (New York: W. W. Norton, 1972), pp. 218–19.

15 Frederick to CG, US Sixth Army, November 20, 1944.

16 Burhans, *First Special Service Force*, p. 299.

17 Burhans, *First Special Service Force*, pp. 316–20.

18 USNARA, NND/760209, Col. Edwin A. Walker, November 15, 1944.

19 Robert H. Adleman and George Walton, *The Devil's Brigade* (1966; repr., Annapolis, MD: US Naval Institute Press, 2004), p. 227; Burhans, *First Special Service Force*, pp. 299–300.

20 Burhans, *First Special Service Force*, pp. 298 and 300.

Chapter 37. "They were best friends for the rest of their lives"

1   PP, Ray Holbrook Papers, Holbrook to his sister Gladys, March 26, 1944.

2   Joe Dauphinais, in Springer, *Black Devil Brigade*, p. 177; PP, Ray Holbrook Papers, "Medal of Hero Sent to Mother," undated newspaper article; Email to author from Janice Harshbarger (Ray Holbrook's niece), September 28, 2017.

3   Email to author from Janice Harshbarger (Ray Holbrook's niece), September 26, 2017.

4   MacKinnon, "Memories of the Battle," p. 11.

5   Springer, *Black Devil Brigade*, pp. 145, 177, 253–54.

6   Author interview with Sharyn DeCamp Jones (Clarence De-Camp's daughter), August 11, 2017.

7   Crichlow, "Questionnaire About Military Service."

8   Larry Piette, in Springer, *Black Devil Brigade*, pp. 168, 214, and 216; Piette, "Lawrence J. Piette," pp. 12–13.

9   Piette, "Lawrence J. Piette," pp. 14–16.

10 Nadler, *A Perfect Hell*, pp. 265–67; Joe Glass, in Springer, *Black Devil Brigade*, pp. 200–202.

11 PP, Joe Glass Papers, Glass to his wife, Dorothy, May 25, 1944.

12 PP, Joe Glass Papers, Glass to his children, October 14, 1991; Author interview with Dottie Glass Maxted (Glass's daughter), Sacramento, CA, August 13, 2017.

13 PP, Lorin Waling Papers, Waling to his mother, August 20, 1944, and Steffie Waling to Lorin's mother, September 14, 1944.

14 Author interview with Cheryl, Jerry, Dave and Valerie (Lorin Waling's children), Sacramento, CA, August 13, 2017.

15 DHH, 145.3009 (D2), "List of Citations for Awards, 1st Canadian Special Service Battalion," Sgt. Geoffrey A. W. Hart; PP, Geoffrey Hart Papers, Geoffrey Arthur William Hart, "Canadian Army World War II Service Records."

16 DHH, 145.3009 (D2), "List of Citations for Awards, 1st Canadian Special Service Battalion," Captain Thomas C. Gordon; Author interviews with Nathan Gordon (Tom's grandson), September 10, 2017, and January 9, 2018.

17 Thomas, "From Auburn to Berlin," pp. 50–93.

18 Becket, "Stars and Jack," p. 174.

19 DHH, 145.3009 (D2), "List of Citations for Awards, 1st Canadian Special Service Battalion," Lt.-Col. Ralph W. Becket.

20 Becket, "Stars and Jack," pp. 175–204.

Epilogue. "They helped save a continent in chaos"

1 Hicks, *Last Fighting General*, pp. 146–47.
2 Becket, "Stars and Jack," p. 173.
3 Hicks, *Last Fighting General*, p. 241.
4 Canadian Armed Forces, "Amongst the Eagles—The Battle of Mount La Difensa," accessed August 24, 2018, https://www.youtube.com/watch?v=cKLG4F4eqkA.
5 PBS News Hour, "Congress Awards First Special Service Force with Gold Medal," accessed August 24, 2018, https://www.pbs.org/newshour/nation/congress-awards-first-special-service-force-gold-medal.

Index